H ~ FLY LOW

First edition
published in 2004 by

WOODFIELD PUBLISHING
Bognor Regis, West Sussex, England
www.woodfieldpublishing.com

© Eric B Morgan 2004

All rights reserved.
No part of this publication may be reproduced
or transmitted in any form or by any means,
electronic or mechanical, nor may it be stored
in any information storage and retrieval system,
without prior permission from the publisher.

The right of Eric B Morgan
to be identified as Author of this work
has been asserted in accordance with
the Copyright, Designs and Patents Act 1988

ISBN 1-903953-55-3

The cover photograph is of the ultimate photo reconnaissance Spitfire – PR XIX
PS915 – flying over Warton, Salmesbury on 19th March 1987.

Fly High Fly Low

The remarkable aviation achievements of
Leslie R Colquhoun DFC GM DFM

~ Spitfire Photographic Reconnaissance Pilot ~
~ Supermarine Test Pilot ~
~ Hovercraft Development Pioneer ~

edited and annotated by
ERIC B. MORGAN

Woodfield

Leslie R Colquhoun during World War Two.

Contents

Les Colquhoun DFC GM DFM vii
Preface ix

1. Early Life and Employment 1
2. Early RAF Service 10
    No.18 EFTS 11
    9 FTS 12
    No.57 OTU 13
    No.603 Squadron 15

3. Photographic Reconnaissance 18
    No.1 PRU 18

4. Malta – March to June 1942 24
    No. 69 Squadron, March 1942 24
    APRIL 1942 25
    MAY 1942 33
    JUNE 1942 38

5. July to December 1942 45
    JULY 1942 45
    AUGUST 1942 49
    SEPTEMBER 1942 59
    OCTOBER 1942 67
    NOVEMBER 1942 72

6. A second tour of PR work 84
    No.8 (Coastal) Operational Training Unit 84
    No.682 SQUADRON 86
    NOVEMBER 1943 88
    DECEMBER 1943 88
    JANUARY 1944 90
    FEBRUARY 1944 91
    MARCH 1944 93
    MAY 1944 94

    JUNE 1944 95
    JULY 1944 97
    AUGUST 1944 98
    SEPTEMBER 1944 99
    OCTOBER 1944 101
    DECEMBER 1944 102

7. **Vickers Supermarine Test Pilot** 103
    7TH MAY 1945 – GERMANY SURRENDERS 103
    14-15 AUGUST 1945 ~ JAPAN SURRENDER 105

8. **Jet Testing Begins** 128
    EMERGENCY 132

9. **Swift flight testing begins** 142
    RECORD FLIGHTS 153

10. **South Marston and Scimitar testing** 166

11. **The VA-1 Hovercraft** 173

12. **The VA.2 Hovercraft** 183

13. **The VA-3 Hovercraft** 190
    A WORLD FIRST ~ 16/9/1962 193

14. **Hoverlloyd and other Business Ventures** 203
    Goodbye to Vickers 203
    Retirement at 61 211
    A final farewell 212

APPENDIX 1 ~ AWARDS 214
    To 126118 F/Lt LR Colquhoun. 214
    To 1377233 Sgt L Colquhoun 214
    To 126118 F/O LR Colquhoun 214
    To 126118 F/Lt LR Colquhoun (Retired) 214

APPENDIX 2 ~ GEORGE MEDAL 215

APPENDIX 3 ~ Supermarine Swift Flight Tests 218
    Flight No. 74 ~ Swift WJ.960 ~ 18th July 1952 218
    Flight No. 75 ~ Swift WJ.960 ~ 18th July 1952 218
    Flight No. 76 ~ Swift WJ960 ~ 18th July 1952 219
    Flight No. 33 ~ Swift WJ960 ~ 7th May 1952 219

Flight No.3 ~ Swift WJ.965, 22nd July 1952 220
Flight No. 4 ~ 22nd July 1952 221
Flight No. 5 ~ Swift WJ965 ~ 22nd July 1952 222
Flight No. 80 ~ Swift WJ.965 ~ 26th May 1953 223
Flight No. 81 ~ Swift WJ.965 ~ 26th May 1953 224
Flight No.82 ~ Swift WJ.965 ~ 26th May, 1953 225

BIBLIOGRAPHIC SOURCES 227

INDEX 228

Les Colquhoun's medals – The Distinguished Flying Cross (DFC), the George Medal (GM) and the Distinguished Flying Medal (DFM).

Les Colquhoun DFC GM DFM

Leslie Robert Colquhoun was born on March 15 1921, at Hanwell, Middlesex, and educated in Ealing. He enlisted in August 1940, trained as a pilot, and in the autumn of 1941 was posted to No 603 (City of Edinburgh) Squadron, an Auxiliary Air Force Spitfire squadron.

In 1941, Colquhoun had being flying fighter sweeps over northern France with 603 squadron when he was detailed to deliver a photographic reconnaissance Spitfire to Cairo. During a stopover in Malta it became apparent that the situation there was desperate. He and his Spitfire were seconded to No 69 Squadron and so hard pressed were the island's defenders that for a while the squadron comprised only Colquhoun and one other pilot.

For nine months during 1941 and 1942, Colquhoun piloted an unarmed and unescorted pale blue Spitfire out of Malta, flying over Italy and assessing the enemy's positions. Travelling at great speed and using considerable guile, he would continuously outmanoeuvre the enemy before landing back at Luqa with his anxiously-awaited photographs.

Not until May 1942 was the squadron reinforced by Spitfires transported in the aircraft carrier HMS *Eagle*. By then, Colquhoun had survived 154 operational sorties, each of which had been flown mostly over the sea, a risky business in a single-engine Spitfire.

Wing Commander Laddie Lucas, the ace commander of No 249 Squadron, summed up the value of Colquhoun's contribution when he noted: "At Luqa, in the face of adversity, photographic reconnaissance was touching the limits of human endeavour. It placed the highest premium upon personal character and integrity." Sergeant Colquhoun was awarded the DFM and commissioned.

Following his exploits in Malta, Colquhoun returned home for Mosquito operational training and in 1943 he joined No 682, a Mosquito photographic-reconnaissance squadron based in Algeria and operating over Tunisia and Italy, moving to San Severo in Italy in September 1943.

He remained with 682 squadron until October 1944, during which time he flew 82 operational trips over enemy territory involving 262 hours of operational flying. He was awarded the DFC for his photographic contribution to the successful conclusion of the North African and Italian campaigns and his part in the preparation for the landings in the south of France during the summer of 1944.

In 1945, after a short period as an instructor, Colquhoun was posted to Vickers Supermarine, where he joined the team of production test pilots. Here he tested the later marks of Spitfires as they rolled off the production lines. He also displayed a special aptitude for putting new types through their paces, particularly the Attacker, an early carrier-borne naval jet fighter.

In May 1950, he was flying an Attacker when the outer tip of his starboard wing folded up. The ailerons locked and Colquhoun began to lose control of the plane. Coolly declining to eject, he stayed put in the hope of discovering the cause of the fault. Flying by rudder alone, he managed to bring the speed up to more than 200 mph. Although this was about twice the Attacker's landing speed, he was able to land at Chilbolton, Hampshire's 1,800 yd runway, with the length of a cricket pitch to spare. By putting his life on the line, Colquhoun, as the subsequent investigation revealed, had enabled the fault to be identified.

Colquhoun's career progressed through testing naval Scimitar jet fighters and early hovercraft - which assured him control, in 1962, of the first hovercraft service between Wallasey and Rhyl.

He was appointed operations manager of Hoverlloyd in 1966, later becoming managing director and operating the company's car ferry between Ramsgate and Calais. After Seaspeed took over Hoverlloyd, Colquhoun ran the company's jetfoil service to Dieppe.

After a period spent as custodian at Chiddingstone Castle, Colquhoun retired to Broadstairs, Kent. He was a great supporter of the Spitfire society, of which he became chairman.

He died in July 2001 and was survived by his wife Katie, whom he married in 1946, and by their four daughters.

Preface

This is the autobiography of a typical British lad who in common with a lot of other young men of his age (including myself!) was mad keen on aviation and wanted to fly the fastest and the best aircraft in the world.

This young lad went on to became one of Britain's ace photographic reconnaissance pilots during World War Two, was a test pilot for British aircraft manufactures Supermarine in the post-war years and in later life became a Hovercraft Pioneer.

I have endeavoured to list all the aircraft he flew, including their serial numbers and appropriate dates, so that other enthusiasts, such as readers of *Air Britain*, can enjoy themselves with the facts I have been able to find out. These also, with the dates, provide an easy reference to the Operational Record books of the various units in which Les served – all of which are now held at the Public Record Office. Thus any of the facts I have entered here can easily be verified by consulting these original sources.

The full co-operation and help of Katie, Les's widow, Jane Wilson, his daughter and family are very much appreciated.

At the time of his death in July 2001, Les had started, but not finished his autobiography. I have made use of all the material that he had completed, and put his own paragraphs in a different typeface so that readers can easily identify his own words, which give an insight into his remarkable career in aviation, especially his amazing work in the Middle East during WW2, where he flew over and photographed pretty much all the major ports and airfields in that region. It called for real cold-blooded courage to do this, flying alone, day after day, over enemy territory, but Les's reconnaissance pictures were so valuable that it is not unreasonable to say that he played a significant part in shortening the war in that theatre. His aircraft had no guns and thus his only defence against the fighters of the Luftwaffe were his guile, height, speed and what he called his "number one eyeball" which he used to evade the unwanted attentions of German fighter pilots or the flak from ground batteries.

Fly High ~ Fly Low

This part of the story is set out in chronological order in monthly (if long) and three monthly (if flying was limited) paragraphs. Photographs supplied are mainly from my personal archive and I have tried to make them representative of the item being written about. In a lot of cases the photo features the specific aircraft mentioned in the text.

Les came from a Scottish family and might have descended from Robert, 1st Laird of Camsyradden in the County of Dumbarton, who was himself the second son of Sir Robert Colquhoun, 5th Laird of Colquhoun by the heiress of the Baroness of Luss.

Eric B Morgan
Horsell, Surrey 2004

1. Early Life and Employment

Leslie Robert Colquhoun was born on the 15th March 1921 at Hanwell, Middlesex, his parents being local to that area. He was educated at Drayton Manor Grammar School…[1]

I suppose that leaving school is the first milestone in the process of growing up. It certainly was for me, suddenly the safe cosy atmosphere of school life was changed to the reality of finding work and in 1936/7 that was not easy. My examination marks excluded me from taking the soft option of applying to join the Civil Service and certainly did not warrant any idea of university life, not that my parents could have afforded the latter. However one of my many job applications proved successful and I joined W.H. Cullen, an upmarket grocery and provision chain with some 100-150 branches in the London, Kent, Surrey areas. My job was a junior clerk in their Head Office near Liverpool Street in London. It involved a 40 minute journey on the Central Line underground between my home in Ealing and Liverpool Street.

Cullen's was an old family business and the old offices and warehouse were almost Dickensian. My first task was sitting on a high stool with a sloping desk adding up countless rows of figures. No computers or adding machines in those days it all had to be done the hard way and I must confess that I was not very good at it. However I soon learned and the mistakes began to get less frequent. I still have the technique but regrettably the speed and accuracy has dropped a little. Despite the low pay I have happy recollections of working there and I built up an understanding of the complexity of supplying the public with the basic necessities of life.

Working took up a great deal of the day, leaving home at 7.30 and not getting back home until seven in the evening did not leave much time leisure activities and in any case even although I was a working teenager, I was not allowed to be out after 10 o'clock. Reading therefore was a major source of

---

[1] At the time of his death, Les had already started his autobiography and I have included most of what he had written. His words have been reproduced in a different typeface so that readers can identify his portion of this history.

relaxation and it gave me great pleasure. I did meet my friends on Saturdays at their homes or at the milk bars that were popular in those days. Drinking and going to pubs was strictly taboo and in any even it was not affordable on the wages that we were paid. Pub keepers were very strict regarding underage drinking and the off licences the only other source of supply would not sell drink to people under the age of 18. However life was not dull and I can recollect many enjoyable times in those days.

However in 1938 the threat of a war with Germany began to grow and a great deal of our leisure time was taken up talking about the danger and trying to understand what we were going to do about it. When Chamberlain came back from Munich with his promise from Hitler that there would be no war the sense of relief was tremendous and he was greeted with great cheers as the saviour of Britain. But the euphoria was not to last and now with hindsight one can understand that all Chamberlain achieved was a delay which gave Britain a chance to prepare for war.

During that year of so-called peace the process of rearming the British Army, Air Force and the Navy went ahead with gathering speed. Perhaps more importantly it allowed time for the radar chain established around the south and east coast of the country to locate and track incoming enemy aircraft at up to 50 miles away to be completed and trial runs made to prove it's effectiveness. This was to prove invaluable during the Battle of Britain, without it, it is doubtful that that battle could have been won.

Production of Spitfires and Hurricane fighter aircraft was made an urgent priority and slowly but surely the front line RAF squadrons began to get their new aircraft and start training to find their most effective use. The Hurricane and Spitfire were a tremendous advance on any previous type of fighter plane in the RAF. They were faster, more manoeuvrable and were able to operate at greater heights than their old biplanes such as the Hawker Fury and the Gloster Gladiator. In this respect the Germans had the advantage since they had already used their Mel10s and Junker bombers in the Spanish Civil war in 1936-1937.

Throughout the latter part of 1938 and the beginning of 1939 most people realised that war with Germany was inevitable. Despite his promises to Chamberlain, Hitler gave no sign that he was going to keep his word. Quite the reverse, in March 1939 he invaded Czeckoslovakia and began to show his intentions of invading Poland. France and Great Britain responded by saying that if that ocurred they would be prepared to go to war with Germany. However this long delay in realising the true intentions of Germany lost Britain and France the support of Russia and Hitler signed an agreement with Russia that they would divide Poland between them and thus avoided the possibility of the Russians opening an Eastern front against Germany.

Ominously for the citizens of Great Britain gas masks began to be issued and bomb shelters were being dug. Volunteers were joining up to serve in the Army, Navy and the Air force and arrangements for conscription were being passed through Parliament. There could be no doubt that Britain was on a war footing.

On 1st September 1939 German troops entered Poland and an ultimatum was sent to Germany at 9.30 that evening asking them to withdraw. This was not heeded by the Germans and a final ultimatum was sent at jam on the 3rd of Sept. stating that if Germany did not withdraw from Poland we would be at war with Germany. France was associated with these ultimatums. At 11-15 that morning Neville Chamberlain made his dramatic broadcast to the nation stating the Great Britain and France were at war with Germany. His broadcast had hardly ended when the first sirens were heard and everybody rushed for the air raid shelters fearing the worst. Some 10 minutes later the all clear sounded and people emerged from their places of refuge uncertain and puzzled but very aware that the war had started.

At that particular time I was at the local Hospital along with many others filling sandbags to be used to protect the hospital from bomb blast. When the sirens went we all stopped work and gradually began to drift towards the bomb shelters. There was no panic, just a realisation that it was the best thing to do. When the all clear was sounded we emerged from the shelters all discussing what might have happened but very relieved that there had been no bombing at least in our area. If it had one result it was that we continued our work with greater urgency and purpose.

To some extent there was a feeling of anti-climax and over the last months of 1939 and the earlier months of 1940 there was no real involvement in ground fighting or in the air, however at sea the threat of the German U-boats became very apparent. On the evening of 3rd September the liner "Athenia" was torpedoed off the north coast of Ireland with the loss of 112 people, some of whom were Americans going home to avoid involvement in the war. Three days later three more ships were sunk near the coast of Spain. Perhaps the biggest disaster was the sinking of the Royal Oak, one of the Navy's biggest battleships, in Scapa Flow, which was presumed to be a safe haven for the Fleet. This sinking was carried out by a German U-boat that got away after the attack. 736 Royal Navy personnel were lost in this disaster.

On the continent Poland was fighting a losing battle against the Germans, the Russians had annexed the Baltic States of Estonia and Lithuania and was preparing to attack Finland. Our own troops were being shipped into France and Belgium to take up their defensive positions, meanwhile to the south the French were manning the Maginot Line considered impregnable by the French. There were a few sporadic German air raids around the Firth of Forth, the Orkneys and down the east coast of England. However it all seemed strangely quiet to the people of England. Life was however changing, the towns and cities were blacked out, long distance rail travel was disrupted by the troop trains, anti aircraft guns were appearing around large towns and cities and over London and other vital areas of defence barrage balloons floated limply overhead. The LDV, (Local Defence Volunteers), later to become known as the Home Guard was formed. The recruits were men over the normal age to join the forces and those to young to join. Their function was to carry out patrols to capture any parachutists or other enemy forces infiltrating the defences. When I joined for a short period prior to joining the RAF they still had not been issued with guns or any uniform. Our main armament was a pick-axe handle. It was as Dad's Army depicts it, serious intent but good fun and comradeship. Everybody realised that Britain faced a real crisis and everybody wanted to help in any way possible. Spirits were uplifted in December when the Navy succeeded in sinking the Graf Spee a German pocket battleship in the mouth of the River Plate in Argentina. This was a major success and not only boosted British morale but it was a serious blow for Hitler. The Graf Spee was one of his latest pocket battleships and it had been wreaking havoc in the shipping lanes of the South Atlantic.

However the overall situation looked bleak. Russia, although temporarily held up by the winter weather in Finland would undoubtedly overrun that country when the Spring thaw started. There was also a problem with Norway and Sweden. Sweden had declared her neutrality but nevertheless was supplying vital iron ore and steel to Germany. German shipping including their naval ships were also using the Baltic Sea to return to safe ports in East Germany. In addition during the winter months when the Bothnia Sea was frozen the Swedish iron ore was being taken overland to Narvik in Norway for shipment to Germany.

Britain and France agreed plans to lay mines in the sea lanes off the Norwegian coast to blockade the ports and also to send troops to Narvik and Trondeim to seize control of the iron ore supplies through Narvik. Both of these operations were difficult requiring a heavy commitment from the British Navy to protect the convoys of troops and equipment during a long sea passage from the English ports to Norway. Into this tricky situation the Altmark, an auxiliary vessel that had been used to keep the Graf Spee supplied in the

South Atlantic before it had been sunk, appeared in Norwegian waters having eluded all efforts by the British Navy to find her on her voyage back from South America. A British destroyer intercepted the Altmark and forced her to seek refuge in the Josing Fiord. The British destroyer was authorised to enter the fiord which was in effect a violation of Norway's territorial rights and board and search the Altmark. Despite the attempts of two Norwegian gunboats to stop this, the Altmark was boarded and searched and in the holds were some 300 British prisoners of war, mainly merchant seamen captured by the Graf Spee. This incident was a further triumph for the British Navy.

However this incident was to have repercussions, as Hitler, enraged by the news and the danger of Norway coming under British influence decided that Norway was to be invaded forthwith and on March 1st 1940 German troops marched into Norway. This made the plans for a British landing at Narvik and Trondeim extremely difficult and although bridgeheads were established north and south of Trondeim and at Narvik the strong German presence made them untenable and the troops were withdrawn. The King and Queen of Norway were also taken off and sent back to England. The withdrawal was made at severe cost in terms of men, equipment and naval losses, the most serious of which was the sinking of the aircraft carrier "Glorious". It was indeed tragic in that the RAF Hurricanes and their pilots who had been supporting the landings at Trondheim from a small emergency landing ground. When the orders for the evacuation were received, the pilots opted for an attempt to land back on the carrier despite the fact that their aircraft were not equipped for such an operation. That they succeeded in doing this, was due in no small measure to their skill as pilots and to the co-operation of the crew of the Glorious in steaming the carrier at full speed into the wind, thus reducing the deck speed when the aircraft landed. The tragedy was that within hours of this highly successful operation the Glorious was sunk and all the aircraft and most of the crew were lost.

Meanwhile the Germans had launched their offensive against Holland and Belgium. Using the blitzkrieg tactics that they had perfected in the Spanish Civil War and against Poland, these countries were quickly overrun and the Germans were able to start their push through the gap between the northern limit of the French defensive fortifications of the Maginot Line and the North Sea coastline. Despite the gallant efforts of the French and British Armies and the RAF and the Navy the great retreat began and on the 28th May it was decided that the British army and remnants of the Belgium and French armies should be evacuated from the beaches at Dunkirk. This evacuation lasted from the 28th May to 4th June and during that period some 340,000 troops were transported from the beaches to ports along the south coast of Britain. Some 861 ships from small pleasure craft to destroyers and cruisers from the Royal Navy were involved. RAF fighters covered the beaches and kept the German bombers and fighters from attacking the troops. Thankfully the weather was fine and calm so that the small boats were able to play their part in the operation, 243 ships of all sizes were sunk and many others were damaged. It was miraculous that so many troops were safely brought back to Britain, but never the less it was a stunning setback. When the French surrendered to the Germans within six weeks it was even more catastrophic and Britain was left standing alone against the might of the German Army and Air Force.

Just prior to the Dunkirk evacuation, Mr. Chamberlain, the Prime Minister resigned and Mr. Winston Churchill took over and formed a coalition Government. Churchill was a totally different character from Chamberlain. Throughout the thirties Churchill had constantly warned the Government against the German threat. Had his pleas for rearmament in the mid thirties been carried out Britain and France would have been better prepared for the war that was to come in 1939. Indeed it is conceivable that Hitler might not have embarked on his crusade to conquer Europe. However Churchill now had a mammoth task, Hitler had total control of Europe and the fate of Great Britain seemed hopeless. Churchill however was a great leader and as far as he was concerned he would continue the struggle against Hitler to the very end. An extract from his speech to the House of Commons on June 4th gave a clear intention of his will to win:

> "We shall fight on the beaches, we shall fight on the landing grounds, we shall fight in the fields and in the streets, we shall fight in the hills; we shall never surrender; and even if, which I do not for a moment believe, this Island or a large part of it was subjugated and starving, then our Empire beyond the seas, armed and guarded by the British Fleet, would carry on the struggle, until in God's good time the New World, with all its power and might, steps forth to the rescue and the liberation of the Old."

Britain suddenly had a new and inspiring leader.

Hitler did indeed offer terms to conclude the fighting but these were not acceptable. In fact they were given very short thrift by Churchill and the Government. With the new mood in the country the emphasis was to re-equip the army and restore morale. This meant that the armament factories had to step up their production to levels previously thought unattainable. Since conscription and recruitment into the armed forces was gathering pace women were asked to work in the factories and to take over jobs normally done by men. The Local Defence Volunteers (LDV) had a new significance and with the issue of rifles a new title, The Home Guard. Thus everybody was involved and doing what they could to help.

For my part I volunteered to join the RAF as aircrew. This was in July 1940 just as the German Air Force started to increase the raids on shipping round the coast of England and on some coastal towns. I was fortunate and was selected for pilot duties and reported for duty in September 1940. This was at the height of the Battle of Britain.

In July 1940 Leslie volunteered to join the RAFVR (Royal Air Force Volunteer Reserve) and enlisted in August 1940 at the height of the Battle of Britain, as 126118 AC.2 Colquhoun. He wanted to be a pilot and had to pass a Selection Committee but by his words he "did not put up a very good show" because his mathematics were found wanting. The Committee passed him as suitable material to be and 'Air Gunner' but on further questioning they changed that to 'Wireless Operator'. There followed more questions about a most out-of-the-way subject – French Somaliland – which had featured prominently in recent newspaper reports. He had fortunately read some of these and was able to speak knowledgably on the subject. This changed their minds once again and this time they changed his prospective trade to 'Pilot'. He said later that this was the most frightening experience he ever had!

The Battle of Britain was a critical battle that Britain just had to win. Throughout July and August the German air raids increased in number and the targets changed. They began to attack the airfields from which the Spitfires and Hurricanes, now becoming more plentiful, operated. The German intention was to eliminate the RAF and having done that, they could proceed with Operation "Sealion", which was to invade Britain. In August the landing barges and accumulation of men and equipment at the German and French coastal ports was a clear indication that an invasion was being planned.

Largely due to the chain of radar stations established round the southern and eastern coasts of Britain it was possible to identify incoming raids some 30 to 50 miles away. This advance information was essential to Fighter Command who were in charge of the Air Defence of Britain. It enabled the controllers to order the fighter squadrons to take off and be directed to the incoming bombers before they had reached their target. The system worked very successfully but the numbers of bombers and their escorting ME109 fighter aircraft were at times overwhelming and the bombers did get through to their targets. At the beginning of the battle the targets were the aerodromes and aircraft factories the object being to knock out the RAF fighters and thus gain mastery of the air over Great Britain.

During some of these raids damage was done to the radar stations, but the Germans clearly failed to appreciate their true importance, otherwise they would have systematically destroyed them. As it was, those that were damaged were quickly repaired. RAF Fighter command had no other sources available, therefore the use of the valuable information provided by the radar chain to optimise the use of their fighter aircraft was vital.

In July when the Battle of Britain, as it became known, was growing in intensity, RAF Fighter Command had 49 Squadrons of Spitfires and Hurricanes available. This amounted to 610 aircraft and crews who were ready at any one time to take off and engage the enemy. By comparison, Germany had 1,015 Bombers, 346 dive bombers and 1,200 fighters and fighter/bombers in northern France. A considerable force! The Germans used their fighter aircraft to escort the bomber fleets and protect them from the English Spitfires and Hurricanes. The RAF plan was to use the slower Hurricanes to attack the bombers and the faster and more manoeuvrable Spitfires to take on the escorting German fighters.

The battle reached a critical stage during the last two weeks in August with the continuous bombing of the RAF Fighter Command aerodromes and control centres. Roughly 20% of the pilots and their aircraft were lost during this fighting. These losses, particularly the pilots, were serious, in that the reserves were being used at an unsustainable rate and pilots had to be used who had not completely finished their training. The first week in September the weather slowed down the activity, but when the weather improved the renewed activity centred on London, a completely new tactic by the Germans. These attacks on London continued and much damage was done to the docklands and the city of London and thousands of civilians were killed or injured. However this change of tactics considerably helped the RAF Fighter Command to repair the aerodromes and control centres and replace the aircraft that had been lost. Thus on 15th September when the Germans mounted their largest attack on London involving hundreds of bombers and fighters, RAF fighter Command aircraft and their pilots were able to take on the opposing forces and at the end of the day Fighter command had claimed 186 German aircraft destroyed for the loss of only 40 of their own. Post war research proved that these figures were optimistic but even the true figures of 102 German aircraft lost against Fighter Command losses of 67 aircraft are still substantial.

This proved to be a turning point in the Battle of Britain. Although attacks by German bombers on London and other targets continued they were not of the same intensity or frequency. Fighter Command was able therefore to bring it's fighter squadrons up to full strength. The production of fighter aircraft had now reached the point that production was higher than the sustained losses so it was possible to re-equip new squadrons with the Spitfire or Hurricane.

More importantly the success enjoyed by Fighter Command against the German onslaught meant that the Germans had to postpone the plans that they had to invade Britain. In fact they were scrapped as by the time the weather had improved in the Spring of 1942 the military situation had completely altered as far as the Germans were concerned as they were planning to break their treaty with Russia and invade them. Although still enduring the German bombing raids throughout the winter of 1941/2 Britain was busy equipping it's armed forces and building up a supply of arms of all kinds in order to be ready to take on the German forces wherever it might prove possible.

2. Early RAF Service

During all this drama I was doing my initial training in the Royal Air Force, having had my summons to join in early September when the Battle of Britain was reaching its peak. My first assignment was at Blackpool where we were issued with our uniforms and given basic drill training.

The weekend before I went to Blackpool I went to London with some friends to celebrate my last night as a civilian. We went to a show at the London Palladium. During the show the air raid siren was sounded and as was the custom the audience was told that if we wished we could we could continue watching the show but if anybody wanted to leave they could do so. We decided to stay, but towards the end of the show we could hear the anti-aircraft guns firing. When we left the theatre at the end of the performance we could hear the guns and see the searchlights. Over to the east there was a huge red glow in the sky. We started to walk towards the glow. As we got to London Bridge we could see that this was caused by huge fires burning in the dock areas below Tower Bridge. The noise of guns and bombs falling was both exciting and frightening. The police and air raid wardens stopped us from getting any nearer so we started to go home, but found that the tubes were not running and we proceeded to walk to Hammersmith. That was my first experience of bombing. It was, in fact, the start of the German air force campaign of bombing London. Previously they had concentrated raids on the airfields.

Blackpool was a safe haven way from the bombs of London. The drilling went on for four or five weeks, after which we were posted to an Initial Training Wing at Torquay in South West England, in peacetime a beautiful holiday resort. We started our ground training as pilots; navigation, airmanship and elementary engineering principles were the prime subjects – with plenty of drill and physical training as well. The hotel where we stayed had no creature comforts. We had about four to six men per room, depending on its size, and were responsible for making our own beds and keeping the room tidy. An inspection was carried out every morning prior to marching to the classrooms. The hotel was at the top of a steep hill and the classrooms were at the bottom – a distance of about a mile and a half. The lectures and drills that took place at the hotel were so arranged that we had to go up and down the hill at least five times a day. By the time I had completed the course lasting six weeks I not only knew a lot about navigation and airmanship but I was very fit as well!

In January 1941 I began my real training to become a pilot. This was at a small grass airfield at Chobham in Surrey. I can still recall the thrill of my first solo flight in a De Havilland Tiger Moth – a great moment.

No.18 EFTS

Les did his RAF introductory course of 'square-bashing' before joining No.18 Elementary Flying Training School at RAF Fairoaks, Surrey, as an LAC on 28th February 1941. Here his first flight for air experience was in a DH82A (No T-7147) on 3rd March 1941, of 20 minutes duration. After 15 hours and 40 minutes of dual instruction on the type he took his first solo on 16th April, flying aircraft N-9445, it was only for 5 minutes, which was to take off, circle and land, but that was normal procedure. F/Lt Devas evaluated the new recruit for the first six flights and then Sgt Barton took over for the next 12, after which W/Cdr Arthur flew with him to assess him and duly passed him fit to continue…

DH82A Tiger Moth T7120 – the basic elementary training aircraft of the RAF.

After this F/Lt Howard took over for the next phase of training, including his solo flight and others later. W/Cdr Arthur assessed him twice more during the course, and F/O O'Duffy took over his training towards the end. Finally on the 5th May he flew his last DH.82A flight in N9346, and was passed out as "Average" on the 6th May, as proficient on that type of aircraft.

"After gaining more experience I was then posted to No 9 Flying Training School at Hullavington. Here we learnt to fly bigger and more powerful aircraft firstly on the Miles Master a two seat Trainer and then on to the Hurricane. The latter was a real bonus. All this was a tremendous jump from the flimsy Tiger Moth but the training methods were very sound and the transition was not so daunting as was first thought".

9 FTS

After his initial pilot training, Les was posted to No.1 Training Squadron of No.9 Flying Training School, at RAF Hullavington on the 19th May 1941, equipped with the Miles Master II advanced trainer, where he took his first flight in N8447 on the 22nd May 1941 with F/Lt Barrett piloting it.

The Miles Master II trainer, fitted with six rocket projectiles on EFTS service.

His solo flight in N8837 on the 24th May was of 30 minutes, and his next major step was to fly a Hurricane on the 5th July for 55 minutes. Here he was taught map reading, cross-country flying, forced landings, aerobatics and formation flying. His course finished on the 31st

July and the following day he was notified that he was Qualified for the Award of the Flying Batch (i.e. his 'wings') from the 2nd August.

These wings were presented to the successful students at the final passing out parade of the course and was a very proud moment for all of them, to know that at last they were fully qualified as a pilot, after all the effort that they had put into obtaining the qualification, and knowing it would be for life.

"At the end of this course we were presented with our RAF Wings and promoted to the rank of Sergeant Pilot. We were then only one step away from service with a front line squadron".

"But first I had to do some operational training and for this purpose I was posted to 57 Operational Training Unit at Hawarden. Here we were taught to fly the Spitfire and to absorb the tactics of aerial combat".

No.57 OTU

His next posting was to No.57 Operational Training Unit at Wrexham on the 10th August 1941, where he had his a flight on the 12th August 1941 in a Miles Master, and followed this on the 18th with his solo flight in a Spitfire LV-D. (LV was the unit identification and D the individual aircraft). One of the odd jobs he had to carry out was to ferry Spitfire IIA 8107 from Kirton to Catterick, probably refuel, and then on to Hawarden west of Chester, for the unit on the 30th September 1941.

Spitfire F.IIA, P7895, like Colquhoun flew whilst with 57OTU.

By the time he left 57 OTU he had flown 68.00 hours on Spitfires, with his last two flights taking place on the 20th October 1941 in Spitfire XO-N. From all of this training he was promoted to Sergeant-pilot.

"On completion of my training I was posted to No. 603, City Of Edinburgh Squadron at Hornchurch Aerodrome in Essex. This was in October 1941, just over a year since I joining the Air Force as a 19 year old volunteer. I could hardly believe that such a change in my life style could have occurred, from a junior clerk in a city office to a fully fledged Spitfire pilot. As a small boy I had dreams of flying an aeroplane but I never dared believe that it might prove even remotely possible.

No.603 Squadron was one of the RAF's elite Auxiliary Squadrons and had achieved a fine record during the Battle of Britain. Now, however the RAF was not so much concerned with defence but with offence. This involved carrying out fighter sweeps over the coast of France to try to bring up the 109s for aerial combat or to do low level attacks on German military installations along the French Coast. These were carried out by 11 Group which controlled the whole of S.E. England. The sweeps involved a Wing consisting of three squadrons of fighter aircraft flying in loose finger four formation along the French coast. Sometimes nothing untoward occurred but on other occasions quite big battles took place if the Germans launched any 109s to defend their territory. Tactically it also kept German squadrons along the French coast to protect their military bases there. When the Germans attacked Russia in the Spring of 1942, this helped the Russians as it meant that the German Air Force was fighting on two fronts.

RAF Bomber Command were also becoming a significant force. With new and larger aircraft they were now able to penetrate into German territory and bomb their factories in the Rhur and beyond. Indeed sporadic raids had been carried out on Berlin and it is believed that one of these carried out on 6th Sept had so infuriated Hitler that he ordered Goering the Chief of the German Air Force to bomb London, hence the change of tactics that had so changed the course of the Battle of Britain.

From my own point of view my experience of carrying out fighter sweeps over northern France was short lived as the Squadron was posted to Dyce in Scotland for an operational rest. This was disappointing from my personal point of view but Scotland proved a very interesting experience. The main task of the Squadron was to patrol the shipping lanes and protect the convoys leaving the Firth of Forth from the threat of German bombers. We had one sighting of these and for the first time I put the safety catch on the trigger to fire the guns to fire. Unfortunately the JU88 which we were chasing dived into cloud before we could get in range. This was to prove my one and only offensive act in an aeroplane".

No.603 Squadron

Les was posted to No.603 Squadron at RAF Hornchurch, as a Sergeant pilot on the 29th October 1941, and flew his first aircraft with them, a Spitfire VA P7692 XT-Q, on the 30th October. His first operational sortie was flying R7226, on the 2nd November, when he went on a Convoy Patrol, another followed on the 5th in R7229 N, another in W3379 S, then the 11th in R7230 Y. He flew from Hornchurch to Fairlop on the 12th, because of the units' relocation, and then on the 15th another Convoy Patrol in W3242 N, then 20th in R7230 Y twice that day, then the 22nd in R7230 Y.

An incident must have happened on, or about the 5th December 1941 at No.9 SFTS, because LR Colquhoun was given an endorsement to his flying licence of:-

"Gross carelessness landing out of wind - harsh braking".

This most unwelcome document was signed on 14th December 1941 by the Group Captain Commanding RAF Hornchurch.

Spitfire F.IIA P7895. This aircraft was received by 72 Sqdn on the 20/4/1941.

A rest until the 6th December with P8585 'S', and another Squadron move to RAF Dyce on the 15th December 1941, where he carried out what was classified as a Patrol in W3110 R on the 18th. On the 31st of the month he flew BL431 on a Convoy Patrol, followed on the 1st January 1942 by another in P5784 V.

Colquhoun's 603 Sqdn mates:- Sgt Thomas, F/Lt Buckstone, F/O Murray, Sgt Waddy, F/O Thomas, Sgt Bush, F/Sgt Hurst and himself, at Dyce.

Colquhoun, Johny Hurst, Cyril Bush, Yankee Jones and "Stoney" Stone.

Les flew to Montrose on the 6th in AD502 Z where once again the Squadron was relocated, and he carried out a patrol the following day. He then flew to Dyce on the 10th in P8585 S, did some dusk and night landings, returning to Hornchurch on the 11th. The Squadron was moved again back to RAF Dyce on the 11th. He flew AD502 Z on a Patrol on the 12th, after which he had a spell off, until the 8th February when he took out AD502 Z on a Convoy Patrol (which was classified as non-operational), though he had flown for 2 hours on operational flights up to the present. He carried out three more Patrols on the 14th in W3833 R, 16th in BL386 P and 18th in AD502 Z, and flying his last flight with 603 Squadron in AD502 on the 23rd. A posting had come through for him to go to No.1 P.R.U. (Photographic Reconnaissance Unit) at RAF Benson, with a brief note in his log book reading:-

> *Very sorry to lose you. Best of luck and send us a close up of Rommel.*
> *Sqd Ldr D. Douglas-Hamilton[2]*
> *OC 603 Squadron*

---

[2] His full title was Squadron Leader Lord David Douglas-Hamilton.

3. Photographic Reconnaissance

"In February of 1942 I was posted from 603 Sqdn to No 2 Photographic Reconnaissance Unit in Cairo. This involved reporting to RAF Benson the Headquarters of RAF Photo Reconnaissance in the UK and pick up a Mk IV PRU Spitfire and fly it to Cairo via Gibraltar and Malta".

No.1 PRU

Les's spell at No.1 PRU was very brief; he moved there on 2nd March 1942 and his first flight was in AB309 on 5th March, this was a Supermarine Spitfire PR-IV followed by eight other PR-IV aircraft which he air tested and carried out camera tests on, until the 25th of the month, when he was notified (as one of a party) that he was to deliver a PRU Spitfire to No.2 PRU at Cairo. At No.1 PRU he had flown a total of 15 hours in the PR-IV aircraft including 5hrs 15mins on BP885. Up to now his total flying hours were 285.30.
1942-03-25: Posted to No.2 PRU Cairo.
1942-03-26: Flew Spitfire PR.IV BP885 from Benson to St Meryn, Cornwall, continuing on the 28th to Gibraltar and then on the 1st April flew into Malta, an overall flying time of 9hrs 40mins.

Spitfire PR.IV BP888 actually of No.8 OTU in 1943.

"I was somewhat devastated by this news. Firstly, I had had no experience of taking photographs from a Spitfire and the thought of flying from Cornwall to Gibraltar and thence to Malta and then Cairo was as good as asking me to fly to the moon. However, in the RAF you have to do as you are told, so I reported to Benson to pick up my Spitfire PRIV. These Spitfires were specially adapted for photo reconnaissance work. There were no guns fitted, the space in the wings being taken up with extra fuel tanks. The aircraft had a range of over 1,000 miles, compared with the fighter Spitfire, which was 2-300 miles. I was allocated Spitfire PRIV No BP885 and after a few test flights I was cleared to set off on my trip to Cairo via Gibraltar and Malta. My first stop was at a small aerodrome in Cornwall called Trebelzue or St Meryn. At the time it was the setting off point for reinforcement aircraft going to the Middle East, however these aircraft were mostly Wellington bombers with full crews and navigation equipment. I found out at Trebelzue that the Spitfire I was taking was only the fifth to set off on the route. I found this out at the navigation briefing just before take off for Gibraltar. The briefing Officer gave the departing bomber crews substantial information concerning winds at various altitudes, courses to steer and various turning points on route to make navigation easier for them. Myself, and another officer also flying a Mk IV Spitfire to Cairo, were the last to be briefed and the Briefing Officer admitted that he could not help us very much as we would be flying at 25,000 feet and he had no information on wind speeds at that altitude. He merely suggested a course to steer, gave a warning to keep well clear of the Brest Peninsula and not to fly over Spain. For good measure he advised us to make sure that we fired off the colours of the day when we entered the landing circuit at Gibraltar as the navy gunners there were likely to think that we were German ME109s and, being trigger happy, would greet us with a salvo which would not be a pleasant reception!

I am pleased to report that in the event the flight was not too bad. After taking off from Trebelzue in rather nasty weather I broke through the cloud over the Bay of Biscay and shortly afterwards I could see the north coast of Spain. Being at 25,000ft, I decided to ignore the instructions about flying over Spain but edged towards the Spanish/Portugal border to give myself a better approach to Gibraltar. Without further incident I entered the circuit at Gibraltar, firing off the colours of the day and fervently hoping that the navy gunners would identify me as a friendly aircraft. Thankfully they did, and I landed and taxied to a dispersal, where the aircraft was refuelled and serviced ready to take off for Malta the next day. My night in Gibraltar was a new experience. For a start there was no black-out, as in the UK, and the bars and restaurants were filled with soldiers and navy personnel hell-bent on having a good time. It was very fertile ground for the Military Police and soldiers and sailors in substantial numbers were being marched off to detention centres to cool off the excesses of drink.

My trip to Malta went off without incident; the weather was fine and I could see the island when I was some 50-60 miles away. It was late afternoon when I arrived over the island and, having read of the bombing that they had suffered, I flew round the Island to see for myself the damage that had been inflicted. It was appalling and I counted myself lucky that I would be away to Cairo the following morning. Little did I realise the news that awaited me when I landed a few minutes later… Having touched down and taxied to the end of the runway I was met by a corporal on a bicycle. He signalled me to follow him, which I did, and a merry dance he led me! By the time he indicated me to stop, the engine was at boiling point and so was my temper. The corporal, having jumped on the wing to help me unstrap, told me the devastating news that the reason he had led me to this seemingly remote spot was that I and the aircraft would be staying on the island and that, as from that moment, I was a member of 69 Squadron.

I subsequently learnt that No.69 was a light bomber and reconnaissance squadron flying Maryland aircraft. Their problem was that they had no aircraft – all their Marylands had been either lost in action or damaged beyond repair by the German bombing of the island.

As I have said, this news devastated me. I realised that I would really be in the thick of the battle for Malta. I found out the next day that there was only one other operational aircraft in the squadron and that was another photo-reconnaissance Spitfire like my own and like me it's pilot, Flying Officer Colbeck and his aircraft had been hi-jacked. Colbeck was a New Zealander and quickly explained to me our duties, which were to carry out reconnaissance flights over Sicily, to photograph the airfields that the Germans had built up on the island and to carry out reconnaissance flights over the large ports in southern Italy to monitor the movements of the Italian navy and to search the west coast of Greece and the Tunis peninsula for German convoys carrying troops and reinforcements to North Africa.

During 1940, Italy had reached an agreement with Hitler and had entered the war. In November 1940 the Italians invaded Greece and moved troops into the Abyssinian and Libyan countries that they had captured in the 1930s. This threatened our position in Egypt and troops were rushed to Egypt and Greece to help fight off the Italians. These efforts met with success. British troops occupied Crete and in the Western desert the Italians were routed and many prisoners were taken. However, these successes were relatively short-lived and when the German troops arrived to help the Italians the battles along the coast of North Africa surged to and fro and the Germans recaptured Crete. But to supply the German and Italian troops in North Africa ships were required to sail from Italian ports across the Mediterranean to Tripoli and other ports along the North African coast. It was in this context that Malta became so important to the Allied cause.

In 1940 and 1941 the air defence of Malta was carried out by three Gloster Gladiators that had been left on the island by the Royal Navy. They were in crates and RAF and Royal Navy engineers had to assemble them and make them ready to fly before they could be used to attack the Italian aircraft that were sent over to bomb the island. They were very successful and a good many Italian aircraft were shot down. Maltese legend has it that they were named Faith, Hope and Charity.[3]

In the latter half of 1941 [June actually] Hurricane fighter aircraft were flown to the island. They took off from Royal Navy aircraft carriers that steamed under naval escort as far along the Algerian coast as they dared, because of the threat of attack by units of the Italian Navy. The Hurricanes were fitted with drop tanks which gave them sufficient range to reach Malta from their launch point. However, at the same time, units of the German Air Force were moved to Sicily with orders to eliminate Malta and by doing so, allow the supply ships ferrying reinforcements to the German Army in North Africa, to take the direct route free from the threat of attack from the Royal Navy submarines based at Malta. As a consequence the Hurricanes were confronted with ME109s as soon as they reached the island and suffered severe losses and were therefore unable to stem the rising level of bombing that had started with the arrival of the Germans in Sicily.

Situated just south of Sicily it was in an ideal spot to carry out attacks on the Italian convoys taking supplies to the German troops in North Africa. It was also an ideal staging post for British reinforcement aircraft proceeding to the Middle East. The British Navy had a strong presence on Malta, mainly submarines; the 10th Flotilla was stationed there. The larger capital ships of the Navy including the aircraft carrier *Illustrious* remained at sea and were serviced from Alexandria in Egypt. It was thought that the risk of bombing from the German

---

[3] Four Gladiators, N5519, N5520, N5524 and N5531, arrived Malta in April 1940 and their first combat was on the 11th June against Italian Air Force SM79s bombers and CR42 fighters, on the day after Italy entered the war against us. One Gladiator crashed, and then there were three…

Air Force stationed in Sicily was too great. During the period from 1941 to 1943 the 10th Flotilla of submarines destroyed more than 1,000,000 tons of German and Italian shipping. Unfortunately they lost 26 submarines in the process. This harassment of the German convoys both by the submarines and later by Wellington bombers and Beauforts carrying torpedoes ensured that none attempted the direct route. Even using the relative safe routes through the Greek islands, the convoys still incurred losses. In our Spitfires Colbeck and I would locate them and report back their position and that night either the submarines or the Wellingtons would go out to attack them. This caused delays of reinforcements to Rommel's German and Italian troops by up to five days – something that Rommel could ill afford.

As a result the German Air Force in Sicily was strengthened and Malta was subjected to some of the most severe bombing ever experienced by any target. The frequency and severity of the raids started in the latter part of 1941 and reached its peak in the spring of 1942. These figures give some idea of the pain and suffering that the Maltese people endured".

- In the first 3 months of 1942 there were 2,000 raids on the island, more than 20 per day.
- 1,000 tons of bombs were dropped on Malta during February 1942.
- In February to April more bombs were dropped on Malta than Bomber Command dropped on Germany in the whole of 1942.
- In March 1942 the number of bombs dropped on Malta was greater than the total dropped on UK cities throughout the war

All this on a small island less than 20 miles long and 10 miles wide! How the Maltese withstood this battering is almost beyond belief. Awarding the Island the George Cross for their courage, endurance and loyalty was just a small token of the country's esteem.

Throughout this period Colbeck and myself carried out our sorties over Sicily and southern Italy, bringing back vital photographic information, taken with the special cameras installed in the fuselages of our aircraft. When photography was not possible a visual report was made. By the end of April the squadron had hi-jacked two more PRU Spitfires and their pilots, so we had four pilots and aircraft available. This eased the workload.

On 9th February 1942 SS *Cape Hawk* set sail from Liverpool loaded with the first 16 fighter Spitfires for Malta, together with 16 pilots of No.249 Squadron and 100 groundcrew under the command of W/Cdr Maclean. These Spitfires were in crates in pieces, together their associated ground equipment and would have to be assembled on arrival. They arrived at Gibraltar on 21st February and anchored near the aircraft carrier HMS *Eagle*. It was here that the Spitfires were transferred to the *Eagle* and assembled, but fuel flow problems to the long-range tanks delayed delivery of them to Malta. Fifteen of them were able to fly off on 7th March 1942 and the 16th, which had been cannibalised for spares, was left behind. This was the first delivery of Spitfires to Malta.

4. Malta – March to June 1942

No. 69 Squadron, March 1942

The British Government, aware of the need to keep Malta operational, took the decision to send Spitfires to the island using the same technique that had been used by the Hurricanes. The first of these arrived at the beginning of 1942 [on 7th March, 15 flew in from HMS *Eagle* and HMS *Argus*] and a further attempt was made in March, shortly after I arrived on the island. [On 21st March nine from HMS *Eagle* and on 29th March seven more from HMS *Eagle*]. The number of aircraft on each delivery was 36 [no] but these early attempts met with the same fate as had befallen the Hurricanes. They were attacked by German Me109s as they arrived and shortly after they had landed, the German bombers came in to inflict further damage. Despite these setbacks the Navy submarines and Wellington bombers continued their harassment of the German convoys making their way to North Africa and the damage done to them was considerable.

P/O Colbeck and I played our part in this in that we were flying over Sicily and southern Italy on a daily basis, keeping watch with our cameras on the movement of German aircraft and shipping. [Colbeck had flown to Malta in Spitfire PR.IV AB300 and his first mission was on 15th March on a PR to Catania, but no mention of his original arrival in the ORB or in his book, *The Maltese Spitfire* published by Airlife in 1997). There were several occasions when we could not land at our base aerodrome at Luqa, due to German bombing. Sometimes we had to land at one of the other airfields, but on other occasions we would fly south of the island and circle until the bombers had departed. In April the situation became even worse, in that the ammunition supplies for the Bofors guns used to defend the aerodromes had become so low that the guns were allowed just one clip of five shells per day. In effect, this meant that they were almost useless in deterring the 109s from strafing the airfields and other military targets. To boost morale every member of the armed forces was issued with a rifle and instructions to 'have a go' at the enemy fighters. Of course, the chances of actually hitting an aircraft roaring down the runway at 300-400mph was minimal, but at least it gave everybody a feeling that they were 'doing their bit'.

By this time the effects of no Allied convoys getting through to the island were beginning to be felt. Food was scarce, especially for the Maltese people, and attempts at introducing rationing were not very effective; it became a case of queuing and scrambling for what little was available. With the intensity of the German raids reaching a peak, life on Malta became very uncomfortable the British armed forces and was scarcely bearable for the civilian population.

APRIL 1942

It was AVM Hugh Pughe Lloyd and the AOC-in-C MEAF who called in at the Air Ministry in January 1942, asking for a few experienced fighter pilots to be trained for PR Spitfire operations from Malta. As can be seen above and below, action must have been taken almost immediately, and must have been one of the better decisions taken in this war.

Colquhoun had barely arrived in Malta before the intelligence officer delivered a Form Green teleprinter paper with the orders for his first mission on 4th April in BP885 – to photograph the docks at Tripoli, Medenine and Gabes. He returned almost immediately, owing to bad visibility, after only 15 minutes flying.

As previously mentioned, the Spitfire PR-IV was an unarmed aircraft and had to rely on its 300mph cruising speed, its operating altitude and the continuous use of "number one eyeball" for defence. Les's missions were all at a height of about 25,000ft, so he would have had to wear an oxygen mask continuously, which cannot have been comfortable, but at least his altitude kept him out of the way of the enemy fighters. At this height the external temperature was about minus 20°C but the internal was about +18° C because of the necessity to keep the cameras from freezing up and the windows from misting, so it was reasonably comfortable for the pilot.

The following day Les completed the sortie successfully in 3hrs 15mins in BP885 to the area of Tripoli, railway to Medenine and Gabes. In Tripoli harbour were 3 destroyers, 14 merchant vessels, 3 motor landing craft, 6 seaplanes, 1 aircraft at Gabes, a merchant vessel aground 20 miles west of Tripoli. Having taken off at 10.40 and landed back at 13.55hrs.

Fly High ~ Fly Low

BP885 with "Bill" Burrows, Ernest Ludlow, Meadows and Gasgoine.

Two views showing crew consisting of Gascoigne, Meadows and Cruxall.

Fly High ~ Fly Low

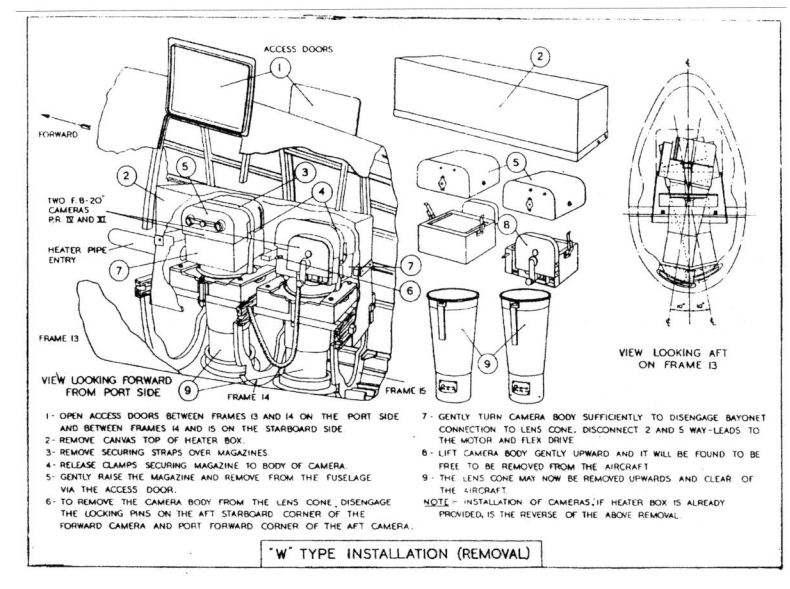

"W" TYPE INSTALLATION (REMOVAL)

1 - OPEN ACCESS DOORS BETWEEN FRAMES 13 AND 14 ON THE PORT SIDE AND BETWEEN FRAMES 14 AND 15 ON THE STARBOARD SIDE.
2 - REMOVE CANVAS TOP OF HEATER BOX.
3 - REMOVE SECURING STRAPS OVER MAGAZINES.
4 - RELEASE CLAMPS SECURING MAGAZINE TO BODY OF CAMERA.
5 - GENTLY RAISE THE MAGAZINE AND REMOVE FROM THE FUSELAGE VIA THE ACCESS DOOR.
6 - TO REMOVE THE CAMERA BODY FROM THE LENS CONE, DISENGAGE THE LOCKING PINS ON THE AFT STARBOARD CORNER OF THE FORWARD CAMERA AND PORT FORWARD CORNER OF THE AFT CAMERA.
7 - GENTLY TURN CAMERA BODY SUFFICIENTLY TO DISENGAGE BAYONET CONNECTION TO LENS CONE. DISCONNECT 2 AND 5 WAY-LEADS TO THE MOTOR AND FLEX DRIVE.
8 - LIFT CAMERA BODY GENTLY UPWARD AND IT WILL BE FOUND TO BE FREE TO BE REMOVED FROM THE AIRCRAFT.
9 - THE LENS CONE MAY NOW BE REMOVED UPWARDS AND CLEAR OF THE AIRCRAFT.

NOTE - INSTALLATION OF CAMERAS, IF HEATER BOX IS ALREADY PROVIDED, IS THE REVERSE OF THE ABOVE REMOVAL.

Spitfire PR.IV "W" Camera installation with two F.8 20-inch lenses.

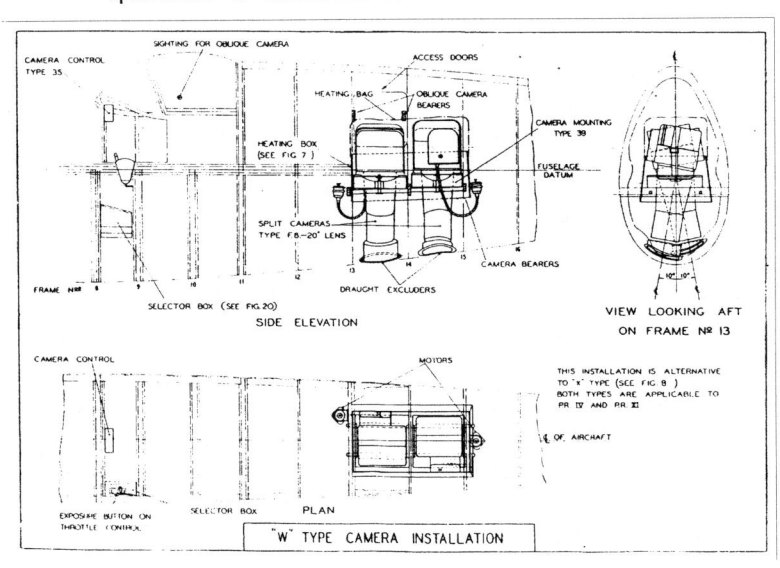

"W" TYPE CAMERA INSTALLATION

THIS INSTALLATION IS ALTERNATIVE TO "X" TYPE (SEE FIG 8). BOTH TYPES ARE APPLICABLE TO PR IV AND PR XI

~ 27 ~

Fly High ~ Fly Low

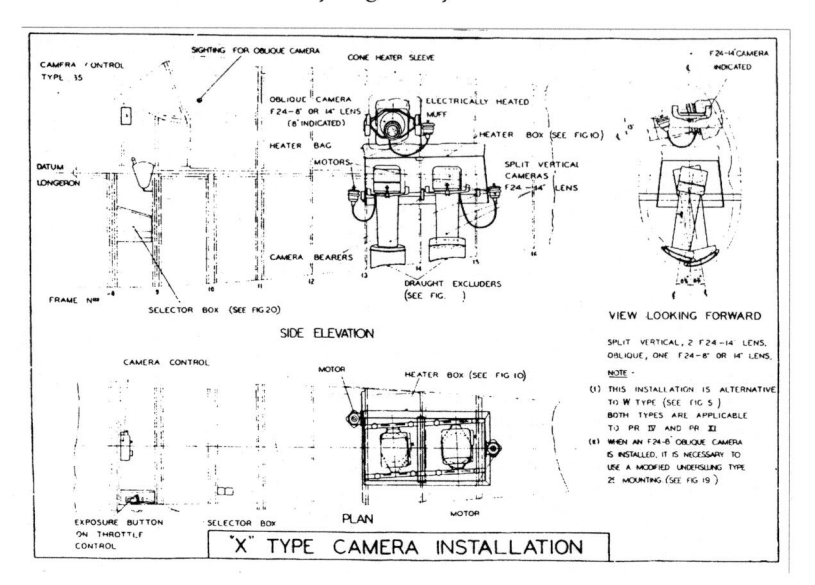

The "X" Type camera installation top and the Universal fit of two F.52 cameras in a later Spitfire PR.XI. Note the overlap of 6½° on the "X" type and 5"20' on the F.52s.

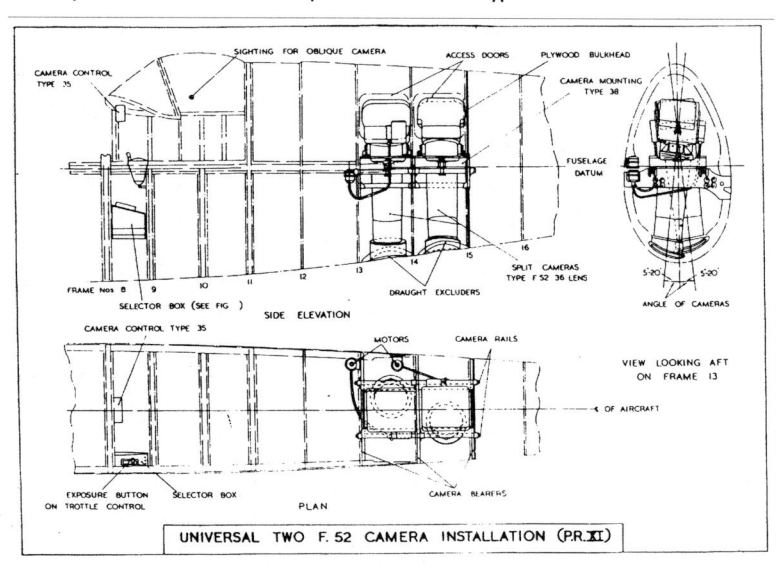

Using BP885 Les carried out a photographic reconnaissance on the 9th April of the East Sicilian aerodromes: Syracuse had 4 Do.26 flying boats and 1 sunken merchant vessel; Augusta had 8 torpedo boats and 37 seaplanes; Catania 2 merchant vessels; Catania aerodrome 47 aircraft; Gerbini showed an increase of 4 or 8 Ju.88s; Gela had 33 aircraft. He also took photographs of Biscari and Comiso.

He took BP885 on the 10th to cover the Sicilian aerodromes: at Augusta there was a hospital ship and photos of Comiso showed 22 bombers and 71 fighters; Biscari had 33 aircraft but he took no photos of Catania, Reggio di Calabria or Vibo Valentia, owing to cloud.

On the 11th he took off in AB300 at 11.20 and landed at 14.20hrs, having carried out a reconnaissance of Sicilian aerodromes: Catania had 78 aircraft, Catania Harbour had one merchant vessel; Reggio di Calabria 39 aircraft; Messina 1 battleship, 2 cruisers, 5 destroyers, 3 torpedo boats, 2 submarines, 1 tanker, 3 merchant vessels, 3 train ferries and 6 small merchant vessels. At Trapani there were 2 destroyers, 5 merchant vessels, 1 oiler, 7 small vessels. Trapani aerodrome had 1 aircraft visible; Boeizzo 3 aircraft; Marsala 27 seaplanes; Castal Vetrano 69 aircraft; Pantelleria and Vitro Valentia not covered owing to cloud; 4 destroyers 3 to 5 miles off Trapani heading for harbour and 3 ships 30 miles SW of Marsala.

All-in-all this amounted to a considerable amount of information to have been gathered in a single sortie by a single aircraft.

On his return to Malta, Les was stood off for 1 hour awaiting a raid to subside. The runways were damaged at Luqa and he landed at Ta Kali after a sortie lasting 4 hrs 5 mins. The aircraft was flown back to Luqa later that day.

A major event happened on 16th April 1942 when King George VI awarded the George Cross to the entire population of Malta for what they had endured in the defence of the island, the only time this award has been presented in such a manner.

Another major event happened on the 20th April when 47 Spitfire fighters were flown off the United States carrier *Wasp* and landed on Malta. USS *Wasp* had been specially requested from the USA by Winston Churchill to carry out this reinforcement. 46 aircraft landed with just one missing, but the Germans knew they had arrived and within two hours sent out Ju.87 and Ju.88 bombers to attack them on the ground in Malta. Many of the new Spitfires were damaged and 17 were rendered unserviceable. German and Italian aircraft made some 308 sorties that day and further bombing on the following day resulted in only 18 of Malta's 54 Spitfires being available. As a result their numbers were decimated within a few days of their arrival and so the German bombings increased in intensity.

Les wrote:

"My own personal experiences during one day in April give some indication of the pressure under which one was expected to live and work. At the time we were quartered in what was the old leper colony and rumour had it that the Germans believed that their own prisoners were sheltered there, so despite all the bombing none ever fell on the leper colony or anywhere near it. As a consequence we ignored any air raid warnings.

On this particular day, our complacency was severely shaken. The warning went about 6 am and as usual we ignored it and, although awake, stayed in bed. My peace of mind was shattered by the unmistakeable noise of a bomb coming down fairly close to us. It was, in fact, very close; the church some 100 yards away, which I could see from my bedroom, disappeared in a cloud of smoke. A fragment of rock flew in through the window and ricocheted round the room. Shrapnel must also have come in too, and when I leapt out of bed I must have put my foot on a piece, as I suffered a slight burn. Indeed, I need hardly say that we rushed down the stairs to the air raid shelter in the basement. The all clear went after about an hour and we dressed and went to the sergeant's mess, this was a wooden building on the airfield. After breakfast the air raid warning went again and we dashed into the slit trench, which was a ground level shelter from which you could see out. We saw the bombers approaching and saw one strike of bombs coming down that looked as though it would be close to us. It was in fact very close, one bomb fell short of us, and a second passed over us and hit the sergeant's mess some 100 yards away. Again we were showered in debris, and when the dust settled we realized how lucky we had been.

Some of the 'Colquhoun boys': Cpl Morton, Souter, Parker, Cpl Hoggett, Farrell, Cruxall and Meadows.

Bob Wells strapping in Les Colquhoun.

The sergeant's mess was totally destroyed. In the afternoon the air raid sirens sounded again and this time, we decided to seek shelter in a slit trench a little further from the airfield. Again, we waited the bomber formation approach and watched the bombs hurtling down. Fortunately we were not directly in line this time, but they fell close enough for us to be covered in dust and dirt. So ended a day in April".

During April it was obvious that something was being planned. Colbeck and I, together with our new colleagues were doing extra flights to cover the Italian and Sicilian ports to establish the position of the various units of the Italian Navy. Further urgency was given to the situation by the fact that our coverage of the Sicilian airfields revealed evidence that the Germans were building glider strips at some of the airfields. This could only mean that they were preparing to invade the island. But activity on Malta was also increasing. Large squads of Army personnel were sent to the airfields, their task was to fill the empty jerry cans, which originally contained aircraft fuel, with sand. These were then used as building blocks to construct three sided blast pens, which would protect aircraft parked in them from the German raids. This work was proceeding day and night. There was a persistent rumour that all this work was in preparation for a large delivery of Spitfires.

On the 21st April 1942 a reconnaissance of the Sicilian aerodromes was carried out with BP885 in a time of 2hrs 10mins, checking up on the bombers and fighters that were now available to the German High Command to bomb Malta. This was done again on the 24th using AB300 in 2 hours. BP885 suffered its first major bomb damage on this day being caught in a hangar that was hit by a bomb and the falling roof, respectively. The windscreen hood was smashed and other minor damage, but the damage was soon repaired by the maintenance personnel.

The 25th April 1942 and BP885 was back in service again, when it flew to photograph the Sicilian harbours and it was on this day also that there were several air raids on Malta when a lot of damage was done, and aircraft damaged. On the 30th the photography included the Catania Basin and its aerodromes. The total time for these last two missions was 4hrs 35 mins.

As soon as the films were processed, they were scrutinized by two photographic interpreters, Flt/Lts Howard Colvin and Raymond Herschel, and it was these two that discovered that the Italians were building what was described as "a potential glider take-off area". One of the photographic coverages of Gerbini airfield had overrun and this was the first they knew of the possibility of an invasion of Malta. After this finding, other sorties were carried out to find other possible take-off areas, which meant flying effectively a square search up and down over the same region, covering a strip then returning and covering the next until the film ran out. After a lot more coverage looking for more airstrips it was learned that an invasion had been planned, but Hitler himself had cancelled it. It is thought that this was one of his more costly mistakes, as Malta was not in a very good condition to defend itself for very long.

MAY 1942

This rumour proved correct and on 9th May some 64 Spitfires took off from the US carrier *Wasp* and HMS *Eagle* and set off for Malta. [Two crashed, one went missing and one landed back on board, so 60 landed on Malta]. The day before this event, a Royal Navy cruiser disguised as a merchant ship had crept along the Algerian coast and made a dash for Malta, carrying ammunition and aircraft fuel for beleaguered Malta. The ammunition was used to set up an anti-aircraft barrage so when the German aircraft came over to attack and bomb the incoming Spitfires they were met with a surprise barrage of anti-aircraft fire. This proved a great deterrent against the Ju.87 dive bombers and many were shot down. The Spitfires already on the island were sent up to meet the incoming German raiders and they also met with success and shot down many aircraft. Thus the incoming Spitfires from the carrier were able to land safely and were guided to newly-constructed blast pens where they were refuelled, rearmed and with new pilots made ready to take off and continue the fight against the German fighters and attacking bombers. All this was done in the space of 10 to 15 minutes, thus the German raiders were met with a new wave of Spitfires and consequently suffered heavy losses.

During the period 10th to 14th May some 100 German aircraft were destroyed and the battle for air superiority over Malta was won. On the 10th Malta flew 110 Spitfire and 14 Hurricane sorties, 23 enemy aircraft were shot down, 15 by fighters and 8 by ack-ack; three Spitfires were shot down, but only one pilot was lost.

There were further raids but nothing like the severity of those that had been experienced during the first four months of the year. Another fly in from HMS *Eagle* and HMS *Argus* brought 17 more Spitfires into Malta on the 18th May. Malta's problem now was to break the blockade, which was causing shortages of food, fuel and ammunition. The only means of getting these essentials to Malta was by submarine or light cruiser, such as the one that brought in supplies immediately before the arrival of the Spitfires on May 10th. This cruiser started a regular run, but in no way could the submarines or this lone cruiser satisfy the needs of the island.

The service personnel existed on tinned food, which had been salvaged from one of the ships that had been sunk in the March convoy. These were mostly tins of meat and vegetables and since the labels of the tins had been washed off when the ship sank it was always a surprise to see exactly what the contents were. For the Maltese people the situation was more serious. They were rationed to 10 ounces of bread per day. This was a basic commodity, things like sugar, wheat and cooking oil were desperately short and many Maltese had to rely on the soup kitchens that were set up to ensure that they did not starve. The situation was therefore critical. As a morale-booster King George VI announced that he was pleased to award the Island of Malta and its people the George Cross. This is the highest award for bravery in civilian life and is equal to the Victoria Cross, which is awarded for bravery amongst military personnel. It proved an inspired action, the Maltese were very proud of their honour and indeed they still are.

About this time 69 Squadron received some bars of chocolate and Colquhoun was duly allocated one of these luxuries. Returning from one of his sorties over Sicily he decided that he would indulge himself with this rare treat. He lost height to about 16,000ft so that he could remove his oxygen mask in order to eat the chocolate. He was flying over Cape Passero, south of Pachino and was just beginning to enjoy the taste of chocolate once again when a shadow went over him. He froze. Just behind him was the menacing nose of a Me.109 fighter. However, it did not open fire but just turned and flew away – a happy outcome to this close encounter that would be relived in great detail back in the mess…

A map showing the area of coverage that the PR Spitfires had to accomplish.

A reconnaissance mission to photograph the Sicilian aerodromes was undertaken in AB300 on 2nd May 1942, but after flying for 30 minutes in 10/10th cloud Les concluded that the cloud must extend over the whole of Sicily and so he returned to Malta. The following day in the same aircraft he managed to photograph the aerodromes and the well-defended island of Pantellaria, returning after 2hrs 55mins.

On the 6th, after a rest for a couple of days, he flew BP908 to photograph the Sicilian aerodromes, and again it took 2hrs 10mins. He did the same again on the 8th, flying BP885 straight there and back in 1hr 50mins, checking where the Axis fighters were.

The following day, the 9th, there was another reinforcement of Spitfires to Malta, flown from the USS *Wasp* and HMS *Eagle* and the Allies wanted to know if any of the aerodromes had been reinforced with extra aircraft from Germany. Also on the 9th, BP885 took part in a shipping search for German/Italian vessels that might attack the carriers and 2hrs 5mins was spent doing just this.

The 10th May mission was one of the longest sorties carried out so far – 3hrs 40mins, using BP885, checking for troop movements and shipping off the Tripoli coast. A day's rest and then another trip to the Sicilian aerodromes to check on any build up of aircraft, in BP908 on the 12th, duration 1hr 55mins.

On the 16th May Les made a round trip to photograph Messina, Palermo and Trapani harbours in BP908, lasting 2hrs 35mins. These ports were on the northern coast of Sicily and meant flying over the toe of Italy, along the north coast of Sicily to exit round the west coast of Sicily to return to Malta.

Another sortie was carried out on the 21st by BP885, of 2hrs 15mins, taking in Messina harbour, Catania, Gerbini strip and Gela, Biscari, Comiso and Pachino. During this trip his starboard camera became inoperative, which was very unusual because these cameras were normally very reliable. Les reported that there were five large Italian bombers seen taking off at Gela Co South. There was no subsequent raid on Malta however. It is possible that this was the sortie that the AOC (Air Officer Commanding) Malta sent a telex to the squadron the following reading: *Please congratulate Colquhoun on excellent photo cover carried out yesterday.*

Colquhoun himself wrote of it:-

"A real dicer, (SW, S & G) at Gerbini and District and chased home by Me.109s and Macchi 202s only half the job done, quarry had not left Messina harbour."

BP885 was flown on the 24th May to do a recce of Messina, Catania, Gerbini strip, Gela, Biscari Comiso, Augusto and Pachino LG, lasting

2hrs 40mins. On this raid he saw five "eytie" bombers taking off from Gela, but wrote that there was on no raid on Malta.

The night of the 25th/26th was somewhat noisy in Malta because the Germans/Italians bombed the island. During this bombing Luqa was hit several times and Colquhoun's aircraft BP885 was "well and truly pranged" (as he put it) and probably [requires] "two new mainplanes, besides patches to fuselage and hood".

BP885 was not rendered 'Cat 5' and must have been repaired, because on 1st August 1942 it is recorded on the AHB (Air Historical Branch) Aircraft Cards that it went to the Middle East, being SOC (struck off charge) on 13th September 1945. It is not recorded as being flown by Colquhoun again.

Instead he took BP908, which he had flown before on missions, on his 26th May reconnaissance of Catania, Gerbini strip, Gela, Biscari, Comiso and Pachino landing grounds and an unknown "special mission". He returned immediately, owing to R/T trouble. His R/T equipment was changed and he took off again and successfully flew the mission taking 2hrs 20mins.

His mission on the 28th with BP908, was to Palermo, Trapani, Pantellaria and Lampedusa, the latter two being fortified islands to the west of Malta, taking him a total of 2hrs 45mins. He spotted an enemy convoy south of Pantellaria containing 3 merchant vessels and 3 destroyers and passed it back to base. When he returned he carried out an air test on AB300 for 45 minutes.

To finish the month of May he flew BP908 on the 29th for a PR of Pantellaria, Lampedusa, Trapani and Palermo. He spotted an enemy convoy south of Pantellaria (presumably the same one he had spotted the previous day) consisting of 3 merchant vessels and 3 destroyers. Photographs taken showed that they had cargoes of MT material. On the 30th his mission was to take pictures of Messina and Palermo harbours, a task which took him 2hrs and 45mins.

The British commanders had a pressing need to know what shipping was at the various ports and what aircraft were at the aerodromes. On 26th May 1942, General Rommel had started a new offensive in Libya, breaking through the British lines and causing havoc, so any disruption to his supply lines from Sicily and Italy was very welcome.

During May a third member arrived to join No.69 Squadron, Flight Sergeant J.O. Dalley and a fourth member arrived in June, Sergeant Frank Gillions.

JUNE 1942

Colquhoun continues:

"At the beginning of June, I and my colleagues in 69 Squadron became very active. Our instructions were to photograph all the Sicilian and Italian airfields and also the naval ports of Naples, Taranto, Brindisi, Messina and Palma. By the 10th June we were covering these targets at least twice a day and sometimes three times. It was obvious that something big was in the offing. On the 12th June we heard officially that two convoys were on their way to Malta, one from Gibraltar and the other from Alexandria. By this time Malta had squadrons of Beauforts and Beaufighter aircraft ready to attack any enemy shipping. These were in addition to the submarines, so Malta had a significant strike force. The Spitfire squadrons were also carrying out sweeps over Sicily, thus keeping some German aircraft on the ground.

Our reconnaissance of the Sicilian ports showed that two large Italian cruisers were in Palma together with their escorting destroyers. On the 14th June, the day before the convoys were due to reach the island, I was ordered to make a flight to Palma at last light to make sure that the naval ships were still there. They were still in the same position as established in earlier sorties but there seemed to be some intense activity around them, as if they might be making ready to sail, which indeed they did later that night. However, my coverage established their whereabouts and the submarines were alerted to the fact that they looked as though they might sail.

However there was worse news. The convoy from Alexandria had been forced to turn back. They had come under heavy fire from Italian naval units and had been bombed incessantly by German aircraft based in Crete. All Malta's hopes rested therefore on the convoy from Gibraltar. Our Squadron flew out to find this convoy and had a first sight of it south of Sardinia. It was obvious that it had received a severe battering from the Italian Navy and the German bombers. Of the six ships that had set out only two could be seen, plus their escorting destroyers. They had been heavily bombed and attacked by units of the Italian Navy to the west of Sardinia. As the surviving ships rounded Tunisia they came under the protecting umbrella of firstly the Beaufighters and, as they got even nearer to Malta, of the island's Spitfires, and were thus able to sail safely into Valetta Harbour, where they were quickly unloaded. This major effort to break the siege of Malta was only partially successful. The tanker that had been part of the convoy was sunk as had been three other merchant ships, two destroyers and one cruiser. Three destroyers and a minesweeper had been damaged and had returned to Gibraltar.

However the island's Spitfires and Beaufighters had shot down 14 German aircraft and several units of the Italian navy had been damaged. The minimal success of the operation did not warrant any letting up of the Island's rationing of food and fuel – if anything things got worse. There was only one relief in that the bombing of the island was very sporadic and mostly confined to quick attacks by fighter-bombers. Our reconnaissance of the Sicilian airfields showed that there were fewer German aircraft based there and we heard later that Hitler had ordered some of his air force based on Sicily to proceed to the Russian front, where the German army was having a difficult time.

Life had therefore become a little less grim on Malta. However, due to the shortage of petrol it was not possible to move freely around the island so there was little socialising with other squadrons based on other airfields on the island. The shortage of food and drink also made partying a rare pastime, but life was far from dull, especially at Luqa, where our Squadron was based. Luqa was the biggest airfield on the island and all the reinforcement aircraft en route for the Middle East used it, so we had many visitors in the mess, who kept us in touch with happenings in the UK. They also brought in useful supplies for the bar, so they were very welcome!

Operationally, further reinforcements of Spitfires flew into the island using the aircraft carrier technique that had been successful on previous occasions. These were:-

- 3rd June   HMS Eagle   31 Spitfires launched   27 landed
- 9th June   HMS Eagle   32 Spitfires launched   32 landed
- 16th June HMS Eagle   32 Spitfires launched   31 landed
- 21st June HMS Eagle   30 Spitfires launched   28 landed

Being untroubled by bombing,, the strength of the Spitfire squadrons was steadily building up and they were able to take on German raids on an equal footing and not outnumbered, as had been their previous experience. More offensive aircraft were also appearing on the island; our own squadron had a flight of Baltimores, which were twin-engined American light bomber aircraft. Our Spitfire Flight had also built up to around ten aircraft.

L to R: P/O S T Johnson, BEM of Gillingham, Kent; F/Lt L R Colquhoun DFM of Ealing, London; F/O D Redman of Newcastle-on-Tyne; F/O J A Black of Wishaw, Glasgow. F/Lt Colquhoun is being de-briefed by F/O Black. [Photo K. Colquhoun]

I had experience of one offensive operation when I was ordered to accompany a squadron of Beaufort torpedo bombers on an anti shipping strike just off Pantelleria. The first thing that struck me was how low they were flying; I could see the airstream from their propellers ruffling the surface of the water. I was flying in loose formation on the left of the Beauforts. When we neared the target area, the three merchant ships and their escorting two destroyers loomed up ahead and I was astonished how large they looked. My previous experience was watching from 25,000ft when ships however large, looked small. The destroyers immediately opened up with anti-aircraft fire and I pulled up to about 8,000ft to take my photos of the action. The Beauforts however continued in at low level, splitting into two flights that attacked from different directions before loosing their torpedoes at the enemy ships. Once the torpedoes had been released they turned and began to re-group ready for the flight home. Fortunately, none of the Beauforts was shot down, but several had been hit by the anti aircraft fire. I took the photos of the attack, one of the ships was burning furiously another had obviously been hit and was virtually stopped. The destroyers seemed to be unharmed and were obviously preparing to pick up survivors from the damaged ships. My activities were cut short by the appearance of two Me109s, so I rapidly climbed to a safer altitude and turned for home. An exciting two hours!

The month of June 1942 started, with a trip round Sicily on the 1st in this order: Messina, Catania, Gerbini strip, Gela, Biscari, Comiso, Augusta and Palermo and took 2hes 30mins. A local flight on the 5th in BP300, in visiting Ta-Kali and Halfar, which were neighbouring airfields, was finally accomplished. The next day he flew in BP908, round 'the circus' of Messina, Augusta, Catania, Gerbini strip, Gela, Biscari, Comiso and Pachino in 2hrs 20mins. On the 7th it should have been San Gidjanni, Ctania, Gerbini, Gela, Biscari and Combo but he had to return after 2hrs without complete coverage owing to engine trouble and camera failure. A further trip that day in BP908, accomplished Catania, Gerbin, Gela, Biscari and Comiso in 1hr 50mins. The next day, the 9th, was quiet, in that he only flew an air test on BP915 of 40mins. He used this same aircraft on the 11th to carry out a reconnaissance of the major port of Taranto, which is situated in the heel of the foot of Italy. This was because a big show was going to be tried in order to reinforce Malta, by starting two convoys, one from Egypt and one from Gibraltar, this took him 3hrs 20mins. He followed this the next day using BP908, with another flight to Taranto to do the same thing in 3hrs 25mins. In the event only two ships got through from the West with four others being sunk. The convoy from Egypt turned back because of enemy air attacks and the threat of a major clash with a powerful portion of the Italian Navy. A Beaufort and Fishington (this was a Wellington that dropped torpedoes) contingent did excellent work dropping torpedoes at the Italian naval forces, they had some success and some losses.

To check on this traffic from the ports he photographed the harbours of Cagliari and Palermo on the 13th June flying AB300 for 3hrs 40mins. The following day, the 14th, it was to Taranto using BP908 in 3hrs 10mins, and on his return and using the same aircraft it was to carry out a visual inspection of Palermo harbour in 1hr 20mins. For this, he took off at 2045hrs and landed at 2205hrs, and located 2 C/Rs (Cruisers) and 4 D/Rs (Destroyers) leaving the harbour. A British convoy was on its way through the Mediterranean and this information was vital, and one of these cruisers was successfully torpedoed by one of our submarines and damaged. It was for this report that Colquhoun was awarded the DFM and was later awarded a Commission.

Sometimes a PR mission meant taking photographs of the after effects of previous attacks on axis shipping in the Mediterranean, to confirm or otherwise what the attacks had achieved, and this was incorporated in his mission orders when necessary.

Aerial photo of a successful anti-shipping strike by allied aircraft.

On 15th June Les took off at 06.50 and landed 09.45hrs after flying to Taranto again in BP915 taking 3hrs 30mins. He flew at 25,000ft with the weather really good and the visibility fairly good, there was cloud but only patches of 4/10 cumulus. He took off again the same day in BP908 in 3hrs 10mins, covering the same region as the morning. On the 16th it was to Cagliari and Palermo harbours in AB300 in 2hrs 20mins. The 17th was a very long flight because he had to visit Lecce, Bari, Foggia and Reggio di Calabria, using BP908 and taking 4hrs and 5mins. After this he had a respite because on the 19th he flew AB300 on an air and consumption test for 1hr and on the 21st he flew it again on a 35min air test.

It was back to the grind and flying at altitude on the 22nd when he went to Messina and Palermo harbours in BP908 (2.30) spotting two large merchant vessels in Palermo harbour, and again on the 23rd in BP915, looking for enemy shipping (1.55). He had to use a different aircraft because he had pranged BP809 whilst taxiing out for a dawn take off, causing damage to its propeller and undercarriage. However he spotted two large merchant vessels and destroyers in the straits of Messina. This was passed back to command and Beaufort torpedo bombers were sent out to prang them, but only one m/v was damaged.

A sortie on the 24th June using BP915 was to carry out visual and photographic reconnaissance of Messina, Palermo and Trapani harbours searching for enemy convoys. He had engine trouble starting at Trapani, and struggled back to Malta landing with almost a dead engine. The mechanics found the fault – the float needle of the carburettor had stuck open and was flooding the engine with petrol. On landing it was found that the air intake was full of petrol. The sortie however produced sightings of two lots of shipping, one consisting of one large and one small motor vessel stationary escorted by one large and one small aircraft. The other sighting was in the Straits of Messina of one large and one small motor vessel with one d/r. The actual sortie took 2hrs 50mins, and Colquhoun was very glad to get back without getting wet.

The next sortie on the 25th in AB300 was to carry out a visual and photographic reconnaissance of Tarranto, Foggia, Naples, Messina and the Afrika Korps Depot. This was a long trip, which lasted 4hrs 10mins. An air test of BP915 on the 25th and then on the 26th he used AB300 to carry out a photographic mission of enemy shipping and Taranto harbour. He sighted 3 M/Vs escorted by one D/R and one seaplane off Pt Stilto, also a M/V and 2 MTBs off Constanzaro Marina in 3.05 hrs.

During the second week of June the squadron received Spitfire pilot, Sergeant Dalley, making a total of four, also six Baltimore aircraft complete with crews from the Middle East. The first Baltimore patrols commenced straight away, but at the height of 5,000ft, and it was found to be a very dangerous height, much more dangerous than flying at 10,000ft, and the Commanding Officer, Flying Officer Patrick, was lost as also was Sgt Baum, who failed to return. Later in the month another Baltimore was lost when AG727 was written off on the ground when a neighbouring Beaufort burned and its torpedo exploded. Thus at the end of June the squadron strength was 3 PRU Spitfires and 3 Baltimores with four crews.

It was a somewhat hectic time for all.

Spitfire PR.IV BP904, believed to be of No.2 PRU Middle East during 1942.

5. July to December 1942

JULY 1942

Les Colquhoun's flying in July started on the 2nd with Les in BP915, doing a tour of the harbours: Trapani, Palermo, Messina, Catania, Gerbini strip, Augusta and Pachino. His sightings were one large M/V escorted by one D/R and one floatplane off Riposto and he covered all these in 2.55hrs. This was followed on the 3rd with a search for enemy shipping in the Zante / Cephalonia/ Patras area and to report their position back to base. He sighted 3 large M/Vs, 5,000, 6,000 and 3,000 tons at 33° off Papas at about 20 miles, on a course of 120 degrees travelling at 7 knots. There was also a medium sized merchant vessel in Patras harbour. Photographs were taken from 24,000ft with the weather clear, and the convoy position was reported over the R/T and an answer received from base when approximately 100 miles away. This took him 3.50 hrs.

On 2nd July 1942 he was awarded the DFM (Distinguished Flying Medal) for "shipping reconnaissance during one of the convoys to Malta". He was awarded a commission in the field and was promoted to Pilot Officer at about this time and Sgt Dalley was promoted to Flight Sergeant with effect from 1st July.

Les probably celebrated somewhat and had two days off flying, but on the 6th July he was off again doing his 'round' of Catania, Gerbini strip, Gela, Biscari, Comiso, Pachino and Nota Arga, in aircraft BP915 in a fast time of 1.50hrs. The following day he had a change, in that he had to photograph Benghazi harbour and district using AB300 taking him 3.20hrs. On the 8th he flew BP915 and did the same for Palermo harbour in 1.45hrs, repeating this on the 10th again in BP915 in the same time exactly. It was Benghazi harbour and district on the 12th in BP908, where he found a hospital ship of 7-8,000 tons just outside the harbour entrance, loading up, with 4 lighters alongside, also a probable destroyer, 5 merchant vessels of 2,000 to 6,000 tons and a 500-ton coaster 21 miles off Benghazi, another coaster 3 miles off Benghazi and photographs taken of harbour district, including aircraft on Berka aerodrome and satellite. He returned to Malta after 3.25hrs.

It should be remembered that high altitude reconnaissance work involved its own peculiar difficulties. For instance, when flying at 35,000 feet, wearing an oxygen mask with all its connections, it was very difficult to see any detail on the ground, bearing in mind that this is a height of approximately seven miles.

On the 13th Les took off at 06.30 hrs and headed for Messina, after which he was to search for shipping along the coast of Italy in BP915. But the washer on the filler cap of the main plane petrol tank blew out on arrival at the Messina area and has a consequence, petrol started to splatter over his windscreen, so he returned after 2.00hrs flying. Back at base the fault was rectified and he took off again in the same aircraft and flew to Cagliari and Elmas aerodromes, but met strong winds which had not been forecast and had to be vectored back to base, which he reached without trouble, though his total flying time was 4.05hrs, a long trip.

An uneventful trip in BP915 to Benghazi harbour in 3.30hrs was a welcome relief the following day.

To try to reduce the amount of equipment reaching Rommel a good watch had to be kept on all of the reinforcing ports in Sicily and Southern Italy, which is why Colquhoun was doing the rounds almost every day to check on this traffic. On the 15th July he covered Messina harbour to Naples, C/Rs still in Messina harbour. He flew 3.30hrs in Spitfire PR.IV AB300. On his return to base he refuelled and flew to photograph the island of Lampedusa searching for tank carrying "t" boats, but saw nothing in 1.50hrs. (This "t" is not known). The next day, the 16th, he flew AB300 again to fly to photograph the harbours of Catliari, Palermo and Trapani in 3.45hrs. There was no let up and on the 17th he flew BP908 round Pachino, Comiso, Gela, Biscari, Gerdini Strip and Catania and also Tunis harbour and aerodrome on the way back in 3.45hrs. The next sortie was on the 20th flying AD300 to Cagliari in Southern Sardinia, to photograph a suspected new aerodrome and also Trapani and Palermo photographed in 3.55hrs.

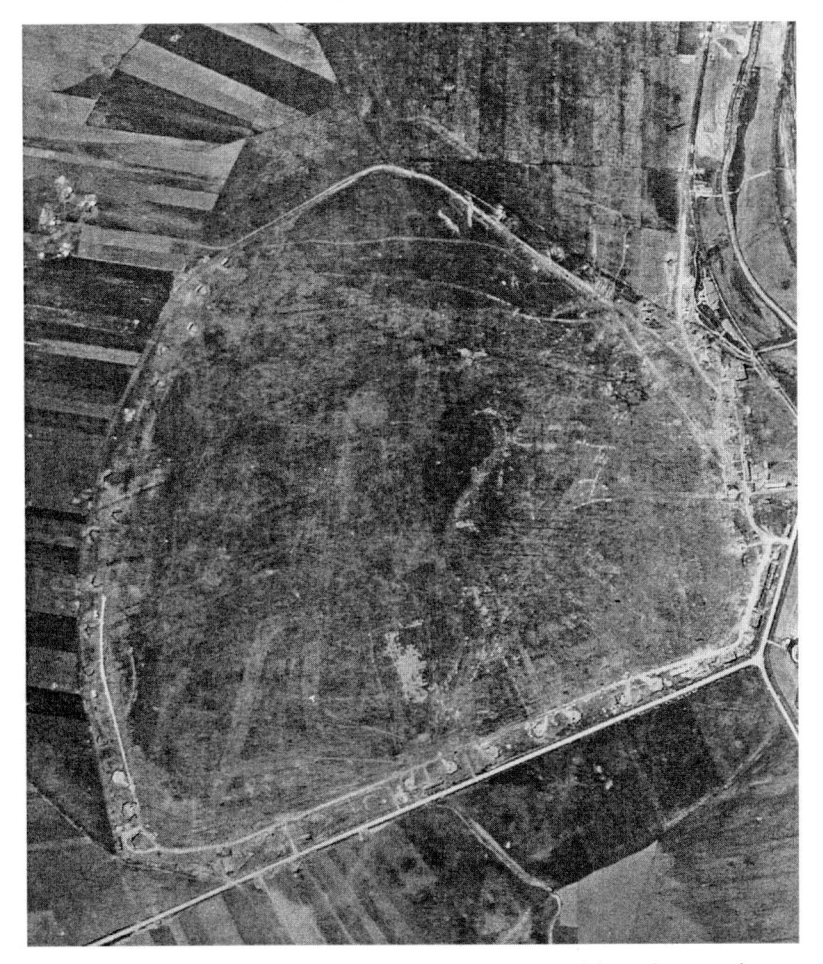

The airfield or aerodrome of Gela with signs of construction around the perimeter and only four aircraft can be spotted on it.

The 21st and flying BP915 he went searching for a M/V pranged by Beauforts off Cephalonia, only sighted a D/R steaming north west, the M/V probably was sunk, returned after 3.45hrs. The next mission was on the 24th with AB300 to photograph Benghazi harbour and Berica aerodrome. One enemy aircraft was spotted at about 5,000ft climbing out to sea, and Colquhoun returned in 3.30hrs. The 25th he took BP915 and photographed Sciacca, Castal Victona, Borizzo, Trapani, Bollo si Falla and Palermoand on this trip he had to play cagey having to orbit the island to allow the passing of enemy aircraft but he still returned in 2.05hrs. A rest until the 29th

when he went to Catania, Gerbini and strip, Gela, Biscari, Comiso, Palkino Noto area, and had a slight scare when two Me.109s passed 500ft below the aircraft over Comiso. The last trip for July was to photograph Navarino harbour on the 31st using BP915 taking 3.40hrs to return.

In July, the PRU flight had no problems but the Baltimore flight lost another aircraft on the 11th leaving them with only one serviceable aircraft, AG734, and AG746 requiring an engine change.

The same aerodrome about a fortnight later, showing what the Germans had accomplished in that time, a new runway, a complete perimeter track and the many individual hard standings.

AUGUST 1942

Colquhoun continues his narrative as follows:

"In the middle of August we had news that another large convoy was going to attempt to break the siege. Our photographic reconnaissances of Sicily and Southern Italy were stepped up and showed considerable aircraft and naval activity, that clearly indicated that the Germans were aware that a convoy was expected. There were some 15 merchant ships including the tanker "Ohio" in the convoy and these were heavily escorted by the Royal Navy. This escort comprised three aircraft carriers, one battleship, four cruisers and several destroyers. As soon as the convoy passed through the Straits of Gibraltar it came under fierce attack first by U-boats. At this stage one of the aircraft carriers was sunk, a major loss to the navy and to the convoy at such an early stage. There was a lull in enemy activity until the convoy negotiated the gap between Tunis and the southern tip of Sardinia. Here the convoy was under continuous attack by German aircraft, E-Boats and submarines and units of the Italian navy. Of the fifteen merchant ships only four made it to Malta. The tanker "Ohio" was abandoned three times by her crew."

The Ohio had been severely bombed and torpedoed, but the captain and crew returned to the ship and lashed it to two destroyers, and it slowly started to make its perilous journey to Malta. Thankfully as it passed to the east of Tunis it came under the protection of the Beaufighters from Malta and as the stricken ship continued slowly east towards Malta the Spitfires maintained a continuous patrol and on the morning of 15th August it sailed into Valetta Harbour where the ecstatic Maltese were waiting to cheer it in. The task of unloading the precious oil that it contained started immediately since the ship was in such a dreadful state that it was barely afloat. In fact shortly after the fuel had been unloaded the ship broke it's back and sank in the harbour. The captain received the George Cross for his gallantry and awards were made to other members of the crew".

VALETTA HARBOUR

The tanker "Ohio" entering the Grand Harbour, Malta with its two escort destroyers.

November 1942: another convoy reaches Malta and is surrounded by small boats for unloading. Nearby is a wreck that the Maltese did not have the equipment to remove.

Two more reinforcement missions were accomplished in August as follows:-

- 11th August HMS *Furious* – 38 Spitfires launched 37 landed.
- 17th August HMS *Furious* – 32 Spitfires launched 29 landed.

So Malta had its fuel, ammunition and food reserves improved but the cost was horrific. Nine merchant ships and their crews - sunk, one aircraft carrier, two cruisers and one destroyer all sunk and one aircraft carrier, two cruisers and one battleship damaged, some severely, but Malta was still there inflicting equal damage to the German convoys trying to get supplies to Rommel who was still battling it out with the British 8th Army in the Western Desert. The RAF in Malta were carrying out daily attacks on Sicily with great success and the Beaufighters continued the good work at night by carrying out intruder patrols. The German shipping losses mounted and Rommel was beginning to run short of vital supplies.

August was another busy month for Colquhoun who carried out 28 missions in 31 days, which must be good going for anyone. The following are listed as they were carried out.

The first mission was on the 2nd flying BP915 "D", (the first time that an individual identity is given), to Sciacca, Bocca di Falco, Palermo, Trapani, Borizzo, Castel Vetrand and Pantellaria covering all of these places in 2.25hrs. He carried out an air test on AB300 of 45mins, on the 5th, which was OK but he damaged the airscrew when he taxied the Spitfire into the hangar. A mystery entry in his flying log book then appears for the 6th which reads:-

"Special mission. Maybe details later [none were recorded, so it remains a mystery]. Plotted back as a 6 plus raid."

This special took 1.55hrs, flying in BP908.

The 7th was a photographic reconnaissance of Taranto, Augusta Harbour and strip and Gela southwest to coast, taking off at 07.00hrs in AB300 and taking 3.30 hrs. Les sighted a merchant vessel of 3,000 tons at 100 degrees of Taranto about 20 miles away but heading for Taranto at a speed of 10 knots. In Taranto harbour were 4 battleships, 5 destroyers, 1 8,000 ton tanker, 1 white ship near tanker, at Augusta there was 1 Hospital ship. Photographs taken of Taranto, Augusta from 24-25,000ft. Mosaic of Gela to coast from

22,500ft. Sighted a large oil streak stretching from Cape San Vito 30 miles Eastwards, 7 miles off coast. Visibility was 30 miles with 5/10 Strato-Cumulus at 15,000ft. P/O Coldbeck and F/S Dalley also flew missions that day.

A Spitfire being loaded by an RAF Leading Aircraftsman, with an F.52 PR camera, and it takes an experienced hand to do it.

Another trip on the 9th in AB300, was to cover Catania aerodrome and harbour, after which he saw two aircraft apparently climbing to intercept. He arrived back safely after 1.30hrs so presume he was able to outpace them. On the 10th he flew BP908 to photograph Taranto and Augusta harbours taking 3.05hrs. Another funny experience on the 11th flying BR432 "D" (so what happened to BP915 "D" of the 2nd August?). He on his way to photograph the Eastern Sicilian aerodromes and Messina, when his hood got blown off, so he had to return immediately after only 15 minutes flying. On his return he got into AB300 to cover the mission but did not cover Messina or Catania due to cloud conditions even though he flew for 2.30hrs. His third trip on the 11th was in BP915 (the original "D") to Taranto harbour, where he sighted one large M/V, one small M/V, 6 "E" boats and a D/R just going into the harbour. He returned after

3.15hrs. It seems that things were hotting up, because next day, he had to fly BP915 to photograph Trapani, Palermo, Messina, Catania, Gerbini, Comiso and Gela that took 3.00hrs. After his return, he had to take off again after BP915 was refuelled and the film changed in the camera, to photograph Catania aerodrome and its harbour that took 1.30hrs. The 13th was another double trip day, the first was in AB300 to Taranto harbour where he saw something and the second when he took BR665 to Messina, Naples and Palermo harbours, both trips took him 3.10hrs.

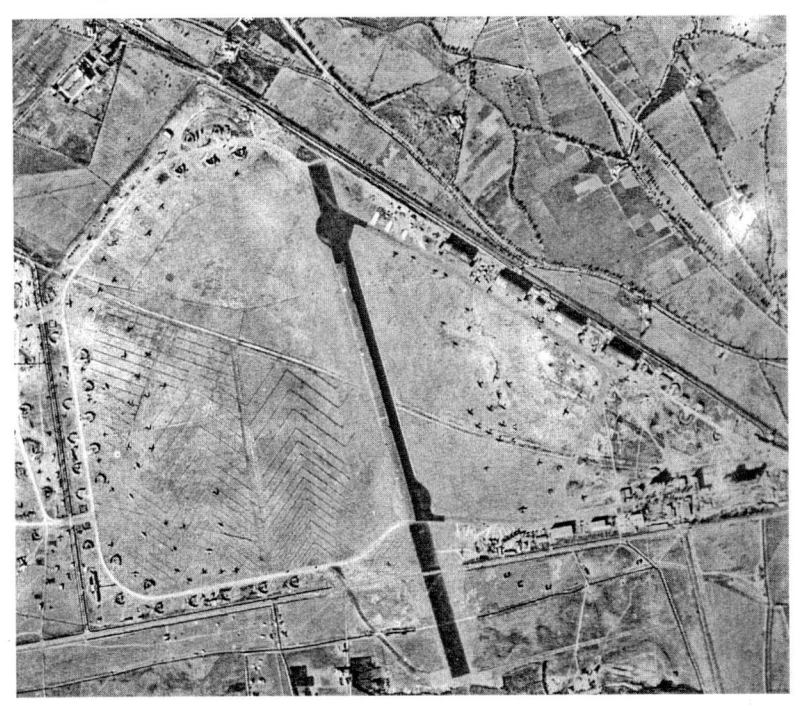

Catania aerodrome with about 72 aircraft visible

On the 11th August 1942 S/Ldr A. Warburton was posted to No.69 Squadron to take over command, and also Martin Baltimores had arrived to form A flight for anti-shipping sorties, B Flight was Spitfire PR.IVs and C Flight with the remaining Marylands and Wellingtons for night time anti-shipping missions.

Arerra Aerodrome, buildings in top of photograph compose the new Alfa-Romeo factory, though a lot of it was underground. 18 aircraft can be seen.

It was at this time that we were using decrypted enemy wireless messages that were received by the Government Code and Cypher School, telling us of the ships that were being put into convoys to cross Mediterranean Sea to Tunis, and of course we sent out our aerial spies to confirm this, closely followed by other aircraft to try to destroy them. Sometimes when the co-ordinates were arrived at, there would be a convoy there, and on the way back to base a radio call would be made in plain English, back to base, saying its position, so that the Germans would know that we had found it using the

Spitfire. This way the secret of the Enigma machine's use was hidden from the Germans.

Capodichina Aerodrome showing a huge number of transport aircraft bound for North Africa, I count about 84 aircraft present.

On 14th August 1942 Colquhoun took out BR431 "D" on a photographic reconnaissance of Messina, Palermo and Trapani harbours returning after 2.35hrs. The next time he went out was on the 16th in AB300, to do the same over Pantellaria, Cagliari, Sardinia and Trapani, Sicily, taking 3.45hrs. On the 17th it was a photographic reconnaissance of a Beaufort and Beaufighter strike on a merchant vessel south of Pantellaria scoring at least one hit, the vessel was left smoking from the starboard side and down by the stern, patrolled by 3 Ju.88s at 5,000ft and 2 single engined aircraft fighters approaching from the north at 3,000ft. At 13.45hrs he saw a large merchant vessel and 2 destroyers line abreast at 180 degrees off Pantelaria at 40 miles course 180 degrees at 12 knots. Left convoy at 16.10hrs, Destroyer heading north. The information was sent out to the Beauforts and then he returned to base after 2.30hrs.

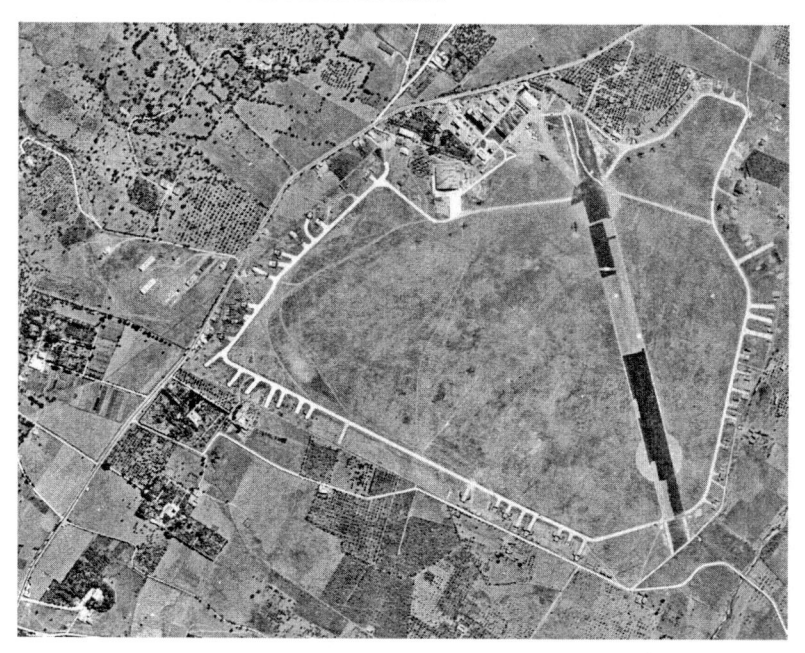

Trapani Aerodrome with at least 19 aircraft, some in the dispersal pens.

The 18th it was BR431, for a PR of Messina, Catania, Gerbini, Comiso, Pachino and Biscari in 2.15hrs. The 19th in BR662, was a shipping search of Mazzaro, Trapani, Palermo, Magettino, Capebon, Kuritt and Pantellaria. From all these places, only one tanker was spotted in Palermo harbour, and he returned after 2.05hrs. A flight round Messina, Catania, Gerbini, Gela, Bucari, Comiso and Pachino but its landing ground was not taken because of the very close proximity of a Me.109, so he returned with BR431, to base after 2.20hrs. A long search was executed on the 21st in BR662 "D" for shipping, especially looking for a tanker at Corfu, but there is no report of him having found it, returning after 3.25hrs.

The following day he went out again searching for this tanker in BR665, this tanker had been pranged by Beauforts, but he had to turn back because of the atrocious weather, even at 32,000ft it was not much better, and in a time of 0.45hrs nothing could be seen. On the 23rd it was a simple sortie in AB300, just Photograph Tripoli harbour, a trip of 2.10hrs was the result. He was still searching in BR663 on the 24th for this missing tanker at Sacarda Bay, but returned after 10mins because his generator was unserviceable. He then took off in BR431 but again had to return, this time having just taken off because his R/T was inoperative. The aircraft R/T was replaced and he took off for the third time and this time he found the tanker that they were looking for, beached in the bay, his trip of 3.30hrs was worth it.

Biscari Aerodrome with whisps of cloud and only seven aircraft seen.

The next day, 25th, he carried out a shipping search in BR665, of Djerba, Kerkenna and Kuiat but sighted nothing of importance except two wrecks (he wrote that it was possibly from the Malta Convoy and landed after 2.40hrs. The 26th he carried out photographic reconnaissance of Sirte, after which he did a shipping search coastwise to Homs taking him 3.35hrs.

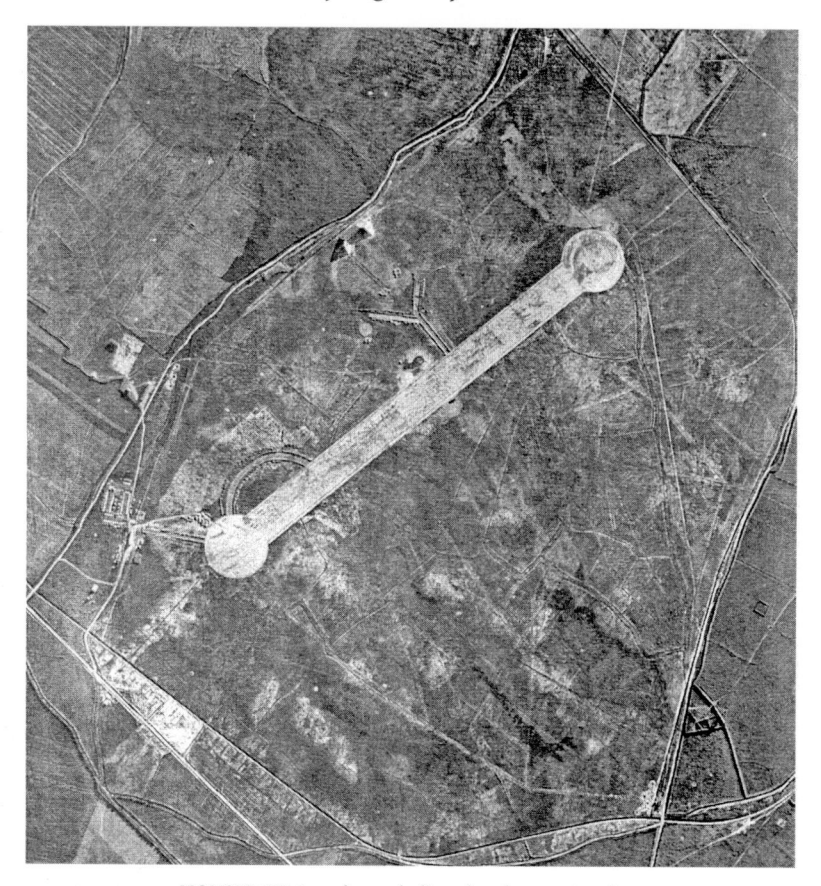

MONSERATO Aerodrome believed under construction.

He used BP662 "D" on the 27th to carry out a photographic reconnaissance of Gela, Biscari and Comiso, some of our fighters carried out offensive sorties at the same time, he noticed that one aircraft was left burning on the ground at Gela, returned after only 1.20hrs. A PR of Navarino, and Warbour flying BR662 on the 28th, resulted in the spotting of a merchant vessel of 2/3,000 tons with 2 D/Rs, and back to base after 3.35hrs. The trip on the 29th in BR663 was another PR of Taranto and Brindisi harbour. At 12.05hrs over Taranto he saw 6 "Battle Waggons" (Battleships in the normal English language), 10 destroyers and several M/Vs being present. 1 "Littorio" battleship across the entrance with tug at either end, another "Littorio" battleship smoking. 1 destroyer and 1 M/V of 5-6,000 tons and 1 M/V of 1-2,000 tons seen leaving harbour of Taranto harbour. He returned at 12.40 hrs to find battleship "Littorio" in same position but convoy in position 280 degrees off Taranto at 4 miles, course 280 degrees speed of 5-10 knots. At 13.30hrs at Brindisi 2 large M/Vs in harbour, 2 destroyers, 1 M/V 6-7,000 tons outside. Photographs taken of all of it. The weather was fine and no cloud except over high ground with a visibility of 15 miles, he then returned after 3.30hrs. The 31st was of BR662 flying on a PR to cover Taranto and Brindisi harbours, resulting in spotting 4 unidentified enemy aircraft just off Taranto, and also smoke rising from a tanker that was pranged yesterday by our Beauforts. This occupied him for 3.35hrs.

Up to now Les Colquhoun had carried out 89 sorties with the squadron, flying 276.40hrs.

SEPTEMBER 1942

General Gort felt that conditions had so improved that in September he arranged that he would hand over the George Cross awarded to the Maltese people by King George VI at an official ceremony in the Palace Square in Valetta. Sir George Borg the Maltese Chief Justice received the award on behalf of the Maltese people. The ceremony was watched by some 5,000 citizens a lot of whom had walked to the Square as there was still not enough petrol to run the full bus service. It was a great occasion.

September 1942 was another busy month, with the first sortie on the 1st flying in BR662 "D" to carry out a photographic reconnaissance of Taranto, Brondisi and Cotrone harbours in 3.25hrs. The 2nd, should have been to take a mosiac of South Eastern Sicily using BR431, but there was cloud over the target and so the mission was terminated after 40mins. The 4th saw BR653 on a PR of Pachino, Comiso, Gela, Biscari, Gerdini strip and Augusta, taking 2.10hrs. BR662 on the 5th flew to photograph a beached enemy merchant vessel near Cotrone, and also covered Taranto, Brondisi where a convoy of 1 M/V and 2 other ships seen, also the strip at Avola and Pachino in 3.30hrs. The 6th saw BR662 photograph Tripoli harbour and a shipping search of Homs - Tripoli but it was bad weather, flying was reduced to 9,000ft through the rain and he returned after 2.40hrs.

Comiso Aerodrome showing only 10 aircraft.

On the 8th he took BR662 again to photograph Pantellaria Castle, Vetrono, Gela, Sorizzo, Palermo, Trapani, Army camp at Castel, taking off at 10.40 hrs. At 12.15hrs found 1 tanker 5-6,000 tons, 1 small M/V 1,000 tons or less, 1 large destroyer and 2 MTBs or E-Boats. 1 floatplane at position 030 degrees off Jaffarano at 30-40 miles on course 170 degtrees, it later turned towards Palermo Harbour at speed of 5 knots. At 11.50hrs position 250 degrees off Cape Granitola at 40 miles was 1 MTB going towards Pantelleria. At 12.40hrs position 200 degrees off Marsala at 20 miles was 1 small M/V of 1,000 tons on course 010 degrees at 10 knots. At 11.40hrs off Pantellaria 2 M.Vs of 1,000 tons, 1 with 2 lighters alongside. At 12.20hrs off Palermo where there were 2 M/Vs of 4-5,000 tons, 1 M/V 1-2,000 tons and numerous small ships. Off Trapani at 12.30hrs several small vessels, 1 enemy fighter 1 mile north of Pantellaria at 1,000ft. Photographs of above from 25,000ft and visibility was 30-40 miles. He landed safely at 13.25 hrs. On the 9th he covered Benghasi, Serfa and Genina in BR663 taking 3.40hrs.

Colquhoun took BR663 out on the 10th for a photographic reconnaissance of Cotrone, Taranto and Grindisi plus the ammunition dumps on Malta in 3.50hrs, this was a change to carrying out PR trips of enemy installations. The next trip was using BR431 on the

12th, for a PR visit to Gela, Biscari, Comiso, Catania, Gerbini and strips and Pachino landing ground. He spotted enemy aircraft up round Comiso, but he had no contacts, and landed after 1.50hrs. His next trip was on the 14th using BR653 to photograph Syracuse, Augusta, Licata, Empedocle, Pantellaria, strips of Agrigents, Canilatti, Caltanisseto and convoy of one merchant vessel and 1 D/R off Cape Santa Roce flying for 2.40hrs.

LECCE Aerodrome showing 16 aircraft in bottom left corner.

On the 16th it was the turn of BR431 to carry out a shipping search off Cape Santa Maria, Pileocia and thence coastwards to Messina. Nothing was found however to warrant further investigation. He landed after 3.40 in the air. The following day, the 17th in BR665, he went on PR to Comiso, Biscari, Gela, Geroni strip, ??omania, Pacino landing ground and from Catania to Belpasso, During this sortie, one of his cameras packed up, and he came back after 1.55hrs.

A photographic reconnaissance on the 19th in BR662, was to Licata, Empedocle, Trapani, Palermo, Messina, Catania and Cape Passers and returned after 2.40hrs. A criptic remark in his log book reads:-

"Gillions started trip but did not return".

This was a colleague of his, Sgt Frank Gillions, and he had Failed To Return in Spitfire PR.IV AB300, from a sortie over Sicily. This just shows one how things happen, one minute you are there and the next minute you are gone. It need not have been enemy action either, it could have been mechanical failure, because machines are not indestructible and are prone to failure. Also, at this time Sqdn/Ldr A. Warburton, DSO, DFC, was posted in as OC 69 Squadron.

The next day, the 20th, he was off again in BR663, taking off at 08.25 hrs for a survey of the Sicilian harbours of Licata, Empedocle, Palerno, Trapani, Messina and Catania strip, from a height of 25,000ft. At 09.30 hrs he was at 140 degrees from Empedocle at 15-20 miles and saw 2 small vessels on course 270 and speed 5 knots. At 10.30hrs he was ½ mile off Cape Orlando where 2 small, unidentified vessels were on course 270, at 09.40hrs it was Palermo where 1 M/V of 6,000 tons was against the outer mole, 2 M/Vs of 3,000 tons against each of two southern jetties, 3 M/Vs of 2,000 tons in northern end of harbour. Ayt 10.00 to Trapani where there were 1 M/V of 2,000 tons in the outer harbour, 1 Torpedo Boat and other small ships. 10.40hrs at Messina 3 cruisers, 2 submarines, other small ships, 10.55hrs at Catania 1 M/V of 1,000 tons. All of the above he took photographs of, returning after 2.35hrs.

For the 21st he changed aircraft to BR431 to search for shipping from Trapani coastwise to Cotrone, and photographed Cotrone and Taranto in 4.30hrs. A note today informs us that his colleague Gillions had become a POW (Prisoner of War). A short trip on the 22nd in BR663 was to photograph Licatta, Empedocle from 12,000ft, during which he experienced light flak from Licata but returned safely after 1.20hrs. On the 23rd he was required to do a visual shipping survey of the Greek Coast, of Patraf and Antipaxes returning after 3.30hrs. The 24th saw a trip to search for shipping around Messina and only took 2.00hrs to carry it out.

The 25th saw a trip in BR662, to photograph Pantallaria, Terpani, Palermo etc taking only 2.50hrs, wheras the sortie on the 27th in BR431 was to photograph the shipping at Taranto, Cape Santa Maria di Leuca (the heel of Italy) and across the Ionian Sea to Corfu, where he sighted some shipping to report back which took him 4.05hrs. On the 28th he flew Navarino harbour for a PR in 3.20hrs, and also the next day, the 29th, he carried out the same sortie in 3.30hrs. The last sortie of the month was on the 31st in BR431, and was a visual shipping search for motor vehicles that left Messina early.
The 25th saw a trip in BR662, to photograph Pantallaria, Terpani, Palermo etc taking only 2.50hrs, wheras the sortie on the 27th in BR431 was to photograph the shipping at Taranto, Cape Santa Maria di Leuca (the heel of Italy) and across the Ionian Sea to Corfu, where he sighted some shipping to report back which took him 4.05hrs. On the 28th he flew Navarino harbour for a PR in 3.20hrs, and also the next day, the 29th, he carried out the same sortie in 3.30hrs. The last sortie of the month was on the 31st in BR431, and was a visual shipping search for motor vehicles that left Messina early morning, these were sighted off Cantanzaro Marina, but he reported no numbers. His flying time on his return was 2.20hrs.

His total number of operations to date were 112 in 342.40hrs, authorised by S/L A. Warburton OC C Flight No.69 Squadron, though Colquhoun himself was on B Flight.

Bocco di Falco near Palermo, used as a base for reinforcements for North Africa. The huge aircraft at bottom left is a Me.323 transport. 51 aircraft in all.

Me 323 'Gigant' -- the largest aircraft used by the Luftwaffe during World War II. 203 of these massive aircraft were built in 1941, 27 in 1942, 140 in 1943 and 34 and 1944.

A Junkers Ju52 German mail carrier, seen here at Habbinaya in December 1938.

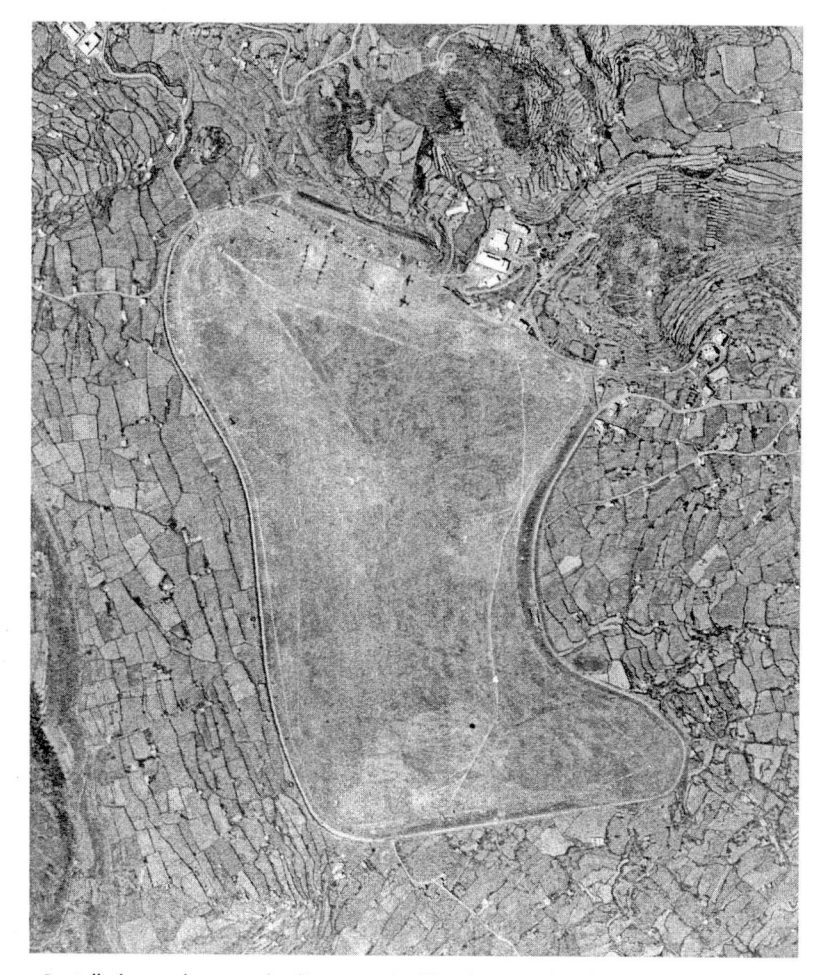

Pantellaria aerodrome, or landing ground, with at least 28 aircraft spread over the area. Rocky surfaces are visible at the top and top right

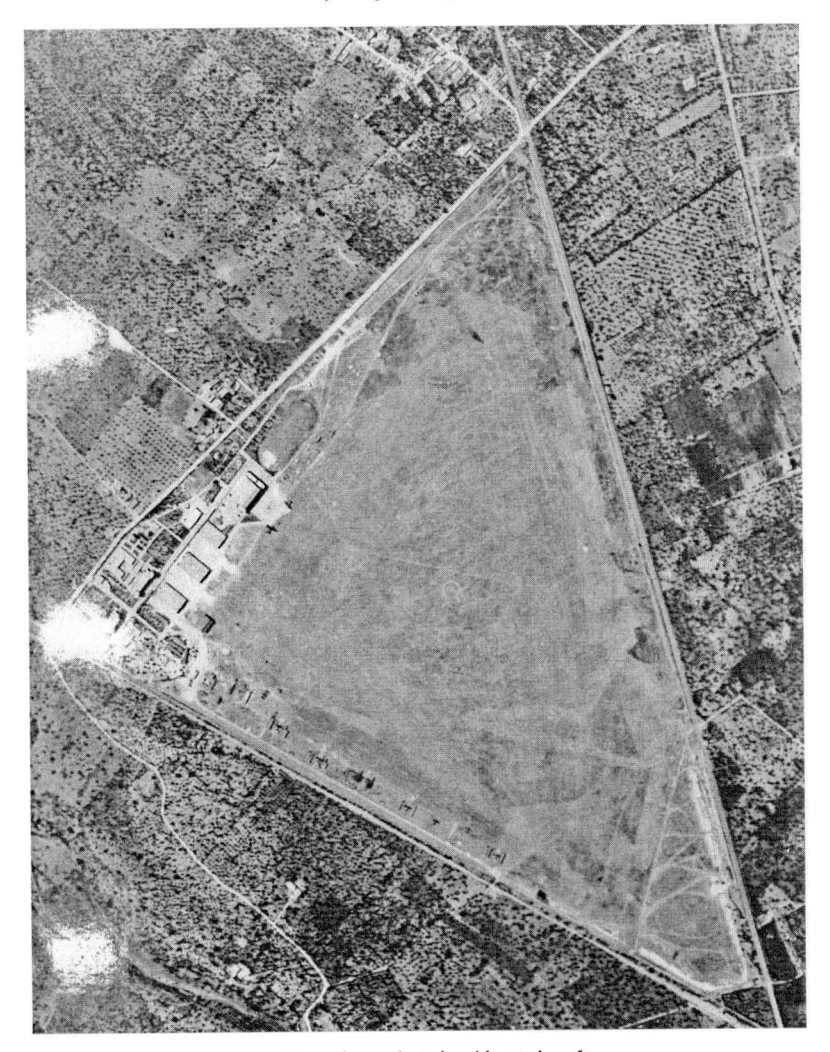

BARI Aerodrome in Italy with 16 aircraft.

OCTOBER 1942

If Rommel was to win his battles in the Western Desert and reach Cairo, his supply routes must be reopened. In an effort to do this the German Air Force started a massive campaign to bomb Malta into submission and on the 11th October, three Ju88s with a heavy escort of fighters attempted to bomb the island. They were intercepted by Spitfires from 229 squadron and all three bombers were destroyed before they reached the island. The following day eight Junkers 88s escorted by sixty to seventy fighters were intercepted over the sea. Seventy German aircraft were shot down, but some got through and bombs were dropped indiscriminately on Malta. The main formations continued to try to break through the cordon of Spitfires and bomb the island, but very few got through and they suffered high losses. Between 11th and 19th October they had lost 131 aircraft. The Spitfire losses were only 34. On the 2nd October 1942 the raids ceased and on the 24th October a final mission was accomplished:

HMS Furious – 31 Spitfires launched, 29 arrived.

This meant that a total of 385 Spitfires had been launched and 367 actually arrived on the island and all during Malta's darkest hours. These aircraft and their pilots were vital to the tiny island throughout the most difficult period in its history.

October 1942 was a quiet month for Colquhoun with only 12 sorties recorded. The first of these was on the 1st using BR431 to carry out a PR of Taranto and Brindisi harbours, and his comment on this was: "What a bind," although it only took him 3.10hrs. On the 2nd in BR431 he was tasked with photographing Benghazi harbour, which he did from 11,000ft in 3.30hrs. On the 4th he flew BP910 – a tropicalised Spitfire VC – on a shipping search around the Cape Santa Maria di Leuca, but he had to return early because of a severe drop in oil pressure. Even so, he was airborne for 4 hours, probably due to nursing the aeroplane back to base at lower revs than normal. On the 6th he used BR653 for a 2.50 hour flight, to search for shipping off Cape Santa Maria, where he found some ships and reported them back to base. His next flight was on the 8th in BR563, a PR to Benghazi but the weather was N.B.G. (as he put it) so he turned back after seeing nothing at his ETA of Benghazi, time out was 2.20hrs.

On the 10th October 1942 the Germans dropped bombs on the island of Malta with six raids of about 120 aircraft. This proved to be the beginning of a sustained and large-scale air offensive against Malta's aerodromes, harbours and other important installations. Until the 19th of the month they maintained the offensive with attacks comprising between 200 and 270 aircraft per day.

During this period the defenders of the island were able to bring down about 100 enemy aircraft, but not without the loss of 30 of the island's Spifires.

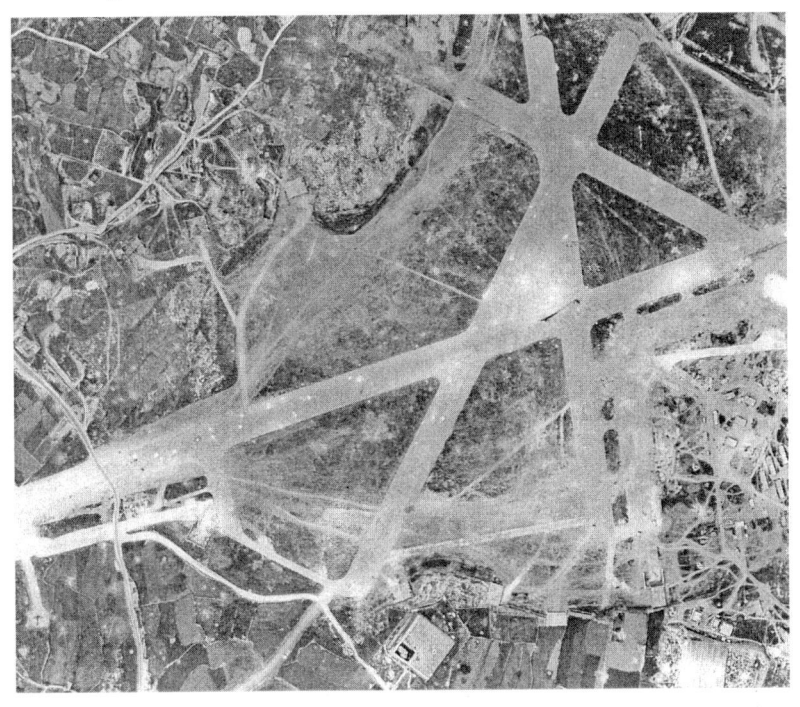

Luqa Aerodrome, Malta. The white blotches are bomb craters and only 5 aircraft can be seen anywhere on the aerodrome.

Colquhoun's next trip was on the 11th using BR431 but was out only 40mins before he returned. The next sortie in BR431 was on the 14th for a photographic reconnaissance and shipping search of Tripoli and surrounding area eastwards where he found one M/V and one floatplane, the mission taking 1.50hrs.

His next trip was on the 11th using BR431 but was out only 40mins before he returned.

The next sortie in BR431 was on the 14th for a photographic reconnaissance and shipping search of Tripoli and surrounding area eastwards where he found one M/V and one floatplane, the mission taking 1.50hrs.

Capodichina Aerodrome, one of the biggest in Sicily with about 127 aircraft, including at least two Me.323 the largest transports in the world.

The 15th saw him flying BR653 on local photography of Hal Far on a flight of only 30mins. On the 16th he was in BR663 on a PR of Pachino, Comiso, Gela, Biscari, Gergini and Catania. On his out trip he passed about 3,000ft over a gaggle of Me109s forming up for a raid on Malta, his time on this trip was 4.10hrs.

On the 22nd of October a convoy had been raised in the U.K. and set sail from the Clyde for Gibraltar, for Operation "Torch", which was to be the invasion of French North Africa (French Morocco and Algeria). The idea was to occupy them and advance to the east to meet Montgomery and the 8th Army advancing from the west.

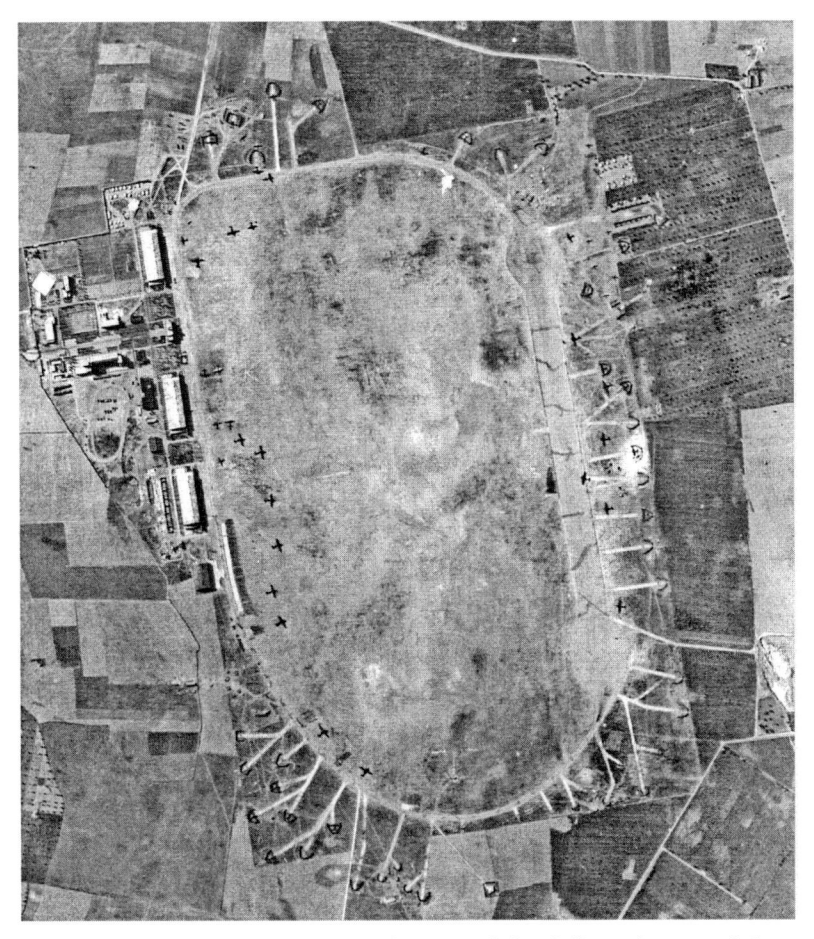

Grotaglia Aerodrome with no runways but hangars and aircraft dispersal areas, and about 28 visible aircraft.

It seems that Les had nine days rest from flying because his next flight was on the 26th, when he accomplished a shipping search of Maria di Leuca area off Italy in BR 653 and found 2 M/V, 3 D/M, 2 floatplanes and 6 fighters, he returned after 2.50hrs.

On the 27th he took off to PR Comiso, Biscari, Gela, Catania harbour, which he did but not Gerbini and Pachina which were cloudy and returned after only 1.50hrs. Once again, he took BR653 on the 29th, when he did a PR coverage of Messina, Catania, Comiso, Biscari, Gela, Pachino and Gerbini in 2.20hrs.

Gerbini Aerodrome – 36 aircraft to be seen.

NOVEMBER 1942

November was a fairly busy month with 23 missions completed. His first mission was on the 1st in BR663 when he managed a PR of Patral, Greece, and a shipping search at Katakolo. He sighted 3 M/Vs in the Gulf of Corinth escorted by 3+ machines. The time taken to return was 4.00hrs. On the 2nd he went on a 'special mission' (as he wrote: 'strips Cagliaki') flying BR431, from which he returned after 3.00hrs. On the 4th was a short one to PR Catania, Gerdini, Gela, Biscari, Comiso and Pachino it lasted only 1.40hrs. The 5th was longer to carry out a PR of Navazino using BR662, his log book also says: 'Start of flap'. He landed after 3.00hrs. On the early morning of the 6th he flew BR662 to attempt PR of Taranto and returned after 25mins. He took off in BR655 later for a PR of Taranto, which was done in 3.30hrs. On the 7th he took BR655 round on a photographic reconnaissance and returned after 2.10hrs.

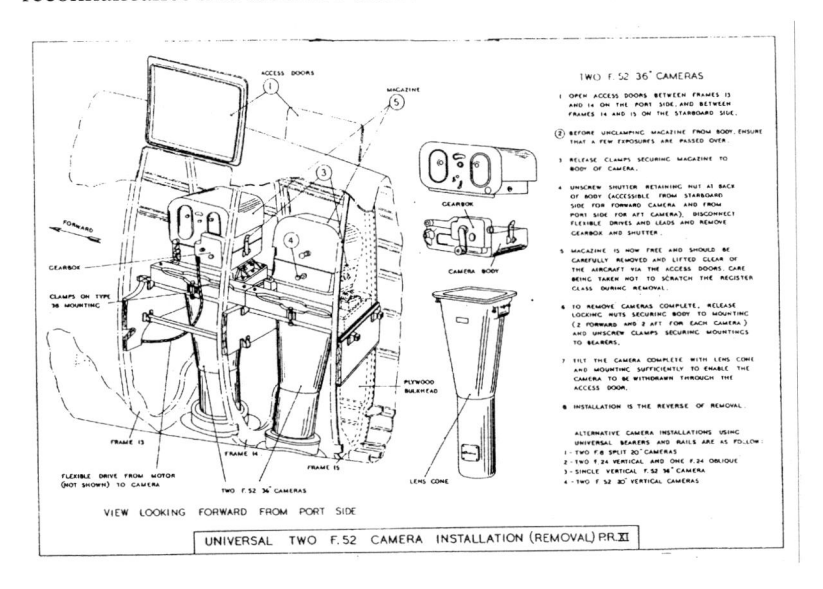

The Spitfire PR.IV and PR.XI camera installations, showing (top) three F.24 and (bottom) two F.52 cameras and how they fit into the rear of the fuselage.

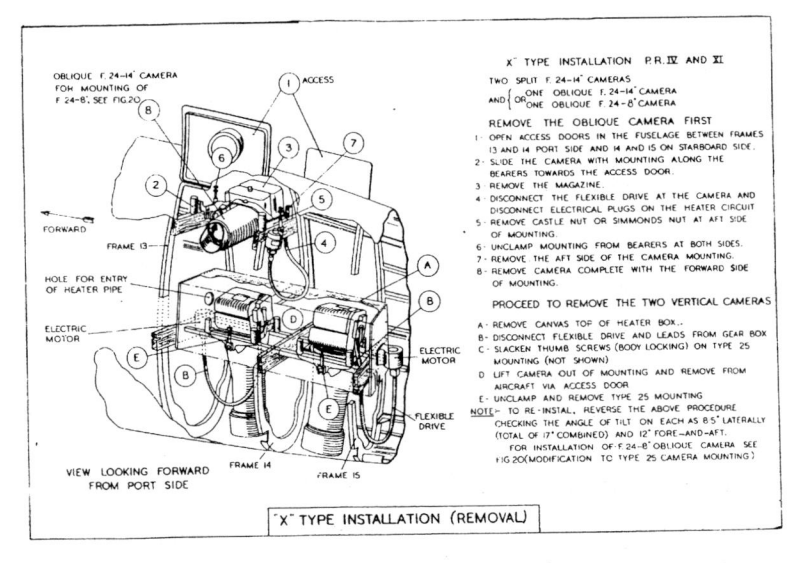

On the 8th he flew a different aircraft, BR662 and carried out a PR of Cagliari, Bizerta, Pantellaria taking off at 05.10 hrs and landing at 08.50 hrs. At Cagliari he saw 5 MVs of 4/5,000 tons and small shipping. Two Me109s climbed to intercept but he had seen them early enough to be able to watch them, and they did not get up to his height. At Bizerta he saw 6 M/Vs of 4,000 tons, 5 D/Rs, 2 probable C/Rs, 2 possible S/Ms and other shipping. There was a little AA and at Pantellaria there was a little small shipping in the harbour. At least 20 twin-engined aircraft on eastern side of drome dispersed about 1 wing length apart. The visibility was good as also was the weather.

In Colquhoun's log book for the 8th he wrote that he would remember it for 'having a cold ride in BR655' because his heating system packed up, though he did carry out his task of photographing Taranto, Messina and Augusta in 2.50hrs. {NB. Something is wrong here. The above flight was of 3.40hrs duration, the aircraft was BR662 and his mission is the wrong one; the Operational Record book reads differently}.

Operation 'Torch' commenced on the 8th November 1942 with the United States Forces beginning landing operations in the early hours of the morning at several points on the shores of North Africa, these operations being assisted by the Royal Navy and Royal Air Force. The objective of the first landings was to capture Casablanca, Oran and Algiers. Lt/Gen Dwight D. Eisenhower was in charge of the operation, requiring American troops to make the first landings at all three objectives. The British would be allowed to take over from the Americans at Algeria.

Les's trip on the 9th November in BR665 was somewhat warmer when he did a photographic reconnaissance of Naples to Palermo, but there was a storm west of Naples, so came down low to 3,000ft and diced with the AA barrage that was put up especially for him, which he commented on as "N.B.G." He was glad to get back after 3.50hrs. The next day, the 10th, he took BR431 for a PR to cover Cagliari from 17,000ft, Elmas and Monserats in 3.30hrs. The 10th was an unhappy day for Colquhoun, because whilst he did a PR of Messina, Naples and Palermo, a colleague of his, F/L R.G. Goldbeck, was being brought down in flames over Augusta. (Later it was heard that he had become a P.O.W.). The trip of Colquhoun's lasted

3.10hrs. The 11th in BP924, he went on a PR to Taranto and carried out obliques at a low altitude of 6,000ft, then to Messina, Catania, Gerbini, Augusta and Palmino, all inside 3.30hrs. Another sortie on the 11th was in BR653 to photograph Messina from 11,000ft, Palermo from 6,000ft and Naples from 18,000ft (the higher the aircraft, the larger the photographic area of coverage).

Flying BR653 on the 12th, he visited Cagliari, Elmas, Monserats, Secimomrino, Villacidea and a new drome near Oristano in 3.10hrs. He used BR653 again on the 13th when he covered Tunis (at 6,000ft) and Bizerta in 2.40hrs.

Elmas aerodrome and seaplane depot, clearly showing 48 aircraft on the airfield and 11 on the water.

On the 12th November British paratroops were dropped by the United States 12th Air Force on the airfield at Bone, 175 miles east of Algiers. The PR sortie on the 14th November in BR663 was a multi-height effort, in that he photographed Pantellaria from 17,000ft, Sfax from 3,000ft and Gabes from 7,000ft in 3.20hrs. BR653 was used on the 15th to take him to Sfax and Gabes on a PR but it could not be accomplished because of 10/10 cloud down to nil feet. When flying over Lampedusa he found the flak very accurate and the trip took 3.05 hrs with a nil result.

P/O F.C.M. Jemmitt failed to return from the mission on the 15th November. In a Telex message from A.H.Q. dated the 16th November 1942, part of it read:

"P/O L.R. Colquhoun (126218) appointed Acting Rank Flight Lieutenant w.e.f. 16/11/42 on taking over P.R.U. Flight 69 Squadron."

Another photograph of Emas Aerodrome, showing long shadows, so that the picture was taken either early morning or evening, with the aircraft more defined.

He also used BR653 on he 17th to go to Sfax, Gabes, Tunis and Pantellaria but the cloud was again in evidence, his VHF radio decided to call it a day as well and so he returned after a 3.30hr flight with nothing. He went out on the 18th using his favourite BR653, to photograph Naples, Messina, Palermo and Empedocle which he accomplished in 3.35hrs. The 19th he flew BS358 for a visual survey of Taranto where the cloud was down to 50ft, and a PR visit Messina where he could film from 5,000ft, and returned after 3.15hrs.

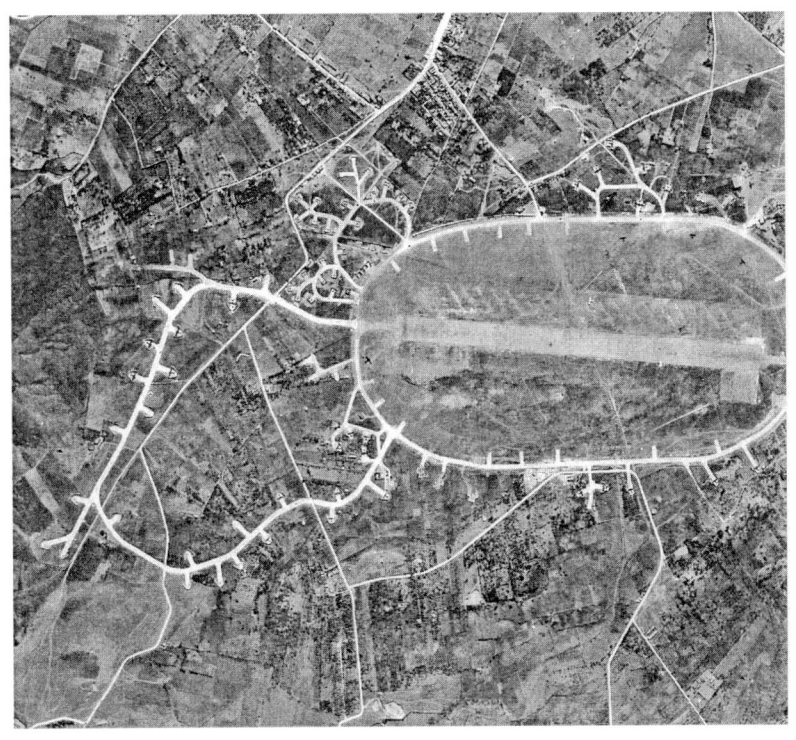

An excellent view of Castel Vetrano Aerodrome, showing 5 aircraft on the airfield and another 39 sheltering in the aircraft bays, in a planned dispersal network.

Les received a telex message as follows from the A.O.C. Malta to F/O Colquhoun after he had returned from Taranto reading:-

"Congratulations to you and your flight for a grand piece of work, especially the Battle Fleet reconnaissances this morning = 2210A/19/11".

As can be seen from this telex he had been promoted to Flying Officer sometime previously.

Tunis Aerodrome with about 60 aircraft dispersed all over the airfield.

He went out in BS424 on the 21st for a visual reconnaissance of Taranto from 5,000ft and oblique photographs of Messina from 2,000ft, he also had a good view of Mount Etna erupting, returning after 3.30hrs.

It was on this day too that they saw W/Cdr Warburton again. He had been shot down by a Me.109 after shooting down a Junkers 88 on his return from Gib. He landed by parachute at Jone with only his pride hurt.

The 23rd was Colquhouns' last flight in BR653 for a while, but he went on a PR of Messina, Naples and sent back a good report, including a 3,000 ton M/V off Messina that he had sighted.

Mount Etna with cloud around the summit, and bare patches indicating heat.

On the 8th November F/Lt R.G. Goldbeck was awarded the D.F.C., but he was shot down by Italian Marine Artillery south of Augusta, Sicily where he had descended to about 4,000ft and his ground speed was about 400mph, on the 10th November 1942. A Marine Artillery shell must have hit his tail because he was catapulted through the canopy slightly injured, but he managed to pull his ripcord and land in the sea. He was rescued by the Italian Navy and made a Prisoner of War. The Italians treated him very humanely, for which he was grateful.

Villacidra airfield showing about 8 aircraft on a hard baked surface.

After all that had accomplished, Les was at last offered the chance to return to the UK for a visit, which he took gladly, and left Malta on the 25th November 1942, in V8222, a Beaufighter IF, which flew to Gibraltar in a time of 5.00hrs. Here he stayed until the 27th when they took off for Perranporth and landed after another flight of 5.00hrs. He did not fly back to Malta in the Beaufighter (which was reported missing on a night patrol with No.603 Squadron on the night of 2nd May 1943). He had a joy ride in a Mosquito on the 1st December. I wonder what he thought of that compared to his Spitfire? On the 4th he flew Spitfire PR.IV BP905 on a camera and consumption test from RAF Benson for 1.40hrs. The following day he flew it to RAF Manston in 1.10hrs ready for staging to Malta. On the 6th he took off and flew to Gibraltar in 4.05hrs, continuing the following day to Malta in 4.40hrs, so only 8.45hrs to Malta.

He was soon back at work, because the next day, the 8th, he was on "his circuit" again, using BS496 to carry out a PR of Taranto from 4,000ft, Messina from 900ft, but it was visual only, because of the weather being so atrocious, he returned having flown for 3.05hrs. An air test of BR426 was carried out on the 9th of 40mins. BR653 was flown by him on the 10th, on a PR mission to Taranto and Messina where 2 c/rs were missing from Messina, returned after 3.05hrs. The 12th was his next flight in BR424 on a PR mission to Messina and Naples in 3.00hrs. A trip in BS426 to carry out a PR of Naples and a visual of Messina from 17,000ft was accomplished in 3.05hrs on the 13th. He was flying BR426 on the 15th on a PR mission to Pantallaria, La Goolette, Tunis docks and Bizerta docks where he encountered a heavy A.A. barrage which did not affect him and back to Malta after 2.45hrs. On the 17th flying in BR424 it was to Lampedusa and Sousse . Aircraft were still burning on the island following an attack by Spitfires on a low level attack, this sortie lasted 2.15hrs only. A happy event in a way happened on the 18th when Colquhoun flying BP905 was on an air test and dinghy search for Sgt Howard who had been shot down. He was overhead when he saw him being picked up and took some photographs of this being done, he was only airborne for 40mins. On the 19th it was BR456 that he flew on a visual mission of 3.05 duration. The 21st was to carry out a PR of Tunis, Sousse and Bizerta but there was 10/10 cloud, so nothing could be done, and nothing was seen, which was 2.05hrs for no results. The 23rd December 1942 was an altitude air test in BS564, all Colquhoun wrote was "O.K." and it took him 1.15hrs.

Another small airfield, Pachino, with only three aircraft in view.

Fly High ~ Fly Low

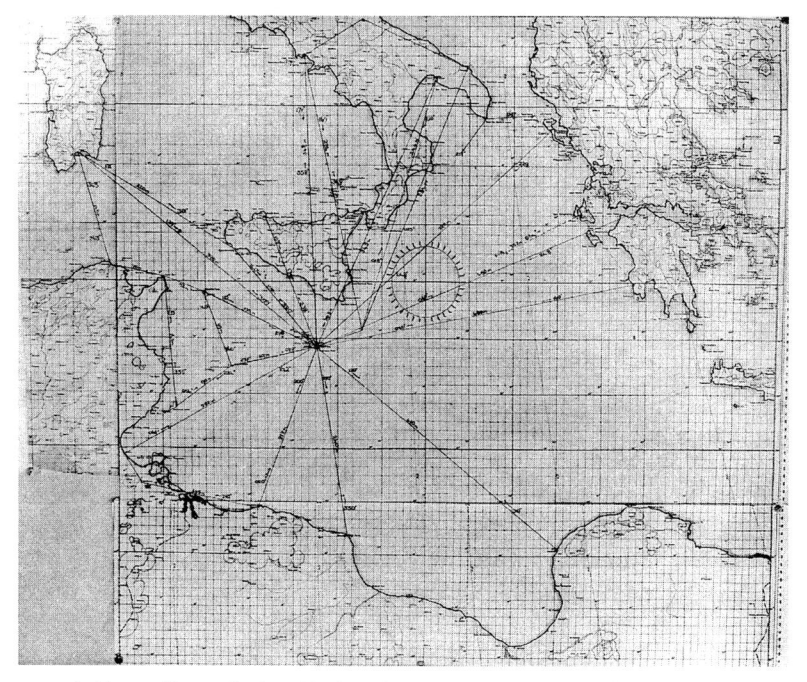

Probably a wall map displayed in the briefing room of No.69 Squadron, showing the places flown to on some of the PR missions and their mileages.

This was the end of the year and W/Cdr Adrian Warburton DSO and bar, DFC and two bars, DFC (USA), OC of No.69 GR Squadron, (this officer had originally been flying Marylands on PR missions from Malta in 1940-41 and had flown over Taranto on the 10th November 1940 flying over the harbour three times at low level bringing back photographs showing 5 battleships, 14 cruisers and 27 destroyers in the harbour. the Swordfish attack the following day sent some of these to the bottom of the harbour, he completed over 300 PR sorties,), wrote his assessment of LR Colquhoun on Posting, with the following comments:

- Proficiency - Above Average
- Remarks - An exceptionally able PR pilot.
- No of sorties flown 154
- No of hours operations 474.15hrs
- Posted to No. 8 C.O.T.U. at Dyce.

Another telex signal was received by the squadron on the 27th December 1942 from SASO AHQ Malta, that read:

"Please convey to Colquhoun, Dalley and Cubb, Air Officer Commanding's appreciation of the very fine work which he has carried out for us in Malta. It is largely due to their courageous and unstinted efforts that recent operations have been so successfully completed. The very best of luck to them in England."

Following this, it is believed about this time, that Les was awarded the DFC (Distinguished Flying Cross) for his PR exploits.

A group of airmen with Les Colquhoun on the extreme left, taken in Malta c1942-43.

6. A second tour of PR work

No.8 (Coastal) Operational Training Unit

Colquhoun was posted to No.8 COTU at Fraserburgh on 5th February 1943, but moved to RAF Dyce on 9th February so that he could have a rest from operational flying and also instruct others on the idiosyncrasies of operational PR flying. He was here from February to October 1943. It had absorbed 'K' flight of No.1 PRU Detling on the 1st August 1942, together with its Spitfire aircraft, and on the 8th February 1943 it officially moved to DYCE. Here its aircraft establishment was 20 +10 Spitfires PRVII/IC/F, 8+2 Spitfire PR.IV and 4 +1 Masters

Colquhoun's first flight at his new unit, was on the 7th February 1943 in Spitfire X4162 'G', a PR 'G' machine (predecessor of the PR.IV) – time airborne 15mins. On the 8th he flew X4335 'F', a PR.IV for 25mins, and then on the 9th he flew X4162 from Fraserburgh to Dyce in 40mins. Next, he flew R7032 on the 11th on a weather test, followed by X4620 on an acceptance test on the 13th for a short 15mins. Local flying with BS357 on the 19th lasted 1.10hrs, whilst on the 20th it was R7032 for a full 1.00hr and another for 30mins on aerobatics and local flying. At last, on the 21st he flew BP925 on a photographic flight to take oblique photographs of the Cairngorms. The flights on the 22nd in X4839, an F.1, and 26th in BR951 (no a/c with this number) were for test and lasted 15mins each. He signed all of these off with the rank of Flying Officer, so that he had lost his Flight Lieutenant on leaving Malta, it was only temporary.

There were a variety of aircraft on the unit and I am sure he must have flown them all in his time with the unit. Here I list the Spitfires he flew for the sake of a few Spitfire enthusiasts:

N3270, N3113, P7324, P8036, P8236, P9385, P9518, R6900, R6902, R6905, R6910, R6986, R7031, R7032, R7059, R7131, R7198, R7234, X4162, X4334, X4335, X4383, X4384, X4505, X4596, X4620, X4832, X4839, X4944, AA784, AA788, AA790, AA794, AB122,

AB302, AB784, AB794, AG122, AR235, AR242, AR257, AR258, AR259, AR261, BP886, BP918, BP929, BR422, BS357, EP395, MB937. Also listed are the other aircraft:- Avro Anson R9808 and EG253.

Miles Master I N7098, N7867, N7992, N8020 and N8022,

Miles Master II W9058, AZ619, DK924, DK964, DL129, DL121, DM133 and DM160.

One other odd aircraft on the unit was a DH Moth Minor HM455, that Colquhoun had to have a flight in, on the 6th March 1943. Other "odd" flights that he carried out whilst he was on 8 OTU included:- 2nd June he flew Spitfire P8236 and took some oblique photographs of Aberdeen, on the 20th flying Spitfire P9518 he did a "Wings for Victory" beat up of Ballater and Braemar, then on the 22nd he did the same again: flying X4944 a "Wings for Victory" beat up of Insch, another of Huntley flying Spitfire R7032 on the 27th. His most unusual passenger that he had ever flown with, was on the 11th July when he flew the Padre in a Tiger Moth to Fordown, which took 25 minutes and bringing him back the same day in 20mins.

X4620 A Spitfire F.1 converted to PR.VII, to No.8OTU on the 4th February 1943 and FACE same day, to HAL 14th August 1944 and finally FACE on the 25th August.

In the meantime, in Malta, B Flight of No. 69 Squadron became a squadron on its own, when on the 1st February 1943 it became No. 683 Squadron under W/Cdr A. Warburton. The following month a new Commanding Officer arrived to take over No. 69 Squadron who was S/Ldr R.C. MacKay.

During 1943 and Colquhoun's absence the following major events took place:-

- on the 10th April 1943 the 8th Army entered Sfax, Tunisia
- on the 18th April there was a "turkey shoot" when British and US fighters shot down 52 of 100 German Junkers Ju.52 transport aircraft off Cape Bon, Tunisia. This was followed on the 19th when 12 more of them were shot down.
- on the 22nd the Germans brought out their biggest and newest transport plane the Me.323 and sent a large formation again to try to reinforce their troops in North Africa, nearly all of these were destroyed as well.
- The allied air forces now had air supremacy, and on the 28th, the allied aircraft bombed Naples and sank ships between Sicily and Tunisia.
- on the 7th May the troops entered Bizerta and Tunis. In the South Mediterranean area, the Axis forces in Tunisia surrendered on the 14th May 1943, and then the Allies had captured Sicily, invading it on the 10th July 1943 with complete occupation by the 17th August, after only 38 days fighting.

The invasion of Italy had commenced on the 3rd September 1943, crossing from Sicily onto the 'toe' of Italy.

No.682 SQUADRON

After this period as an instructor, Colquhoun was posted to No.682 Squadron, which had been formed from No.4 PRU at Maison Blanche, Algeria, on 1st February 1943, for Photographic Reconnaissance in the Western and Central Mediterranean. The squadron moved to La Marsa, Italy on the 6th June 1943 and on the 8th December 1943 moved to San Severo.

On the 20th September 1943, Colquhoun flew down to RAF Benson in Spitfire PR.XI, EP395, for leave, before proceeding on an overseas posting to No.682 Squadron at La Marsa, Tunisia, which was now in the North African Photographic Reconnaissance Wing (NAPRW) of the Mediterranean Air Command, together with the US 3rd Photographic Group. This wing was under the command of Lt/Col Elliot Roosevelt (son of the US President) who had only arrived in Freetown, Africa in April 1942 in a Boeing B.17 Flying Fortress for photographic missions over the Canary Islands, Cape Verde Islands, Senegal and the Ivory Coast. He was accused of resenting any British Domination of the USAAF activities, even though the British were more experienced and had the well tried and tested photographic equipment. No.682 Squadron was commanded by S/Ldr A.H.W. "Freddie" Ball, and in Malta an extra squadron was now No. 683 Squadron under W/Cdr A. Warburton. The NAPRW had distinct boundaries of the area west of longitude 12 degrees East which included the islands of Sardinia and Corsica, the area East of this line was covered by 683 Sqdn and 69 Sqdn

In the meantime, the Italians surrendered in September 1943, but this was not seen as a victory, because the Germans effectively filled most of the important positions almost immediately.

On return from leave, he returned to RAF Benson and flew Spitfire PR.XI MB937 to RAF Portreath on the 23rd October 1943 in 1.10hrs. He flew on the 25th from here to Gibraltar in 3.15hrs, continuing the same day to Maison Blanche in 2.20hrs and then the following day on to El Adjina in 1.45hrs, and he was back in the Middle East.

At La Marsa No.682 Squadron, flew missions over Tunisia and Italy from Algeria, moving to San Severo in Italy on the 8th December 1943. With the advance of the allied forces, it was decided to reorganize the Mediterranean Air Command, and on the 30th October 1943 the British 336 Wing was formed under the NAPRW at La Narsa, Tunisia. No. 680 Sqdn was in Egypt, 682 Sqdn at La Marsa flying Spitfire PR.XIs and PR.IVs, 683 Sqdn in Malta, now with Mosquito PR.IVs and Spitfire PR.XIs and 60 (SAAF) Sqdn at Ariana, Tunisia with Mosquito PR.VIs and PR.IXs all commanded by W/Cdr A. Warburton, who had by now accomplished 390 sorties. He had become our ACE PR expert, and I would have thought that all PR pilots accomplishing greater than 100 missions should have been classified as Aces too.

NOVEMBER 1943

Colquhoun's first flight, and first mission with the squadron, (his 155th), was to cover Coastal pin-points at San Stefano to Greta in Spitfire PR.XI BN422 on the 1st November 1943, which he covered in 4.00hrs.

He flew on the 3rd November in EN677 from La Marsa to El Aouina in 15mins. His next mission was using MB937, on 5th to B.D.A. pinpoints Rome and San Stefano area (BDA I am afraid I have no idea) returning after 4.10hrs. His mission on the 11th, in BN422, were pin points in North Central Italy and Florence in 4.05hrs. There was a spell then, when Colquhoun did no flying until the 22nd. He then flew BN422 from Sidi Amor to El Aouina in 25mins, and on the 25th he flew MB937 from El Aouina to Ajaccio in Corsica in 1.50hrs, (in the ORB it states that he took off at 1010 and landed at 1715 but I cannot see that he flew this length of time, I prefer the log book entry). He flew a PR of Gorgoua Islands, Leghorn, Pisa/Albayow, A/Ds of the town, San Guisto A/D, Viareggio, Spezia Port, Vezzano bridge, NE Shezia, Sarsamo A/D, Lucca A/D, Piastoia A/D and town, Cesina A/D and town, Camfuglia, Marrtina A/D and Piombino Port and M/Y, which shows how restricted the log book entries normally can be). He probably refuelled and then went on a mission to BDA Spezia to Leghorn, Pisa, Pistoria and return El Aouina in 4.10hrs. In BN422 on the 29th he attempted a PR of Pin Points at Gaetta and south of Rome, but actually photographed Ascoli, Teramo town and Picento town, in 3.45hrs, because the weather was completely unsuitable in the first areas. (In the ORB the date is given as the 30th).

DECEMBER 1943

On 1st December 1943 Les flew BN422 on a photographic reconnaissance of Pin Points at Sienna, Rome M/Y, Capronica, Orvieto and Arcidosso A/D, Malignano A/D, Pien del Lago A/D, Asciano RRJ, Arezzo A/d, Castiglione del Lago SPB, Perugia and Lalero RJ in the longest time yet of 4.25hrs. In the ORB he is put down as Flying Officer Colquhoun but he was not gazetted until the 2nd January 1943.

F/Lt Colquhoun with his Operations officer studying the map of Italy and his arm indicating the East coast possibly telling Colquhoun of his next mission. (Photo K Colquhoun)

As is the case when an army advances, the bases are left behind, and so more bases are required nearer to the front line, and in this case it meant that No.682 Squadron had to find a location to set up base again. On the 12th December 1943 the main party of No.682 Squadron left Bizerta Staging Camp and embarked on the HMS LST427 under the command of S/Ldr J. Morgan DSO, and arrived at San Severo the same day, the place selected from which to commence operations.

He started his 161st mission on the 13th in EN331, to El Aouina to Foggia No.7 but had to turn back at Cape Bon because his engine was cutting, but airborne for 35mins. He flew EN331 El Aouina to Foggia No.7 on the 15th in 2.45hrs, returning to Foggia No.1 in 10mins on the same day. In the ORBs for that day there is a different story, which was that he went on a PR to Pantellaria harbour and aerodrome, La Goulet, Tunis harbour and aerodrome. His visual showed 1 M/V of 6,000 tons in dry docks. All were photographed. Bizerta aerodrome, part of the docks and outer harbour were photographed. There was very heavy and accurate flak and smoke screen over the harbour from about 15 generators. Tunis and 30 miles out he saw 3 fleet D/Rs, another about 25 miles North cruising slowly round an oil patch. There was some yellow scum in parts of the oil patch. For this mission the visibility and weather were good.

It was not until the 23rd that he carried out mission No.161 using MB888, when he covered the coastal strip Orbatello and Civalivecchio in 2.35hrs. His last mission of the month was in EN331 to Rome aerodrome and Pin Points, he encountered slight flak at Guildonia returning after 3.00hrs.

JANUARY 1944

On the 3rd January 1944 Colquhoun carried out his 163rd mission, flying EN331 to Pin Points at Pescara, Ancona, Bastia and Spoleto with light flak coming up at him from Guildonia, he landed after 2.15hrs. When he returned he flew EN441 from Foggia No.1 to San Severo in 30mins. On the 6th he flew MB940 to Fiume port and pinpoints in the Alps and Padua (the ORB records to Fiume, Avisio, Dogna, Ossopo A/D, Aviano LG (Landing Ground), Padua M/Y and town, railroads, bridges, ammo dumps and pin points), landing after 3.25hrs.

The 8th, and it was EN414, to Orvirto, Piomouino, Portoforram, Devechia and Rome aerodromes in 2.50hrs. It was to Specia, Ravenna, Anlong, Denedet and Guildonia with BB940 on the 12th, the weather was poor and flak was experienced at Guildonia, he landed afer 3.00hrs. A quick one followed on the 16th, a 1.35hr flight to cover Rome and Mosasc. Two air tests followed, of EN331 and EN414 on the 18th and 20th of 45mins each. A long flight of 3.40hrs on the 21st to Pola, Trieste, Venice, Aviano and pinpoints. One aircraft seen at 20,000ft over Venice but it did not interfere with the return to base.

On the 22nd January 50,000 troops of the Anglo-American Fifth Army landed at Anzio, 30 miles south of Rome and established a beach-head, but on the 24-25th German aircraft sank the British hospital ship "St. David", which was evacuating injured allied troops from the Anzio beach-head, and many of our troops were drowned. The German Air Force were afraid to fly during the day because of the allied air superiority, so had to fly at night, so our troops were being shot up and bombed during night time

He went to Milan on the 25th and the surrounding pinpoints in EN414, but could not take any photographs because of bad weather being 10/10ths, he returned after 2.20hrs. A communication flight using MB888, was flown on the 26th from San Severo to Vasta, Italy, and he then turned around and came back the same day, flying 15mins each way.

FEBRUARY 1944

On the 2nd February 1944 682 Squadron received its first Spitfire PRXI, PA854, which arrived from the UK, followed by another one, MB897 on the 4th. Another item listed under squadron activities was the fact that they had collected £312 for the National Savings Contribution from November 1943 to date.

On the 3rd February 1944 he was able to take a Fairchild 24W-41A Argus FS641 for a flight (this was one of 161 such aircraft, FS500-FS660) obtained from the USA for observation duties. Also with him was S/Ldr Morgan the CO. This flight was only a familiarisation local flight of 15 minutes.

He flew Spitfire PR.XI, PA854, from San Severo to Luqa on the 4th February in 1.50hrs and returned the same day in 1.45hrs. On the 6th he flew PA854 on a mapping run over Pistoia and Bologna areas in 3.00hrs. This was followed on the 10th in the same aircraft by a coastal strips sortie of Zara to South Dubrovnik, Yugoslavia, (ORB as follows:- PR Ulijan Island, strip south of Zara, area north and south of Sibenik, Vela Luka (west strip), Brag (east strip). Makarska (area), Mijet Island (east strip), Dubrovnik area, Gulf of Kotor and port area. 1 MV app 3,000 tons believed 1m south of Tivat (43.25N 18.43E) with tug and small vessels plying between Tiver and Tara, 1 MV 2,000 tons and smaller vessel sighted in Dubrovnik Creek). It was on this trip that Colquhoun was air sick for the first time ever, regardless of this horrible catastrophe, especially if he was using his oxygen mask, he would have to suffer the horrible smell for the rest of the sortie, that you have with this malfunction but he still flew it for 3.05hrs. It does not seem to have affected him, because on the 14th he used MB897 to fly to Celina Bridges, Leghorn and run into a Boeing Fortress raid on Prato, but no results were seen or recorded because of cloud, his flight of 3.10hrs was for nothing. On the 16th he flew MB671 from San Severo to Pomilgliano in 25mins, then took off to photograph the strips of Cassino 5th Army front from 15,000ft, in 1.10hrs, back to Pomilgliano and take off again for San Severo, in 1.10hrs and 20mins.

It was on the 15th February that the ancient monastery on Monte Cassino, was bombed and destroyed by 222 American aircraft and Fifth Army artillery. It was thought that the Germans were using it as a defensive position, which they were not, but immediately after the bombing they moved in. It took until the 18th May for Polish forces to occupy the derelict buildings.

His last flight of the month was on the 25th February, in PA895, into new territory in Austria covering all but two of the twelve targets briefed, which were mainly industrial units. He flew and covered Fiume Port where he saw large formations of Flying Fortresses flying South, escorted by fighters which he thought were Thunderbolts and which turned as if to make a quarter attack.

Colquhoun did not respect the Americans aircraft recognition so took evasive action, flying east into Yugoslavia, when the pursuit was broken off. Also, during this period two unidentified aircraft flew over the top of him making trails at 26,500ft and flying north, a hairy time one way or the other. He continued on to Klagenfurt T.N. Factory where he saw no trace of smoke or recent damage at 12.45hrs. Then to Leuben-Donawitz where he saw 5 groups of Fortresses flying south. Onto Sunjarr Junction, Bruk an der Mur, Bruk-Karfenburg, then to Graz/Thalerhof where he only carried out one run over A.D. due to the presence of a FW.190 fighter, which hampered his photography, but there was no interception. To Donji/Skopje A.D, then onto Leuben to take photographs of the steelworks and blast furnaces, before continuing to Donawitz, and Bruk-Kapfenburg for the gun barrel and cable works, followed by the lead and zinc mines at Bleiburg, and after all this, he returned safely after 3.30hrs.

Mission 170, was in MB888, on the 27th February to Rieti, Terni, Perugia, Siena, Florence, Pistoia and area at Leghorn strip at Castelmauro. He encountered flak over Perugia and his starboard camera packed up after about 100 exposures, he landed after 3.30hrs. On the 28th he flew to Vasta again in MB890 taking 15mins. He intended to fly MB888 on the 30th to Spezia, Pisa, Leghorn, Piomino and Siena but he had to return because of engine trouble landing after only 25mins. He flew MB937 on the 30th as well, this time to Spelia, Pisa, Leghorn, Piomino and Siena. He could only manage photographs of Arcidosa, because in the other targets the weather was 10/10 of Strato Cumulus, time on this one was 2.35hrs.

MARCH 1944

He flew MB940 on the 6th March 1944 to cover a strip south of Genoa and south of Spezia also Orbetello and railway, Monte Castrelto, the weather was terrible returning after 3.15hrs. His last trip for March was flying PA905 to Udine, Ossoppo, Villaoba and Maniago, a radar station at Pula, at Venice there was part cloud cover and Pulo, Trieste and Pola there was complete cloud cover with intermittent flak at Pula. He returned after 3.05hrs.

It was during this month that saw his promotion to the rank of Flight Lieutenant.

He carried out no flying in April 1944, the first complete month without any since he joined the RAF. (It was on the 12th that W/Cdr Warburton, now flying Lockheed F-5B PR aircraft with the USAF went on a PR trip to Schweinfurt in Germany from which he failed to return).

MAY 1944

In May however Colquhoun carried out 10 sorties of varying sorts. The first of these was on the 2nd May when he flew PA911 to Vicenzo, Bolzano, Belluno, Aviano, Ossoppo, Maniago and Villaorbo. No pictures taken because of cloud at 20,000ft but he encountered heavy flak at Villaorbo, but returned safe after 3.35hrs. His 180th mission was on the 4th when he flew PA910 for a PR of the marshalling yards in Florentine plain and Bologna, Rimini and Ancoma in 2.50hrs. The 5th was just an air test of 30mins in PA905, and the 8th he flew PL760, (which was a new PR.XI arrived in the MAAF on the 25th March 1944), to and from Pomigliano in 50mins. The 10th he flew PA911 on a PR of Villafranca, Sergnano, Gedi, Milan on A/Ds and M/Y, Vericelli and Turin. (A/D and M/Y are unknown). He landed after 3.10hrs with no tail wheel, and all he had to write about that was "dam!!!". He flew San Severo to Alghero, Sardinia on the 14th in 1.55hrs in PA905 and on the 16th he flew a PR to Toulouse, France on A/Ds and took 3.30hrs. He used PA905 on the 17th to carry out a PR of the A/Ds of Lyon, M/Ys of Gnonne, St Etienne, Vienn, Valance and Schom in 3.35hrs, and using the same aircraft on the 18th he returned Alghero to Severo in 1.40hrs. This had been in association with the US 5th Photographic Group who were carrying out reconnaissance flights of the south coast of France, preparatory to an invasion by the US 5th Army. The invasion took place on the 14/15 August 1944 with the landings being almost unopposed, because the German troops were fighting the D-Day landings on the north coast.

On the 21st May 1944 he flew Spitfire PR.XI PA760, to Southern France returning after 2.55hrs. He flew MB888 on the 24th to Turin

A/Ds and M\Ys, Alesion, Piacenza Italy, Reggio and Emilia on A/Ds in 3.50hrs. Then on the 26th in PA786 he went to survey coastal strips Niece to Tenca and Piacenza in 3.40hrs. The sortie on the 29th was a visit to carry out a PR of Klatenfurt and Steyk taking him 3.30hrs. On the 30th he started out on a mission to Milan in PA911, but returned with engine plug trouble after 40mins. After he landed he got into PA760 and carried out his mission in 3.55hrs. His assessment for May 1944 now reads:

- PR pilot – Exceptional
- As pilot-navigator above the average.

The squadron was based at San Severo during this time and the station was extremely busy with the photographic staff working night and day, developing the returned films and producing high resolution prints for the different service departments. Besides the RAF photographers, who numbered about 100, there were the No.60 (SAAF) Sqdn with their own department and, also, the San Severo American squadrons had to have their own departments too.

It was also during this month, on the 5th, that American bombers based in Italy attacked and bombed the huge oil refineries at Ploesti in Rumania

JUNE 1944

June was to be a fairly busy month for Colquhoun with 15 missions that he covered. It started off with a simple air test on PA905 of 15mins on the 1st, and then taking it on the 2nd on a PR mission to Cangola, Trento, Bolzano, Joine and Gozilia with M/Ys of Laviano, all this covered in 3.30hrs. Air test on PL760 on the 2nd, of 25mins, and then taking it on mission No.190, a PR of Rome and coastal strips at Orbetello. Last photograph of German occupied Rome, taking 2.25hrs to complete.

On the night of the 4/5th June Rome, was occupied by the allied forces, the Germans had evacuated it previously.

The 6th JUNE 1944 was D-day when the greatest invasion force in history, embarked on boats or were dropped from the air on German occupied Europe to free the oppressed people, some of whom had been suffering for five years. 35 divisions and 4,000 ships assembled in the ports and camps, 150,000 men being available for the invasion. 11,000 aircraft were ready, 8,000 of them available for the immediate assault.

By D+20 the British had 93,000 vehicles and 450,000 men ashore, whilst the Americans had 96,000 vehicles and 452,000 men.

It was also during this month that the Italian city of Rome was occupied by allied troops, so now the noose was around Hitler's neck.

Air test on EN786 on the 7th of 30mins followed on the same day with a PR sortie in PA867 to Vologna, Farli and bridges south of Bolana, but the weather was cloudy but the sortie took 2.45hrs. A visit on the 8th, in PA895, to PR Cividivecchia port where he arrived too late, because the British had captured it, so he returned after 1.25hrs. An air test on the 9th in EN786 of 50mins and on the 10th using MB895 he flew to Venice, Maestre, Joine, Trieste, Plesi and strip on Isle of Rab, and he saw fires still burning at Maestre and Trieste, all this covered in 3.10hrs.

A different mission was called for on 13th June 1944, and MB895 was the aircraft, which went on it, to carry out Mapping of Elba and Pianosa islands, accomplished in 2.45hrs. His next mission was on the 15th flying PA905 on a PR to cover Imperia, Genoa, Spezia and Allessandria but his camera system failed and returned to base after 3.25hrs. On the 16th in PA960 on a PR he visited Padua, Viacenza, Tremto, Bolzano, Morizia and Udine, but had to return after Viacenza because of engine trouble, after 2.30hrs. His next flight was just an air test on PL760 of 15mins. Another operation was on the 21st in PA905 on a PR to Ferrara, Modena, Parma, Reggio, Piacenza, Crescia and Verona on M/Ys and Piacenza, Reggio, Ferrara, Piaggio No.1 and 2, Bovola, Shedi A/Ds roads and Ferrara and coast in 3.30hrs. He went out again in PA905 on the 23rd for a PR to the Poza Peninsular and Undine area but there was 10/10 cloud and he took pictures of Polo and Monofallone only and returned after 2.45hrs. The 25th was a trip in MB890 for a PR of the Arsa Channel, Fiume, Trieste and Yugoslavian islands. He had camera trouble and returned after 3.05hrs.

His 200th sortie was on the 26th June, flying PA960, on a PR to Bad Aibling and Munich A/Ds, Augsburg M/Y and A/D of further targets abandoned owing to presence of enemy fighters, he did fly for 3.35hrs. The 28th he flew PA895 on a weather sortie and attempt PR targets around the Turin area but no pictures were possible, though flying time was 3.00hrs. He took PA895 the next day on a PR to Padua for M\Ys and areas arpund Ravenna and Vicenza and roads around Lake Garda in 3.30hrs. His kast mission of the month was flying PA911 on a PR of Aulla and Levigaldi M\Ys, Airasca, Turin/Aeritalia A/D, Chivasso BDA, Casaibianco landing ground but others abandoned owing to oxygen trouble, his flying time was 3.45hrs.

JULY 1944

During July 1944 Colquhoun carried out another 13 missions, his first being on the 2nd flying PA895 on a PR to Villach, Austria and Klagenfurt, Austria M/Ys and a pinpoint 3 miles south of Klagenfurt, Austria, another target but there was 10/10 cloud and after 3.10hrs nothing to show for it. He used MB938 the following day to carry out a PR mission (No.205) to railways at Belluno, Italy and near Innsbruck, Austria and M\Ys in 3.25hrs. Next day, the 4th, he took PA911 and tried to carry out a PR of the River Danube near Budapest, Hungary and area, but was unsuccessful due to 10/10 cloud in the area, returning in 3.25hrs. The 5th was an air test day when he flew EN658 for 1.15hrs on an acceptance test. The 6th he flew a Fairchild Argus again, FS614, for 10mins, on a checking out test. The 7th he took MB938 on a PR to Zagreb, Yugoslavia A/Ds and M\Ys, Vienna, Austria A/Ds, Graz, Austria A/O and Celje, Slovenia and Kralovdc M\Vs, taking him 3.40hrs. A rest for a couple of days then on the 10th he flew PA910 on a PR of Viacenzo A/D, Bolzano M/Ys to do a clean up of defence surveys and cloud obscured the rest of the targets landing after 3.20hrs. The 11th he just flew an air test on PA905.

PR Aerial Surveys on the 14th, using MB897, of Padua, Vilena and Schid-Asiago areas, Vilenza A/D Trento A\Ds and buildings, the latter taken only, because of 10/10 cloud cover, in 2.50hrs. His 210th mission on the 15 flying PA911 was to the Danube ports Vapuror, Apatin Yugoslavia, Mohal, Baja Hungary, Kis Kan, Haslar and Sjerba on A\Ds, in 3.00hrs. His next mission was on the 19th using MB888, to carry out Mapping of Maestre-Treviso area, Loine, Cariza, Trieste M\Ys and Gorizia A/D in 3.30hrs. On the 20th he flew MB890 on a Cover of B/S lying in Capodistre Gulf from a height of 14,000ft, this took him 2.00hrs. He was tasked on the 24th to cover the roads in the Alps and radar sites in the Udine plain, he flew PA911, but he encountered 10\10 cloud and returned after 3.05hrs. On the 26th in PA911, he flew for 3.45hrs covering the roads in the Alps near Innsbruck. Again using PA911, and on his 215th mission, on the 28th he covered the roads and certain areas in Yugoslavia in 3.30hrs. Changing his aircraft to PA905 on the 31st, he covered the Po Valley on pinpoints, only three were possible in 3.30hrs.

AUGUST 1944

The month of August and Colquhoun carried out 11 further missions. The first being on the 3rd in PA905, to cover pin points and A/Ds in Udine and the Po Valley area of North Eastern Italy, the hydraulic pump sheared, so on landing he had the indignity of landing with his tail in the up position, with slight damage to the rudder as well, his flying time was 3.55hrs. He carried out an air test on EN422 of 1.00hr, on the 4th, followed on the 5th, with a flight in EN414 to cover an 'A' priority target on the Yugoslavian Islands, taking only 1.10hrs. He took PA905 on the 6th, to cover Pola Yugoslavia, Grada, Capodistre and Fiume Yugoslavia, ports, Villaorba A/D and San Pietra M/Ys in 2.55hrs. He flew MB888 from San Severo to Ancona on the 9th in 45mins, and continued on the same day to Ancona where he attempted to cover roads in the Vienna area, but turned back at Pola because of a ropey engine, landing back at base after 1.05hrs safely. He took MB890 on the 11th for his 220th mission to cover areas of Lake Como and north of Bergamo, BDA at Trento and taking 4.00hrs to landing. These surveys continued on the 12th in PA905, flying to areas and roads around Golzao and HXD Lake Garda in 3.30hrs.

Such was the improvement in the Mediterranean area that Winston Churchill, our Prime Minister, was able to fly from Algiers to Naples to see Marshall Tito of Yugoslavia on the 11th August and afterwards flew on Ajaccio, Corsica to see the troops there. At 8am on the 15th August, landings between Cannes and Hyeres, Southern France began, with over 400 gliders taking part and 9,000 airborne troops in the landing. Opposition on the ground was negligible and the landing was a success. 2,000 aircraft had been moved to Sicily for the operation, at least 400 being transport type for glider towing. Churchill knew of this and wanted to be there for the kick off, and watched the landings in St Tropez bay from the British destroyer HMS "Kimberley". He flew back to Naples on the 16th and then visited the battle front along the River Arno in Italy.

He used EN658 on the 13th August to visit Lake Garda and Dolgano Merano areas and roads in 3.25hrs. The next day with the same aircraft he went to Lavariana, Compoformiom, Villaoma for A\Ds, Udine, Norhern Italy, for M/Ys and mapping strips in 3.30hrs. His next mission in PA910, was an attempted sortie to Linz, Northern Austria, but had to return after 30mins because of having no electrical system in the aircraft. The problem was sorted out after he had landed so he took off again on a mission to St Valentin tank works, Herman Goring tank works at Linz, Eferding A/D returns after 3.40hrs. His 225th mission was on the 23rd in EN331 for mapping Arems, Golzano, Lake Garda, Teents area that was accomplished in 3.25hrs. Colquhoun used PA910 on the 26th to take him on a PR of Bros M/Y and oil refinery, Osijek oil ref. Sarajevo, Yugoslavia A/D and returned after 3.00hrs. After he returned, he carried out an air test on PA905 of 15mins. His last mission for August was on the 31st, in PA905, on a PR of Fiume etc which took him 3.30hrs.

SEPTEMBER 1944

September he only accomplished eight missions, targets may have been getting more difficult to find. On the 2nd he flew EN414 in 1.45hrs from San Silvera to Le Luc de Grande Bastiele, returning on the following day in 1.40hrs. On the 4th he carried out another liaison visit using PL857, to fly from San Severo to Bari and back the same day in 30 and 15mins respectively. He went on his 228th mission on the 5th in PA905, on a PR to Paverazzi A/D, Venegona A/D, Strip area Gravedonna–Castella mapping of roads and Ravenna M/Y and Port, He wrote "Cords around Lake Como and Lake Gacoa", in 3.25hrs. He had his first flight in the latest in PR technology, when he took RM640, Spitfire PR.XIX, on a camera test, on the 8th, but the emergency landing oil pressure gauge failed so he landed after only 15 minutes. [This aircraft was delivered to RAF Benson on the 23rd May 1944 but failed to return from operations on the 9th February 1945.] This must have been fixed, because he took it up again on the 9th, on a camera test, which lasted for 40mins.

He used this aircraft on the 10th on a PR to Munich aerodromes, but it was impossible to take pictures in 10/10 visibility in Strato Cumulus cloud, he landed after 2.45hrs. For his 230th mission he took PL763, a PR.IX, on the 11th on a PR to cover Tekkarh M/Ys, Ravena M/Y and Port, Ferrara M/Ys and BDs, Grado, Monfalcone, and Trieste Ports, and Gorizia M\Ys, all in Italy and the other targets were under cloud, which he covered in 2.40hrs.

MB777 required a camera test on the 12th, which lasted for 40mins, and on the 13th he flew PL763 on a DWECHAT on ref. CSPOD A/D Oberhosdorf, Zagreb A/D, Kiriloves A/D and area near Vienna covering it in 3.35hrs. On the 16th he flew a XIX, RM639, to cover aerodromes at Munich, Rheim, Schlesheim, Ingolstadt and Neuberg, Germany, in 3.15hrs. On the 19th he was using MB890 for mapping Gorizia, Trieste area and Graud, Monfalcome, Parenzo, Cantania and Gorizia M/Ys in 3.00hrs. Another mission on the 23rd was in RM639 of an attempted BDA of Munich M/Ys, A/Ds and Allach fty [sic] but no pictures because the weather was 10/10 strato cumulus, the trip lasting for 3.10hrs [the fty is not understood].

Colquhoun's 235th mission was on the 26th September in EN658 to cover Zara, Razanas, Jablanac, Klagenfurt, Jesenice, Zagreb A/Ds and M\Ys in 3.10hrs. A simple flight on the 30 was to fly to Brindisi in PA910, in 40mins.

The allied forces by now were occupying about three quarters of Italy, and on the 21st September they occupied the town of Rimini, near San Marino, which is on the Adriatic coast.

Les's total operational hours up to the present were 734hrs 50mins.

OCTOBER 1944

October was his last operational flying period, and started on the 1st with the worst day that the Squadron had ever experienced with continuous and heavy rain, a Deep Depression was the cause in the Gulf of Taranto. His first flight was a local flight in PL771, and then on the 4th he had to load the aircraft with two 36 inch F.52 cameras for his last operational sortie flying PL763 on a run to cover the Adige River and lower canal in Central Po Valley, that was required for a study of flooding, and Ravanna M/y and the short canal to Porto Corsim was also done, taking 2.40hrs. After he had landed, he took off again on an air test of PL760, of 30mins, and then on the 12th, an air test on PA900 of 40mins.

On his last night on the squadron it seems that the "Mess gave him the usual send off" which of course implied that he was the main reason for it and plenty of alcohol would have been consumed on the premises.

His total tours were two, total trips or sorties were 236 and total operation flying hours were 737.30. His total flying as pilot was 1,077.10hrs daytime and 11.15hrs night flying, and he ended this period of his life with the DFM and the DFC.

With effect from (w.e.f.) 16th October 1944 Les was posted to No.8 COTU Dyce, where he had been previously. Just to show that he was 'back to square one', here are his flights for the month of November 1944…

He first flew Spitfire PR.XI EN154 on the 26th for 45mins on air test, then on the 29th he took up EN652 for 30mins, followed by another flight in EN552 of 20mins, and then he took up a Spitfire F.XIV MV308 for 30mins. His last flight was in a DH Mosquito T.III which was flown by F/Lt Mortimer with Colquhoun in the jump seat as passenger, lasted for 40mins.

A beautiful view above the clouds of a banking Spitfire F.XIV

DECEMBER 1944

December was somewhat similar, in that it seemed as if he was just having fun. He flew in Master II DM133 on the 1st with F/Lt McNillan for 45mins to check his dual rating, and then by F/Lt Spurgeon for 50mins for the same thing. On the 3rd he flew Spitfire EN652 on "A Home Guard beat up", which he probably enjoyed, on the 13th it was EN154 for 15mins air test, followed by EN416 on the 19th for 20mins and BS357 on the 31st for 25mins. His final flight with the unit was on 6th January 1945 in Spitfire PR.XI which he wrote down as number 19 from Dyce to Haverford West in 1.40hrs.

7. Vickers Supermarine Test Pilot

Les Colquhoun was posted to Vickers Aircraft (Supermarine) Ltd at High Post, near Salisbury, as a service test pilot, on secondment, in February 1945, under the Supermarine chief test pilot, Geoffrey Quill, with Spitfire experience, on secondment, because Supermarine were short of production pilots. This was the way that the Air Ministry sometimes worked, by helping out the aircraft factories with experienced pilots. Colquhoun said that this was one of the high lights of his life when he knew that he had been selected for the post.

I shall not be putting down many of his flights from Supermarine, because they built 22,500 Seafires and Spitfires and all of them had to be test flown, and it would only be repetition, so I shall only insert his more interesting flights. His first flight with his new firm was in a Spitfire F.XIV, on the 12th February 1945, which he put down the number only as 851 for a 5min test flight. (This was most probably RM851). He blotted his copy book on the 17th February 1945 (his 6th flight with them) by pranging it on landing, this was Spitfire HF.IX RR206, it was probably repaired without any trouble, and was accepted by CFE on the 10th May 1945. This was probably a pecking, whereby he applied the brakes too harshly or too quickly and the aircraft tipped up on its nose and damaged the propeller, this did happen a lot to inexperienced pilots, so Colquhoun must have felt like an idiot, at the home of the Spitfire too. Actually the airfield was an ex Flying Club airfield and was in a sodden state and Geoffrey Quill also did the same thing, sinking up to his axles, so Les was in good company.

7TH MAY 1945 – GERMANY SURRENDERS

Les was married on the 23rd June 1945 at St Stephen's Church, Ealing to Katie Penty, living in Salisbury for a short time before moving to Chilbolton near Andover. Here, three of their four daughters were born, twins Helen and Jane, followed by Peta, whilst the last one, Sally was born at Blunsdon, near Swindon, after Vickers/Supermarine had moved to South Marston works.

Les and Katie, married on 23 June 1945.

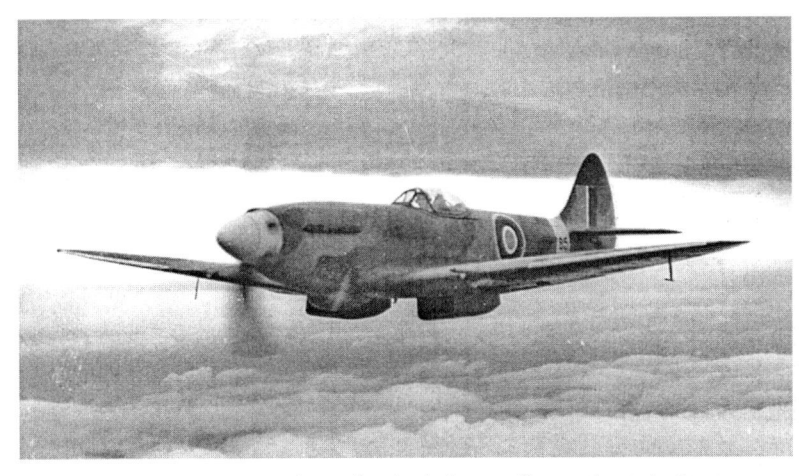

Spitfire FXIV RM785 on air test showing its huge radiators, about 2/12/1946.

14-15 AUGUST 1945 ~ JAPAN SURRENDER

Spitfire FR.XVIII showing oblique camera window in June 1945.

He flew from Aldermaston to High Post, the Supermarine Headquarters, then back to Chattis Hill on the 18th October 1945, then on the 20th it was Eastleigh to Keevil, it was a tour of the Dispersal Unit airfields where Spitfires had been flying from after assembly. In February, (and his first flight was not until the 12th,) he carried out 45 further flights. To transit between the different airfields, Supermarine used various small aircraft, which were probably impressed at the outbreak of the war, such as a DH Hornet Moth, a GA Cygnet HL539, Miles Monarch, Miles Magister, Taylorcraft Auster and Percival Vega Gull.

Spitfire PR.XIX PS925 showing the underneath camera port clearly.

His flights for March 1946, totalled 95, this included multiple flights in some aircraft, like on the 2nd he flew Spitfire F.XIV NH791 six times, and then twice on the 3rd, the flights from 5 to 20mins duration. He flew the Cygnet six times in five days, so that overall you would classify him as a very busy person.

A small internal Supermarine memo dated 12th April 1946 read:

It has been confirmed that Mr Colquhoun's appointment with this Company as test pilot shall commence as and from the 10th April 1946.

The previous flights for April were either production flights or transit flights except:- Spitfire F.XIV 321 (probably JF321) that he flew on the 17th for 1.30hrs of intensive flying fitted with a contra propeller and Mk.IX 299 fitted Passitor fuel gauge on the 17th. In April he flew 56 times, on the 3rd and 5th it was in 321 on contra prop trials for 3.20hrs total, the rest were Mk.XIV except once, on the 23rd when he flew a NA Mustang IIIF FR409 for a short period of 15 minutes only. It was during this month that he was demobilized, and became a civilian worker with Supermarine. He had been in RAF uniform ever since he had joined Supermarine and the only difference it made was that instead of uniform, he had to wear his own civilian clothes. The next month, May, he only flew 44 times, with some different marks added, on production test, including 8 PR.XIXs, mark XVIIIs SM844 on the 16th and SM843 on the 18th both for 50mins, NH872 on the 24th for 35mins.

In June he only flew 34 times, only now it was a mixture of F.XIV, FR.XVIII and PR. XIX, and his last flight of the month was on the 21st. He then he had a fortnights' leave.

He returned to work in July, taking Spitfire FR.XVIII TP408 up for a 50min production test on the 7th and only flying 32 times during the month. August was also a low month, only flying 18 times. In September he only flew 20 times in Spitfires, but clocked up 7.10 flying hours in ferrying flights. In October he flew 30 times, but lists on the 9th, propeller trials on Spitfire FR.XVIII aircraft TP340, TP345, TP347, TP348, TP364 and TP365 against which he just records 40 minutes, was it roughly 5mins each?

Seafire F.XV NS487 prototype with W/T mast, and pointed tail.

On the 15th it was the same again with TP366, TP367, TP369, TP443 and TP444 in 40mins. On the 30th he flew a Seafire F.XVII, PS157 to Eastleigh in 10mins. Then on the same day he flew Seafire

F.XVs PS243 and PR454 on what he termed "partial glides" The last day of the month, 31st, he flew Sea Otter 757 for only 10mins, I wonder what he thought about the amphibian. This was a flying boat used for Air-Sea Rescue similar to the Walrus but the modern version with a tractor engine.

Sea Otter Mk.II, JM977, one of a block of 250 built by Saunders-Roe from January 1943, which saved a lot of people from drowning.

In November, he tested his first Spitfire F.22 on the 1st of the month, in that he flew combat climbs to 28,000ft in PK320. Later on that day he flew PK518 on all out level speeds at 32,000ft, 28,000ft, 26,000ft, 24,000ft to 22,000ft and 21,000ft to 10,000ft, all these in 50mins. To complement these he flew PK518 on the 3rd on all out level speeds 16,000ft, 14,000ft, 12,000ft, 10,000ft, 8,000ft, 6,000ft, 4,000ft and 2,000ft in MS (Moderately Supercharged) gear all in 50mins. On the 9th he flew a DH Domine (this was a twin engined biplane) to Lee-on-Solent and return with three Vickers employees, then to Aldermaston on to Farnborough and Lee-on-Solent, and returning to High Post.

Colquhoun first flew a Seafire F.III on the 14th, November but the only number he wrote down was "C.206" for 30mins on ADDLs (Arrested Dummy Deck Landings) at Eastleigh. He attempted a landing on HMS Ravager flying "E.767" but the ship turned him back. However on the 17th flying "655", he flew to HMS Ravager and made four deck landings and returned taking him 55mins. After this, he returned to the more mundane task of testing FR.XVIIIs.

A Seafire F.III just landed back on board but "pecked" on doing so. As can be seen the propeller is damaged and the undercarriage is also badly damaged. This aircraft belongs to No. 807 Squadron and is possibly aboard HMS "Hunter" in 1944 in the Mediteraean area, for the invasion of Italy.

Another first for Colquhoun was his first flight in a Spiteful F.16, RG518, on the 30th for handling and familiarization in a 40min flight. This was the fastest propeller driven aircraft in the world at this particular time, achieving a level speed of 494mph on plus 25lb boost pressure, with the engine liable to pack up at any time.

December developed into a month of experimental testing which must have suited him more than the production testing that he had been carrying out, because most of his 23 flights were of this nature. On the 3rd he flew Spitfire F.22, PK320, on all out level speeds from 35,000ft downwards, fitted with a set of Supermarine stubs. He carried out three more flights on the 5th on this aircraft, flying levels at 20,000ft downwards, at 28,000ft and at 8,000ft, this took him a total of 2.45hrs. On the 9th he flew the first production Spiteful NN664 flying levels at 20,000ft for 15mins, and again on the 12th for 25mins this time, and the 21st but levels at 26,000ft. He also carried out all out levels at 35,000ft, 31,000ft, 27,000ft and 10,000ft on Spitfire F.22 PK318, taking 1.10hrs on the 13th.

Spitfire F.22 and Seafire F.46

On the 19th of December he flew a Seafire F.46, LA541, on trim curves for 1.05hrs, this was one of the ultimates in Spitfire evolution, this was the first production and built at South Marston, Swindon. Its top speed was down to 443mph at 25,000ft, but it had a ceiling of

41,000ft. He flew this aircraft again on the 27th when he carried out "Stick force per 'G'" experiments flying for 35mins.

January 1946 started on the 1st, with a flight in Spitfire F.22 PK318 on combat climbs in M.S. gear to 30,000ft, landed after 40mins. On the 14th it was a flight in Sea Otter RD876 on delivery from Eastleigh to High Post. Then on the 21st he delivered Spitfire F.22 to Boscombe Down (the first time that he had been here, and where a lot of research was carried out) taking him only 5mins. On the 30th it was a production test on Spitfire F.XVIII TP219, of 1.10hrs, and on the 31st he did the same for TP225 in 40mins, TP223 in 15mins and TP218 in 2.00hrs.

Up to this point in time, he had flown for a total of 1,533.30hrs.

February was the normal production programme with the odd variation. On the 13th he flew Spitfire PR.XIX on a pressure cabin test to 40,000ft, on the 19th he is supposed to have delivered three Spitfire F.22s, PK682, PK717 and VN314 from Castle Bromwich to South Marston. It is quite possible, with a ferry aircraft available each time, but who would be flying the ferry?. (3 journeys to SM & return). On the 27th he flew another Spitfire F.22, PK313, from Castle Bromwich to South Marston.

March was similar with production tests of Spitfire F.XVIII and F.22 and deliveries on the 6th and 8th were:- F.21s PK719, PK720 on the 6th and PK722 on the 8th from Castle Bromwich to South Marston, also Seafire F.45 LA491 from High Post back to South Marston on the 8th. A different test on Spiteful F.14 RB521 on the 27th was a stalling test when fitted with a spoiler fitted on the starboard wing, it was only airborne for 15mins. He delivered a Spitfire F.22, VN324, from Keevil to Aldermaston on the 25th, to which I cannot see a reason for it. South Marston was the production airfield and Chilbolton was the test airfield, these latter two were Supermarine dispersal airfields.

April was just a production test month, and he carried out 16 of them, plus a few flights ferrying. May was somewhat similar, though he did fly Seafang VG471 on the 15th and 21st bringing it back from Boscombe Down each time, Spitefuls RB517 and RB516 on performance trials on the 15th and 16th. He flew Seafire F.46, LA564, on the 15th on an air test, and again on the 19th and 25th fitted with a single 500lb MG bomb (this would be a dummy, probably filled with concrete to simulate the weight). This last Spiteful was not delivered to the RAF until the 9th May 1947, so would be used for testing at Supermarine.

He was very busy in June 1946 with 52 flights in Spitfires and its derivatives, including SX297 a Seafire F.XVII on the 4th June that he flew on tests of dropping the long range fuel tank, making sure that it dropped clean and did not come back and damage the aircraft at all, Seafang VG475 on the 14th on combat climb, and on the 15th air temperature calibration, on the 16th it was Spitfire F.24, VN306, for engine test for vibration and also on the 17th. Spitfire F.24, VN302 used on the 18th for handling with 3 x 200lb bombs, and later on the same day Seafire F.46 LA564, handling with 1 x 500lb bomb. The 19th it was LA564 for handling, fitted with 4 x 100lb bombs and an 80 gallon drop tank. The following day he flew Spitfire F.24 VN302 fitted with 3 x 500lb bombs, and later that day, flew it fitted with 3 x 500lb smoke bombs, on the 21st he flew it for handling with a full rear fuel tank, on the 24th he flew it fitted with a 50 gallon drop tank and 4 x 100lb bombs. Tests like this were required, so that a service pilot would have no trouble with handling if he got involved in evasive manoeuvres or action, and the handling performance with these external stores was within the authorised limits.

July was a fairly busy month with 37 flights with the same type of aircraft as last month. On the 1st he took the Prototype Spiteful NN664 on Mach number dives fitted with a camera, probably looking at the ailerons to check for flutter at high speeds. (the prototype Spiteful, NN660, had been lost in September 1944 when Frank Furlong dived into the ground at low altitude for no apparent reason).He flew it for 50mins and again on the 2nd for 55mins. Another experiment on Spitfire F.22, PK320, was when it was flown on the 3rd fitted with 6 x 25lb rockets.

August he flew only 23 times, the first time being to fly Spiteful RB518 back to Chilbolton from RAF Colerne, (this aircraft had to force land with Mike Lithgow flying it when the engine failed for the seventh time, and he undershot at Chilbolton and the two main undercarriage legs went up through the wings. When it was being salvaged the crane dropped it from its maximum height, and no one was sorry), another Spiteful, RB520 was used on the 9th to check aileron measurements.

Supermarine Type 322 "Dumbo" R1810 and Spitfire F.24

September he flew 31 times, 30 of them for production flights on Spitfires or Seafires. However on the 11th he flew "Dumbo" R1815, the second prototype, a special experimental aircraft built fitted with an unusual variable-incidence wing that enabled it to fly at a ground

Fly High ~ Fly Low

speed of only 57mph. Colquhoun only flew it on landings and familiarisation for 35mins.

Below I insert a transcript of the page from the South Marston Flight Log for the month of September 1946, just to show that of the other pilots, S/L Morgan, Lt/Cdr Lithgow and JK Quill, he was the only pilot flying that month.

A/C	Date	Pilot	Duaration	No	Total
PK685	5/9/46	F/Lt Colquhoun	0.15	1	0.15
PK713	5/9/46	F/Lt Colquhoun	0.10	1	0.10
PK713	6/9/46	F/Lt Colquhoun	5,5,5,15	4	0.30
PK685	6/9/46	F/Lt Colquhoun	0.10	1	0.10
LA554	7/9/46	F/Lt Colquhoun	10,15	2	0.25
LA554	9/9/46	F/Lt Colquhoun	15,10,20	3	0.45
PK313	12/9/46	F/Lt Colquhoun	10,5,5	3	0.20
PK722	12/9/46	F/Lt Colquhoun	0.25	1	0.25
PK722	14/9/46	F/Lt Colquhoun	20,5	2	0.25
PK689	17/9/46	F/Lt Colquhoun	25,10,10	3	0.45
PK717	19/9/46	F/Lt Colquhoun	0.25	1	0.25
LA555	19/9/46	F/Lt Colquhoun	10	1	0.10
LA555	21/9/46	F/Lt Colquhoun	25,10	2	0.35
PK716	21/9/46	F/Lt Colquhoun	0.10	1	0.10
PK719	23/9/46	F/Lt Colquhoun	25,15	2	0.40
PK716	23/9/46	F/Lt Colquhoun	10,10	2	0.20
PK716	24/9/46	F/Lt Colquhoun	0.10	1	0.10
PK719	24/9/46	F/Lt Colquhoun	0.10	1	0.10
PK718	26/9/46	F/Lt Colquhoun	0.10	1	0.10
PK716	25/7/46	F/Lt Colquhoun	0.10	1	0.10
PK716	26/9/46	F/Lt Colquhoun	0.10	1	0.10
PK719	26/9/46	F/Lt Colquhoun	10,15	2	0.25
PK718	26/9/46	F/Lt Colquhoun	0.20	1	0.20
PK720	27/9/46	F/Lt Colquhoun	10,20,10,10	4	0.50
PK687	27/9/46	F/Lt Colquhoun	0.10	1	0.10
PK687	28/9/46	F/Lt Colquhoun	0.10	1	0.10
PK687	30/9/46	F/Lt Colquhoun	10,10	2	0.20

Spiteful NN664 2nd prototype and the only Spiteful F.16, RB518.

In October Colquhoun was extremely busy flying 50 times in the month mainly on production flights, but there was one different type of Spitfire that he managed to fly. This was N-32, a Spitfire F.VIII, that had been converted to take two seats and became known as the Spitfire Trainer. He flew it on the 8th for 45mins for photography purposes carrying Mr Dickenson and on the 11th for 25mins.

November was a very quiet month with only 20 flights recorded, with no special flights or tests. December was slightly better with 32 flights recorded. Spiteful RB525 was flown to Brize Norton on the

3rd, as was RB530 on the 5th, also Seafang VG477 on the 19th and Spitfire PM659 on the 30th. What was at Brize Norton for them?

The Spitfire T.VIII, converted from MT818 an F.VIII, in Class 'B' markings as N.32 and later registered as G-AIDN.

January 1947 was more of the sameness, except for the ferrying and demonstration at Wisley of Seafang F.32 prototype, VB895, on the 9th and the 10th,

Flying time was 1.00hr and 45mins respectively. This was not a Spitfire even though it was developed from the Spitfire, with a brand new fuselage and tail, and with a special laminar flow Supermarine designed wing and fitted with a Rolls-Royce Griffon 89 engine of 2,350hp.

The Seafang F.32 prototype VB895, with a top speed of 475mph

February 1947 was the easiest month yet for Colquhoun, because he only managed to fly 8 Spitfire type aircraft, his flying time being only 4.50hrs. However the Supermarine Experimental Flight moved from the grass runway at High Post, near the western end of the huge Boscombe Down Air Ministry test aerodrome, to its new base at Chilbolton, Hampshire, where there were already three concrete runways with a good hangar complex and with a good access by road to Hursley Park, during February. Test pilots consisted of JK Quill, the Chief Test Pilot, Lt/Cdr Mike Kithgow, Guy Morgan the Chief Production Test pilot, John Derry and of course Les Colquhoun. Others followed being S/Ldr Dave Morgan, Peter Robarts, Chunky Horne and Pee Wee Judge.

CHILBOLTON Aerodrome, where an office block was built for the Flight Test Department, which was now seconded from Hursley Park with all the test pilots and the Works Manager.

March was an improvement with 14 flights. These flights included two familiarisation flights in the DH Vampire F.1 TG282, his first flight in a jet-powered aircraft. He did not even bother to put any comments down either. Also, this month he flew a Supermarine Walrus from Eastleigh to Chilbolton in 20mins flying time.

April was another quiet month with just 12 flights but nothing unusual. However, in May, he again flew only 12 flights but he flew the Spitfire Trainer on the 13th to Belgium for a demonstration, staying there for a week, and then returning on the 20th, and on the 25th he flew the Seafang VB895 for 50mins from High Post to Chilbolton. The flying of the Spitfire Trainer continued in June, when it went to Brussels again for a demonstration from the 4th to the 8th, total flying time was 2.40hrs. On the 13th it was again demonstrated but this time to Argentinian pilots, and on the 16th it was flown for 20mins on a practise demonstration. Colquhoun got involved in the "Dumbo" S.24/37 R1815, when he had to carry out a practise demonstration on the 18th for 1.35hrs and on the 23rd for 50mins. Then the same day he flew it to Lee-on –Solent and carried out demonstrations on the 24th, 25th and 26th of 20, 10 and 5mins. Also, in June he carried out production tests on three Eire Seafires, RX210, PX941 and PX929 in 2.45, 0.15 and 1.00hr respectively. Three more were flown on a production test in July, 150, 152 and 153 but, Colquhoun did not put down an actual date. The Irish Government had ordered 12 de-navalised Seafires in August 1946.

August was another learning curve for Colquhoun, and to start we have a familiarisation flight in the 2nd prototype Supermarine Attacker, TS413 on the 17th, another flight in S.24/37 Dumbo for PE calibration with the Attacker on the 21st, a RATOG (Rocket assisted Tale off gear) flight in Seafire F.47 PS948 on the 26th followed by an air test for delivery, which he accomplished next day to the RAE Farnborough, he also carried out a production test on a Seafire F.III No.154 for Eire on that day.

Sometime during this period at Chilbolton both Les and Katie (his wife) were voted in as Parish Councillors for the town of Chilbolton, Katie had been surprised when the local people had suggested that she put up for a seat, and more surprised still when she was elected. When Council meetings came along, she had to get a baby sitter to look after the children. There were eight seats vacant on the Council and the following were voted in with their number of votes in brackets:-

A. Painter (120), Major FL Schwind (104), LR Colquhoun (101), Commander IMN Mudie (86). Mrs FM Abery (85), G Smart (78), Air Commodore G Scarrott (76) and Mrs KM Colquhoun (70).

It was during 1947 that Les Colquhoun moved into "Penn Acres", in Branksome Avenue, Chilbolton with his wife Katie, there were only two neigbouring houses and RAF billets or hutted accommodation, for the aircraft technical people. It was Katie also that lobbied for a GPO letter box in Branksome Avenue, and it is still being used today. Many a social event was held in the local pubs, the New Inn, Seven Stars and Peate Spade. Les colquhoun was a fair fast bowler and one day he delivered a very fast one and knocked out the manager of the Vickers' Newbury Works.

DH.100 Vampire F.3 VV195

September was quite a busy month, it was also Radlett SBAC Display time, and Supermarine let Colquhoun display the Civilian Sea Otter G-AIDM. He flew it from Eastleigh to Chilbolton on the 5th, before delivering it to Radlett on the 7th. It stayed there the whole week, before being flown back by Colquhoun on the 15th. He was also able to fly the prototype Attacker, TS409, on the 17th and 19th on handling, and handling at altitude, airborne for 30mins each time. He carried out his first delivery flying a Seafire F.47 PS953 to RNAS Anthorn on the 23rd in 1.00hr. Last but not least, he carried out production tests on Seafire F.IIIs for Eire as follows:- 155 on the 4th, 154, 155, 156 and 157 on the 26th and 156 again on the 27th, (these are the Irish identifying numbers).

Walrus ASR.1 W3008.

October 1947 was a fairly quiet month with 9 production tests, the Spitfire Trainer, G-AIDN, flown from South Marston, and then on to Boscombe Down, and returned the same day of the 2nd. He flew Seafire F.47, PS957, (this type was the heaviest Spitfire derivative of them all, weighing in at 10,200lb compared to the Mark Spitfire at 5,800lb normal loaded) to Anthorn on delivery on the 16th in 1.10hrs. The next odd job was to fly Spitfire F.24 VN302 on vibrograph recording tests on the 22nd, 23rd and the 27th for 30, 20 and 20mins respectively. He also flew the fastest aircraft, RB518 on the 22nd on an air test of 5 mins. On the 31st he carried out a jettison fuel flow test on Seafire F.47 PS945 of 25mins. November was quiet with only 16 production tests carried out, and December was the same with only 11 production tests and Spitfire F.24, VN324 being flown on a 10 minute flight for an air test and vibration assessment on the 11th.

January 1948, and he flew Seafire F.47, PS944, on the 5th on a 45 minute test of spinning whilst fitted with combat tanks, somebody had to do it first and he was the test pilot selected. The 15th he flew another Seafire F.47, PS948, on a climb to 30,000ft which took him 30mins. One item that all pilots appreciate, is to fly a different aircraft, and on the 14th he did just this, with Wellington B.X LP573 for a production test. He must have found it rather hard, difficult to control and sluggard, cold, noisy and really smelly, this is the impression that the Wellington left with me. In February he carried out 18 production tests, one of which was Wellington B.X LN228 for 10 minutes, rather short as the Spitfires he flew varied from 15mins upwards. He flew Seafang F.32, VB895, on the 6th twice carrying out speed power curve test, with the drop tank on and second flight with it off for comparison, in 45 and 50mins respectively. Attacker TS409 was flown on the 9th for performance measurements at 5,000ft taking 35mins.

On the 27th February 1948 M.J. Lithgow, Colquhoun's boss, set up a new 100 kilometre closed-circuit International Speed Record in the Attacker prototype TS409, at 564.881mph (909.063 kmph), which shows the speed that these Supermarine test pilots were flying at, and were some of the fastest in the world.

March 1948 was a real quiet month with only 5 production tests including Spitfire Trainer now registered G-15-1 on the 3rd in a flight of 35 minutes. Also on the 3rd he delivered Seafire F.47, VP439, to South Marston. He also flew Attacker 2nd prototype TS413 on an attempt at stalls for 15mins and Seafang VG474 for 20mins on handling with servodyne ailerons for 15 minutes. In April there were only 3 production tests of Seafire F.47s VP459 on the 15th, VP460 on the 22nd and VP461 on the 27th. Then there was Spitfire F.24, VN324 on check for vibration on the 12th, Spiteful RB518 for level speeds at 36,000ft on the 13th, also Seafang VG474 for handling with the servodyne ailerons for 50mins this time, Spitfire VN302 for propeller vibration on the 16th, Seafire F.47 PS952 air test with rudder overbalance, and then two aircraft delivered to RAF Boscombe Down Seafang VB895 on the 27th and Spitfire F.XVIII, TP423 on the 29th. The Spitfire Trainer now registered G-AIDN was flown the 21st on an air test.

TS409 prototype Attacker and below the Supermarine test pilots:- Les Colquhoun, Mike Lithgow, Jeffrey Quill, Guy Morgan and John Derry.

Everything changed for him in May 1948, with his first flight being to fly Spitfire F.XVIII TP423 on delivery to Boscombe Down on the 3rd, and then he had a familiarisation flight in Viking LV-XFM, with W/Cdr Boyd, flying it for 50 minutes.

Then he flew as co-pilot with W/Cdr Boyd as follows:-

Vickers Viking I Type 620 LV-XEN for Argentine Government, re-numbered to T.1.

This aircraft was the last of an order from the Argentine Civil Aeronautics Board of 27 Type 615 Viking IB aircraft. LV-XFM first flew 22nd April 1948 and was officially accepted on the 11th May. It was used as a Presidential transport on a few occasions until it went to the Argentine Air Force as T-64 and crashed 27th October 1952 at Moron Air Force base.

The route and date flown were as follows:

11th	Wisley	to	Prestwick	2.10	
12th	Prestwick	to	Keflavik	4.35	Iceland
12th	Keflacik	to	Blue West 1	4.35	Greenland
12th	Blue West 1	to	Gander	4.40	Newfoundland
13th	Gander	to	La Guardia	6.45	New York
16th	La Guardia	to	Nassau	6.00	West Indies
17th	Nassau	to	Kingston	2.35	Jamiaca
17th	Kingston	to	Trinidad	6.20	
18th	Trinidad	to	Belem	6.40	Brazil
18th	Belem	to	Natal	2.00	Brazil
19th	Natal	to	Rio	6.25	Brazil
20th	Rio	to	Montevideo	6.40	Uruguay
24th	Montevideo	to	Buenos Aires	0.55	Argentina

Colquhoun returned to England, on the 31st May 1948, in a British South American Airways "Starliner" "Star Vista" and was awarded the crossing the line certificate when he flew from Natal to Dakar, flying at 175 knots at 11,000ft.

Vickers Wellington T.X, the post war trainer.

He was back at work by the 3rd June 1948 test flying Seafang F.47 VP463 on Rate of Roll tests. During June he flew 17 production tests, including Wellingtons NA912, NA981 and NA713. on the 15th he flew Seafire F.47 VP463, for handling with a 90 gallon jet tank for 25mins. He flew Spiteful F.16, RB518, five times, on the 10th on air test, 16th for performance at 36,000ft, and the 22nd, and the last two on the 28th for performance at 38,000ft. From the fastest aircraft to the slower biplane Sea Otter, JM909, on the 22nd for jettisoning RATOG tests.

In July 1948 there were 13 production tests, once again, including three Wellingtons PG401, NC976 and NC668, Seafang VG474 on the 2nd and the 6th on Rates of Roll tests, Spitfire F.24 VN324 on the 5th and 30th on prop vibration tests and Sea Otter JM909 on stalls with Air Sea Rescue container on the 5th and 6th. The only flight he carried out in July was a ferry flight in the DH Rapide aircraft on the 31st.

August he was very busy with 12 production, three air tests, on the 12th , 16th, 18th, 19th and 24th cooling tests with Seafire F.47, 13th and 16th flying Seafire F.47 VP463 for handling with external stores. On the 26th August Colquhoun air tested the Spitfire Trainer and also flew it from South Marston, the following day he demonstrated the aircraft to Tugese at Wisley (the airfield near Weybridge, the Vickers main Works).

On the 28th he flew it to Lympne and then took part in the LYMPNE HIGH SPEED TROPHY RACE, organized by the Cinque Ports Flying Club in which he came in first, flying the Spitfire Trainer G-AIDN, round four laps of an 80 mile course at an average speed of 324mph.

The Spitfire T.VIII registered G-AIDN and sporting the number 99, and RJ Mitchell on its nose. This was ex MT818 a Mark F.VIII and first flew after conversion in August 1946.

This was a handicap race and the first four of seven crossed the line within 25 seconds, the second home being Wing Commander J. Cunningham in the DH Vampire III fitted with an improved "Goblin" engine at an average speed of 472mph. A record was set in this race by Miss Lettice Curtis flying a Spitfire PR.XI, of a new women's record for the 100km closed circuit, at a speed of 313.07 mph, even though she only came in fifth. He was awarded the Trophy and a cheque for £100 by the Dunlop Rubber Company Ltd. The following day Colquhoun returned to base.

He is supposed to have flown Wellington B.X HS396 on the 29th September but this number only relates to a Swordfish II. And on the same day he flew Spitfire Indian Trainer HS536 for 20 mins, which is quite alright. He did 5 production tests and flew Seafire F.47 VP464 on the 8th, 20th and 24th on cooling trials, VP463 on the

20th (2) and 22nd (2) for cooling trials and then on the 28th (2) and 29th (2) on stability and stick force per 'G' tests.

LRC has just received the Lympne High Speed Handicap Trophy on the 28th August 1948, plus a £100 cheque from Dunlop Rubber Company Ltd.

In October 1948 he started carrying out production tests on some of the Spitfire PR.XIXs that the Swedish Air Force had purchased, they had ordered 50, ex RAF and reconditioned, to be delivered in 1948 – 1949. Three of them were 31007 flown 25th, 31008 on the 27th and 31019 on the 28th for 2.30hrs whereas normal production flights were for between 20 and 45mins. This continued with 31009 on the 9th November and 31020 on the 27th. Another foreign sale was to India of Spitfire Trainers, HS641 flown on the 20th for 1.35hrs. Another 10 Swedish PR.XIXs were flown in December:- 31011 on the 2nd, 31010, 31012 and 31021. On the 3rd, 31022 13th, 31014 16th, 31015 20th, 31023 21st, 31013 24th and 31024 on the 31st, 31010 was flown for 4.05 to check on endurance. Also on the 31st was a Spitfire XIX HS694 for India of 40mins.

Spitfire PRXIX, 31040, of the Royal Swedish Air Force at Nykoping, and was a reconditioned ex RAF PS875.

8. Jet Testing Begins

January 1949 started slightly differently, in that he flew Meteor F.IV VT338 12 times starting on the 3rd on stick force per 'G' measurements. The only Swedish Spitfire he flew was 31025 on the 6th. Spiteful RB518 had had some thing done because it was again on level speeds at 33,000ft and 32,000ft on the 18th, this time it was flown for 50mins, and again on the 20th at 36,000ft, 35,000ft and 34,000ft. It is odd that tests were required at such precise altitudes. Also on the 20th Colquhoun had another first, that of landing on the water in Sea Otter JM909, it must have been a shock to him of the noise of water impacting the hull, when he alighted on the water, it was to me when I landed in a Sunderland for the first time.

The prototype "Seagull" Amphibian, PA143, showing the huge flaps that meant it could fly at about 50mph, the single RR Griffon engine with its contra rotating airscrews, the retractable undercarriage and the underslung ASR container under the wing. Photograph taken in March 1950.

On 1st February 1949, he had an introduction to the Seagull PA143. This was the last of the Supermarine flying boats and was designed initially around Specification S.12/40 for an advanced fleet reconnaissance amphibian for ship stowage. Three of them were ordered in 1943, PA143, PA147 and PA152. PA143 first flew on the 14th July

1948. He only flew it for 15mins but it must have been down on the River Itchen, Southampton. It seems as if Colquhoun was allocated to the testing of the Attacker, TS409, in March, because he flew it 11 times during the month, solely on trim curve tests. He also flew Sea Otter VR-SOL on the 14th on its Air Registration Board test, which took just an hour. In April he flew Attacker TS409 7 times still on trim curves. Of his 5 Spitfire PRXIX flights, 3 were for foreign powers, 31046 on the 29th for Sweden and HS702 on the 13th and HS705 on the 25th for India.

May 1949 was when he really went into the Seagull ASR (Air Sea Rescue) amphibian test programme, when he flew PA143 15 times, starting on the 9th for familiarisation for 35mins, the 10th on for performance, with a total flying time of 12.35hrs including one flight on the 12th devoted to the photographing of the Swift. June was a month dominated by three different types:- the Spitfire Trainer G-AIDN with 4 flights on the 9th, first with Eastleigh to Chilbolton, 2nd a demonstration with Lt Bailey a passenger, 3rd flight Chilbolton to Eastleigh and 4th Eastleigh to Chilbolton. Seafang VG474 flew Chilbolton to South Marston and return, and lastly Seafire F.47 PS952 with 4 flights on test for neg 'G' oil tank test and neg 'G' oil pressure tests. On July 13th a second civil Spitfire Trainer, G-ALJM was flown on air test for 25mins, and another flight on Seagull PA143 for cooling drag lasting one hour, also on 22nd and the 26th for what he described as:- "Investigation of Chain Load on incidence gear". He flew the prototype Swift, VV106, on the 25th July for familiarisation for 10mins, on the 26th for trim curves at 20,000ft and again on the 27th twice for same tests of 40 and 15mins. This aircraft had been first flown by MJ Lithgow, on the 29th December 1948.

On the first few days of August he was flying the Seagull ASR, on the 5th it was checking rectified temperatures and operation of the incidence gear, later that day another flight checking trim curves, both 1.00hr flights. On the 7th it was trim curves, on the 8th 3 more flights doing the same, and 2 more on the 9th with the same again, with 5 more flights that month. He flew Swift VV106 twice on the 16th, the Attacker TS409 six times from the 20th, the last one on the 31st was a delivery flight to Boscombe Down. This meant that he flew three different prototypes in the same month, not many pilot can say that. In September he flew the Seagull PA143 15 times carrying out stick force per'G', demonstration at the SBAC Show on the 11th, trim curves, camera recorded landings on the 14th, oscillatory stability measurements and straight side slips and rates of roll. He also flew the Attacker prototype, TS409, from Boscombe Down to Chilbolton on the 6th and then to Farnborough. He carried out demonstrations at the SBAC Show on the 7th, 8th, 9th and 10th returning to Chilbolton on the 10th. Which means that he demonstrated two aircraft at the show.

There was less work to do in October with only two Attacker flights, Seafire/Spitfire flights, two Wellington flights and a Sea Otter, G.15-76, on air test of 2.45hrs. The first aircraft to be flown in November was another Sea Otter G.18-4 on the 1st, for only 35mins. (These were Class B Registrations G.15 for Supermarine and G.18 for Bristol Aeroplane Co.). Seafire F.47, PS952, was test flown on he 25th, 29th and 30th (twice) to test out new light alloy radiators, flying 1.00hr, 1.00hr, 40mins and 35mins respectively. December 1st PS952 flew again for 40mins and twice on the 5th. He then flew Attacker TS409 on wing tip camera tests on the 6th for 25mins, later that day he flew it for handling drop tank empty. Then on the 9th fitted with drop tank filled with 100 gallons, then later with drop tank filled with 180 gallons and finally on the 12th with drop tank full, this test took him 1.00hr. On the 16th he flew it with tank empty and cut back seal, on the 19th with tank full and cut back seal, on the 20th it was performance checks with tank on, and on the 20th and 21st with tank off and then on the 22nd it was for take-off measurements.

January 1950 started off with five Attacker flights, first on the 4th for air test, and then later for take off measurements with the drop tank on, the next day it was tank jettisoning day and the drop tank separated safely and fell away successfully. Later that day he flew it on take off measurements with the tank off. On the 6th he delivered it to Boscombe Down for them to carry out some of their tests. It seems as if he then attended a course on night flying, because his next log book entries from the 10th to the 23rd are concerning night flight in Airspeed Oxfords G-ALTR and G-AITF and Consul G-AIXF. Flight instructors were S/Ldr Webb and F/Lt Croskell, and the syllabus included General Instrument Flying, SBA Approach (Standard Beam Approach), let downs and more instrument flying. His last flight was in the Consul flown by Capt. Belson on a MCA Instrument Rating test. Colquhoun's last flight in January was to fly Sea Otter G.15-77 on an air test of 1.15hrs.

Airspeed Oxford, one of the twin engined aircraft flown by Colquhoun.

All he did in February was to fly Auster G-AHLI on ferry business for 4.00hrs. March was an improvement in that he flew two ferry trips, Seafire F.47 PS951 on the 24th, Attacker on the 27th on delivery to Boscombe Down, Wellingtons PG136 and LP361 on the 30th and Seagull PA143 on the 31st on a check for tail wheel shimmy and also Spitfire Trainer 684 (ex RAF conversion for Egypt) on compass check and long range drop tank check. On the 5th April 1950 he carried out the "Initial Air Test" on Attacker F.1 WA469, (60 were ordered WA469 to WA534), this phrase probably means first flight, he flew it again on he 11th and 12th on air tests of 30 &35mins. He also flew Seagull PA143 now fitted with an enlarged rudder on handling test. April was also a quiet month with 7 flights in total, 4 of them ferry, two on the 27th were in Attacker TS409 for spinning tests tank off and tank on. May was a different proposition with 27 flights being carried out. Attacker TS409 flying 5 sorties on spinning trials, WA469 using 4, the last of which was an emergency landing, starboard wing tip folded in flight.

Attacker F.1 WA469, the first production aircraft and the aircraft whose wing tip folded in flight with Colquhoun at the controls, and he touched down at about 200mph, and in so doing saved the aircraft, his life and it also meant that the fault was found very quickly.

EMERGENCY

Les Colquhoun was flying WA469, the first Attacker production aircraft, built at South Marston, on the 23rd May 1950, carrying out experiments with the dive brakes, under normal conditions. He was making a high speed run close to Chilbolton airfield at 450 knots (520mph) when there was a loud bang, and immediately to his astonishment he saw the starboard wing tip, a section measuring 3 ft 6 inches, was now in the vertical position, as it would be on an aircraft carrier deck, ready for descending in the lift. He did think about ejecting, and of course his first thought was about carrying out an ejection, but the aeroplane was still flying and he could keep it level. His aileron control had vanished, because when the wing folds up, they are automatically locked in neutral, because you should not be flying it under those conditions. He could however keep the aircraft flying level by astute coarse use of his rudder and also control it in a limited way directionally. He made a wide circuit of the airfield and kept his approach high at about 230 knots (265mph). Then he began to realise his difficulties and one of them was that it would mean a very fast touch down, because below the 230 knots speed, he could not keep the aircraft in line with the runway, and it was exceedingly difficult to keep it laterally level as well. So at this speed he crossed the runway threshold and touched down just over the threshold of the runway at about 200 knots, he juggled the elevator and brakes to keep the aircraft on the ground. He finally pulled up, he says, 10 yards short of the end of the 1,800 yard runway, and the aircraft only suffered a burst port tyre, which was due to Colquhouns' excessive braking, that he had to apply, to stop the aircraft, some testimony on the tyres that were fitted to this aircraft.

This is a photograph of Attacker F.1s, WA493 J:106 foremost, both aircraft on HMS "Eagle" of No.800 Squadron, clearly showing the wing tips raised ready for stowage below deck. Just imagine one of these only, raised in flight and the effects of it on the flying characteristics of the aircraft (photo: Ray Williams).

A Mr Denis Le P Webb (author of *Never a Dull Moment* published 2001) was outside a hangar at Chilbolton and saw this event and wrote: "with its starboard outer plane very slowly waving up and down – it very obviously having come unlocked at the wing fold". He continued: "that with the wing partially folded Les Colquhoun's ailerons were locked and he therefore had no lateral control".

As Denis drove Colquhoun back to the office he asked, "God Almighty, Les, why didn't you use the ejector seat?"

"Lord no, Webby! Those things put the fear of God in me!" was Les's reply.

This saved his life, however, because he was too low to have ejected safely. He also saved his aircraft and so the fault could be found and rectified and make sure that it did not happen again. This saved Supermarine and the Air Ministry a lot of work and expense if the aircraft had crashed, and the production of the Attacker was not delayed as would have happened if it had been written off, the fault located, rectified and authority to recommence flying give.

For his achievement on this day he was awarded the George Medal, which was presented to him at Buckingham Palace some time later by HM King George VI.[4] Another test pilot, Bill Waterton, also received the George Medal when he crash-landed a Gloster Javelin at Boscombe Down on 2nd June 1952. The Javelin had encountered a severe case of flutter, which was so bad that he lost his elevators. He had to land fast, like Colquhoun had to, and his undercarriage legs broke and ruptured a fuel tank in the high speed touchdown, it burst into flames, but he managed to escape and the fire was successfully extinguished.

Of the many congratulatory letters and sundry telegrams that he received, one was from The Royal Society of St George at 4 Upper Belgrave Street, London, SW.1. Also in the letter they offered him Honorary Membership of the Society. The General Secretary went on to say:-

"The Society, as you can see from the enclosed, is composed of large numbers of those who love England, and we feel that if you accept this invitation you will be doing the Society a great honour. I need hardly say that this will impose no obligation on you".

The next time he flew an Attacker was on the 26th May 1950 when he simply took TS413, the second prototype, for a 5 minute flight. By the 1st June he seems to have got into his stride again and flew Swift VV106 from Farnborough back to Chilbolton, and on the 5th flew it back there again. He also flew the Seagull PA143 on the 1st, on P.E. trials – Trailing static, and on the 2nd he did water landings and rudder angle measurements whilst carrying passengers of:- Messrs Beer, RA Harvey and Stewart, he flew again on the 5th on a flight

---

[4] For a full list of Les's awards see Appendix I, at the back of the book.

from Chilbolton to M&AEE Felixstowe, but landed on Southampton owing to hydraulic failure with passengers of Dickinson and Austin. It was probably tax ied up to the Itchen Works and moored there for repair over night because it was the 6th when it took off Southampton Water for Felixstowe with the passengers. On the 7th, he flew Sea Otter G.15-86 to Eastleigh and on the 10th and 12th he flew Attacker TS413 on air tests.

The second prototype Attacker TS413 that he flew on the 12th June.

July 1950 was a very busy month as he flew 43 times including ferry flights. He had flown WA469 again on the 27th June, and in July he flew it again 24 times, just as he put it, on "air test". On the 7th he used RATOG on Attacker TS413 for the first time, must have been interesting. He flew Seagull PA147, with the number 54 painted on its fins, the second prototype, on the 20th July, followed by 5 more flights with Mr Dickenson and Stewart each time. The first of these on the 21st was to fly from Chilbolton to Sherburn-in-Elmet, Yorkshire, in 1.30hrs, followed by 55mins of practise for the Air League Challenge Cup Race. On the morning of the 22nd he flew it for another 40mins on practise, then in the afternoon he flew it in the race.

In this race he set up a 100km closed-circuit World record for amphibians of 241.9mph, (previous record was 209.46 mph), but only came in fourth and flew the second lap at a record speed of 241.9 mph.

The World Record aircraft, PA147, here fitted with a short middle fin.

Only two of these amphibians were built and technology overtook it, in that helicopters were able to do what the Seagull had been designed for, in Air Sea Rescue. Also at this race, Mike Lithgow flying the prototype Attacker, TS409, won the Society of British Aircraft Constructor's Challenge Cup at a speed of 533mph over the 100 kilometre closed circuit, S/Ldr J. Derry was second in a Vampire V at 472mph with S/Ldr T.S. Wade third in a Hawker Seahawk. On the 23rd Colquhoun flew the Seagull ASR back to Chilbolton. His last

July flight, on the 31st, was in Attacker WA469 on an air test of 50mins.

Something different on the 1st August 1950 was to fly the Rapide G-AHJA, whilst someone else was photographing South Marston, taking 45 minutes. These aircraft were also used for General Travel Purposes for Directors and Officials to visit Meetings and Conferences as well as meetings abroad. Les flew Mr Denis le Webb of Supermarine to Germany on two occasions so that he could investigate the appalling defect rates on the FR Swifts. However Les did not enter these into his Log book as such, as he was inclined to just lump these flights together for the whole month.

A DH89 Dominie (in civilian guise as a Rapide). These twin-engined biplanes saw a lot of service. They were used as taxi aircraft by Supermarine, flying pilots between airfields. They were six-seaters so could carry five passengers plus the pilot.

A decision was reached by Vickers that a demonstration tour of the Middle East with the Attacker, might produce some sales, so about two months were used to organize the trip and ensure that any countries Vickers thought might be interested were well informed – especially their Air Attachés. Also, the right fuel had to be made available, because most of these countries had no jet aircraft whatsoever. The main servicing team was flown out in a Valetta and Mike Lithgow was the pilot of the Attacker. On the 9th with Brian Powell as pilot and Les as co-pilot they took off for Baghdad in another Valetta (VX541) as a backup aircraft.

Vickers Valetta C.1, VL263, on an early evaluation flight.

The flights were:-

9th	Chilbolton	Wisley
9th	Wisley	Northolt
10th	Northolt	Rome
10th	Rome	Nicosia
10th	Nicosia	Baghdad (3.1 hrs at night)
12th	Baghdad	Sharjah
13th	Sharjah	Baghdad
13th	Baghdad	Nicosia
14th	Nicosia	Malta
14th	Malta	Nice
15th	Nice	Eastleigh

Total flying time was 35.40hrs.

The rest of August was tame, with 8 ferry trips and Wellington NC497 two air tests. However he flew Attacker G.15-110 on a production test on the 25th for 30mins, the 26th 35mins, 30th 35mins and 31st for 25mins, and twice on the 1st September. Attacker F.1 WA471 was flown on production test on the 4th and that afternoon flown to Farnborough for the SBAC Display. The 5th he flew Spitfire 692 and afterwards the first Attacker R.4000 for Pakistan, and another 7 times in the month. Seagull PA147 that had also been at Farnborough was flown down to Chilbolton on the 11th. In September Colquhoun flew 46 times in all including Swift VV106 on delivery to Farnborough on the 20th.

The first Pakistani Attacker R.4000 which first flew as G-15-110. (photo: F. Underwood)

The next three months were devoted to the Pakistan Attacker R.4000, starting on the 3rd October 1950, when Colquhoun gave it a flight test of 15mins at South Marston (The Home of the Attacker), and he flew to Chilbolton the same day, followed by another air test. The following day, the 4th, he started flying R.4000 to Pakistan as under:-

October			
4th	Chilbolton	Manston	30mins
4th	Manston	Nice	1.35hrs
4th	Nice	Malta	1.45hrs
5th	Malta	El Adem	1.30hrs
6th	El Adem	Nicosia	1.25hrs
7th	Nicosia	Baghdad	1.40hrs
7th	Baghdad	Bahrein	1.35hrs
8th	Bahrein	Sharjah	0.35hrs
8th	Sharjah	Mauripur	2.00hrs.

There are NO entries in Les's log book for November, so no flights.

In December he returned to the U.K. after air tests on the 2nd and 3rd as under:-

9th	Mauripur	Returned (R/T u/s)	1.00hr
10th	Mauripur	Jiwani	1.30hrs
10th	Jiwani	Sharjah	1.20hrs
10th	Sharjah	Bahrein	0.50hrs
10th	Bahrein	Habbaniya	1.55hrs
11th	Habbaniya	Nicosia	1.45hrs
11th	Nicosia	El Adem	2.00hrs
11th	El Adem	Bennina	0.40hrs
15th	Air Test		0.15hrs

15th	Bennina	Malta	1.30hrs
16th	Malta	Nice	1.50hrs
16th	Nice	Blackbushe	1.45hrs
16th	Blackbushe	Chilbolton	0.10mins

January 1951 was just a testing month for Attackers TS409 4 times, TS416 3 times, WA471 deliver to Boscombe Down, R.4000 deliver to South Marston, Spitfire G.15-129 twice and one Wellington. February flights were:- Ferry flights 4, TS409 twice, Wellington NC917 twice and Spitfires G.15-133 twice and G.15-136 once. These Class B registered Spitfires were Mark XIVs for the Royal Thai Air Force as U14-23/93 and U14-26/93 and were not allowed to fly under these registrations. February was quiet, he carried out 11 ferry flights, 10 Attacker production tests, Seagull PA147 test flight on the 9th and flew Spitfire G.15-143 from Eastleigh to Chilbolton taking 5mins.

On the 5th February 1951, a colleague of his, P. Robarts, was flying Attacker F.1 WA477, doing dives up to Mach 0.78, when the aircraft dived straight into the ground, and he was killed. No logical explanation was really found for the accident. This is as bad as being in the services and one of your friends failing to return. It leaves a lasting impression on you, that you might be next.

April was a slight improvement but he still flew 18 ferry flights, 9 Attacker production tests, Wellingtons PS960 and NA597 production tests, Spitfire SG108 delivery Chilbolton to Blackbushe on the 16th and SG104, VP451, SG113 and SG109 on production test.

May was a very busy period when he flew 58 times, 28 of these were ferry flights to the different aerodromes that were making or modifying Supermarine or Vickers aircraft, and they required a pilot to fly one, that was the idea of having shuttle or ferry aircraft to get the pilots quickly to each airfield. The three airfields in the Supermarine orbit were Chilbolton, Eastleigh and South Marston, Blackbushe being used as a transit field for some types of aircraft. Attacker were 18 production tests, the Seagull PA143 was flown on he 18th with Messrs Burnett, RA Harvey and Stewart as cooling and electronic experts. There were 12 Spitfire/Seafire production tests, six Seafires were FAA and the others were:- SG.103 on the 1st, SG120 22nd, Spitfire Trainer 158 24th, SG123 26th, SG122 30th and Spitfire Trainer 169 on the 31st.

June was another very busy month 67, flights being made, 27 being ferry, 22 Attacker production test with 10 with R.4000 and 3 TS416 for handling. Whilst flying WA485 on the 13th, and on taking off at 500ft, he lost his hood. After landing he went to search for it in the Auster G-AHLI but did not find it, but the following day using Auster G-AHLK they found it, no mention is made whether it was damaged or not. Spitfire F.22 PK542 was flown 6 times, and one on the 22nd is the phrase:- "Practise for race". On the same day he flies Rapide G-AHKB from Hatfield to Chilbolton, returning the next day to Hatfield in the same aircraft. He flies Spitfire PK542 to South Marston and then to Chilbolton on the 25th. Export Spitfires he flew were:- SG.121 on the 4th, SG.118 15th, SG.124 19th and SG.115 on the 27th, Spitfire Trainers:- E.160 on the 19th and E.161 on the 27th.

Up until January 1952, and not counting Swift aircraft which are not mentioned, the Aifield Flights of South Marston from January 1948 to January 1952, list Les Colquhoun as having flown 843 test flights. I think Supermarine got value out of this number of flights, and he must have enjoyed his time whilst with them and vice versa.

9. Swift flight testing begins

In July 1951 he flew 59 times, 12 of them using Attacker F.1 WA485 on cockpit heating trials, 12 on Attacker F.1 R.4000 but not entered what test, 18 on the new VV119, Type 535 Swift, 2nd prototype fitted with a nose wheel undercarriage and reheat, which would give it a completely different taxiing and performance characteristic. Colquhoun first flew this one on the 3rd July (it had first flown on the 23rd August 1950 at Boscombe Down). He flew it on level speeds at 5,000ft and 35,000ft, throttling back tests, handling and air brakes and throttling back tests combined, on the 23rd he was asked to pose for photography by the Crown Film Unit, on the 25th it was air brake assessment and gun sightings, and finally on the 27th for air brake tests at altitude. Seagull PA143 was flown 3 times, the 4th, 13th and 17th on cooling trials.

The TEAM of actors, actresses, stage hands and Supermarine workers, Ann Todd is in 2nd row from top and Les Colquhoun is in bottom row 7th from right.

Nigel Patrick who plays the test pilot in the film "Sound Barrier" receiving first-hand instruction from Les Colquhoun, on the actual aircraft, which was VV119 "Prometheus", note the special foot hold and the special set of steps.

It was also during this time that a film unit invaded the sanctuary of Chilbolton, from where Colquhoun was testing the Type 535 Swift. This was *The Sound Barrier*, starring Ann Todd, Ralph Richardson, Dinah Sheridan, Nigel Patrick and John Justin, directed by Alexander Korda and produced by David Lean. The aircraft which was the star in the film was the Supermarine Type 535, VV119, which for the film was named "Prometheus". The film crew took longer than anticipated to finish because of the incessant rain and were there from the end of 1951 until well into 1952. The film was shot during the day, and rushes of it were shown in the nearest cinema, which was Andover, and shown after the last film. The Andover people flocked to the cinema to see the days shooting, which were projected for them to see and comment upon, after the main performance had finished.

Ann Todd, Les Colquhoun, unknown and David Lean on location.

The people who produced this film, British Lion, allowed the Royal Air Force Association to fly a copy of the finished film "Sound Barrier" over to Brussels, Belgium, on the 13th November 1953, so that they could have a premier of it over there. Before this however, on the 12th Ann Todd and her husband Film producer David Lean with other representatives of the film empire flew out to Brussels and were greeted by General Le Boute, Chief of the Belgian Air Force, and a guard of honour plus the usual press people. A cavalcade of a dozen cars escorted them into Brussels to the Town Hall where a band played a fanfare to the people in the crowded Grand Place. Here a reception in their honour was presented by the Burgomaster, M. Van De Meulebroeck and later in the evening a party was held for them in the British Embassy by the British Ambassador Sir Christopher Warner.

The following day, the 13th, a crowd gathered at the Brussels airport to see Les Colquhoun land in the "Prometheus" carrying a copy of the "Sound Barrier" and before landing carried out a demonstration of the aircraft's capabilities before the crowd. The film was taken to the Palais des Beaux Arts where it was shown before H.R.H. Prince Albert of Belgium and two of the Supermarine pilots were presented to the audience, they were Geoffrey Quill and Michael Lithgow, Les Colquhoun was presented to the Prince afterwards.

The Air Ministry had also authorized that the Crown Film Unit visit Chilbolton, so that they could take some photographs of VV119, it was already bedlam without having this crew, Colquhoun flew one flight on the 23rd July to pose for them. It was the other pilots who flew the film series, and Colquhoun had to settle for the mundane jobs. The photograph shows the whole team at the end of the filming. The film showed excellent views of "Prometheus" in the air-to-air role and no undue tricks were used to enhance any of the scenes, it was all real photography of the real thing. There were no model aircraft and no stunts used in the film; what you saw, was always the real thing.

August was another extremely busy month with 70 flights, 29 Ferry, 33 Attacker, including R.4004 on the 9th, R.4005 22nd, 23rd and 25th, Swift 535 VV119 on the 10th for rate of roll and camera gun tests, and twice more on the 16th. The others were mundane production tests. Two aircraft not given a date were Spitfires G.15-167 and 168. His last flights for August was Attacker R.4000 having two air tests of 55 and 50mins.

On 8th September 1951 Dave Morgan whilst practicing for the SBAC Display in WJ960, Dave Morgan experienced a loud bang, and he lost all power in the engine. He raised the undercarriage and flaps to 30 degrees, and managed to fly safely under some power cables, but a house got in the way and he tried to fly the between the house of Charity Down Farm and a barn but it was too narrow and his left wing hit the outside lavatory and he landed slightly damaged in a field just beyond it.

Colquhoun's next flight was on the 17th September when he picked up Swift 535 VV119 and flew it from Farnborough to Chilbolton, with a flight the next day for lateral control checks. On the 19th it was airbrake check tests, 20th, 21st and 26th(2) it was lateral control tests, with a final one on the 28th of gun sighting test, the longest flight lasting for 55mins. He flew Seagull PA143 twice for cooling trials with Messrs Burnett, Hodgson and Austin for 1.15hrs on the 19th and with Burnett, Miller and Stewart on the 28th. His workload for October was somewhat reduced, in that he only flew 31 times, 15 of which were ferry flights, 10 were with Attacker R.4000. He flew Attacker R.4009 on the 9th and 10th for 35 and 45mins respectively and R.4010 on the 30th for 30mins. In November he flew 51 flights, 21 were ferry, 31 Attacker with the following included:-

12th	R.4008	South Marston	Nice	1.55hrs
12th	R4008	Nice	Malta	1.30hrs
13th	R4008	Malta	El Adem 1.25hrs	
13th	R4008	El Adem	Nicosia	1.20hrs
13th	R4008	Nicosia	Baghdad returned	
14th	R4008	Nicosia	Baghdad returned	
14th	R4008	Nicosia	Baghdad	1.25hrs
15th	R4008	Baghdad	Bahrein	1.25hrs
15th	R4008	Bahrein	Sharjah	0.50hrs
15th	R4008	Sharjah	Karachi	1.45hrs

This was the delivery of one of the 36 Attackers that had been ordered for the Pakistan Air Force, and as can be seen, took 13.05hrs to get there. He returned to Chilbolton by the 20th so he did not do much sight seeing. Other Pakistan aircraft test flown were:- R.4012 on the 25th 3 times for 1.40hrs total.

In December he again flew Attacker R.4012 on the 5th for 1.05hrs, R.4000 for 6 flights, R.4013 14th for 45mins, R.4013 18th for 1.05mins and R.4014 for 50mins. His total flights for the month were 24, including 8 ferry trips.

January 1952 and he flew 47 flights including 18 ferry trips, 19 Pakistan Attackers including 17 on R.4013, R.4017 was flown 31st for 1.05hrs. February, a rather quiet month, only 16 flights with 7 ferry trips. One of these trips was in Rapide G-AHKB, to look for Attacker

F.1 WA485 that had crashed on the 7th February 1952 between Leckford Village and Fullerton Junction Railway Station, South of Andover, and Lt/Cdr M.R. Orr-Ewing lost his life. It had only arrived down from South Marston on the 5th for manufacturer's trials. Swift 535 VV119 was flown by Colquhoun on the 22nd twice. In March he flew 40 times, 18 of them being ferry, and the rest were Attacker production flights. April was even worse, only 8 flights with 3 Ferry and 5 Attacker, one of them was WT851 which he flew for 45mins on the 12th, this was a replacement aircraft for a previous one that had crashed before delivery.

L.R. Colquhoun with WJ965 Type 541 Swift, behind him, probably taken on the 13th August 1952 with his test pilot's knee pad in his hand.

May 1952 it was 16 flights with two ferry (these times are now one time only, the different ferry flights are all added into one). On the 7th he flew Swift 541 WJ960 (first flown 1st August 1951 by MJ Lithgow) for 30mins, and again on the 9th and 16th for air intake tests for 45 and 40mins respectively. In June, Colquhoun went to Belgium to check out their Spitfires and ended up flying them for one hour. July he started on the 2nd with Attacker F.1 WK319, and flew it another 6 times on the 4th, 7th and 8th. On the 12th he was given the Type 508, VX133 (first flown 31st August 1951 by MJ Lithgow) fitted with two Rolls-Royce AJ.65 of 7,500lb. st., each, twice the power of the aircraft he had

been flying, which would have given him a completely new experience, and a transonic capability, and he flew it for 25mins. The same day he flew the Type 535 VV119 for air test, and then a demonstration practice, followed by a demonstration at Lee on Solent of 30mins. He flew WJ960 3 times on air intake tests, and WJ965 3 times on general handling (this is the first and second prototype Type 541 Swifts).

Les Colquhoun, with helmet and oxygen mask, similar to the one he used in the Middle East, ready for take off.

August was quiet in that only two Attacker and 6 Swift flights were flown. He flew WJ965 five times, one on the 13th being to provide a photograph for the "Times", which took 50mins, the other were for handling tests. September there were 7 flights, Attacker

WK319 for C(S)A trials for 2.00hrs, Swift VV106 handling 5th and 18th and WJ965 for Demonstration at the SBAC Show on the 2nd, 4th and 6th, flying to Chilbolton from Farnborough on the 10th. October there were only six production tests of Attackers, including R.4028 on the 21st and R.4029 on the 23rd. November there were 15 flights, 11 with Type 535 VV119, it flew to Blackbushe on the 20th, and then on to Brussels in 55mins, returning on the 22nd in 40mins. December only eight flights, Attacker R.4031 18th and 5 RN Attackers, Seafire F.XV G.15-124 flown from Gatwick and Spitfire F.24 PK481 on air test.

Swift prototype VV119 flying off the South Coast of England.

January 1953 consisted of 7 Attacker flights, R.4032 on the 22nd and R.4033 on the 29th, and 5 RN Attackers on production test, also Swift F.1 WK195 the second production, on the 20th for 25 and 30mins.

February he flew 15 times, the Type 535 VV119 on he 16th, Swift WJ960 on the 5th for handling with a V.I. Tail, (This means variable incidence), and he flew it again on the 23rd for 25 and 30mins respectively. All the other flights were with Swift F.1, WK194 for handling and development. Of his 17 flights in March, he flew 4 in WJ960, 2 in WJ965, 9 in WK194, and a solitary one in WK196. It was during this month that Dave Morgan flew the first Supermarine aircraft to go Supersonic, and he was flying WJ960 on the 26th February 1953 when he thought he had only got to Mach 0.96 but the people at Chilbolton had heard a supersonic boom. Later it was proved that the instrumentation was slightly out and he had gone faster than sound. Mike Lithgow followed suit the following day. On the 24th May Mike Lithgow flew WJ965 past Mach 1 and Les Colquhoun also accomplished this feat on the 26th May, the Mach meter only had an indication of M 0.96, however, which was very deceptive.

Les tries out new flying helmet – nicknamed a "bone dome". (K. Colquhoun)

The word Mach means nothing to a lot of people, but to pilots it meant the true meaning of speed. (Mach was an Austrian physicist who died in 1916). This is a combination of Air Temperature, Density (height) and of course actual speed. At Sea Level the speed of sound is at 760mph but the temperature decreases at the rate of 2 degrees per 1,000ft., up to 36,000ft, and then remains constant up to about 100,000ft. To show some examples of this is the easiest and an indicated speed of 400mph at sea level works out at M = 0.53, at 20,000ft it is M = 0.78 and at 30,000ft it is M = 0.97. The Indicated

Airspeed (IAS) is also incorrect, because it is not corrected for changes caused by Temperature and Barometric Pressure and also for the instrument errors, and is mainly only used for low altitude and low speed use.

April he flew 17 flights, consisting of 8 Attacker production test, 3 Swift WJ960 VI tail tests on the 16th and 23rd, Swift F.1 WK194 on the 1st, WK195 on the 15th for reheat tests and Spitfire F.22 PK481, on the 24th an air test, then on the 28th and 29th air firing of the LOCKIE gun for 50 and 40mins respectively. (This was a special 34mm cannon made by Vickers with some special features believed designed by S/Ldr Lockie). These gun-firing tests with PK481 continued on the 4th and 5th May of 45, 45, 45, 35mins until it forced landed at Tarrant Rushton after a further 50mins flying, which caused these tests to be discontinued. Also in between these tests Colquhon carried out gun firing tests with Swift F.1 WK194 of 30 and 30mins on the 1st May, also on the 17th, 19th and 20th.

Mike Lithgow, clad in civilian clothes in a prototype Swift.

17th April 1953 was a red letter day for Chilbolton, because on this day The Duke of Edinburgh flew in on the Viscount 700 G-AMAV aircraft accompanied by the Duke of Kent, Major General CAL Dunphie (Managing Director of Vickers-Armstrongs aircraft division), Mr T Gammon (director) and Air Commodore, Sir EH Fielden, Captain of the Queen's Flight. To receive the Royal Party was Joe Smith, the Chief Designer of Supermarine and all of the test pilots:- Jeffrey Quill, Mike Lithgow, Dave Morgan, Les Colquhoun, Chunky Horne and Pee Wee Judge. The Duke then entered the Flight-test hangar and looked at the Type 508s VX133 and 136, Swift F.1 WK194 and sat in its cockpit and then went on to view Swift prototype VV119 and Mk.IV Swift WK198 together with the prototype Spitfire Trainer G-AIDN. The Duke of York was also interested and had most things explained to him by Les Colquhoun. He then went on to visit Hursley Park and South Marston.

WK198 a Swift F.IV with wing and nose pitot tubes for test purposes.

His total flights for May were 27 with Swift WJ965 being used for photography on the 26th for 1.20 and 1.20hrs.

June he had only 10 flights, 2 Ferry, WJ960, WJ965 6 times for handling, these flights taking 40, 35, 35, 50, 50 and 55mins respectively, on the 4th, 8th, 9th, and 10th and WK196 for an air test. It is also reported that he flew Swift F.1 WK197 on the 4th June 1953 on a demonstration flight for the Turkish Prime Minister, who was on a visit to Wisley and Vickers, and he went through the sound barrier, indicating Mach 1.05 via the wing mounted boom pitot head, (not the nose type of pitot as on WJ965), and the Prime Minister heard the associated boom and was suitably impressed. This flight however is not recorded in his log book, so who slipped up?

Three flights of Swifts in July being WK197 on the 2nd and 21st when it was flown from Boscombe Down back to Chilbolton and WK200 on an air test. In August he flew Swift WK197 10 times on intensive flying, Attackers WA491 twice on cabin heating, the 24th and 25th and WZ292 on the 18th on production test.

RECORD FLIGHTS

In 1950, with the success of the Type 510, Supermarine and its pilots were thinking about taking back the World Speed Record from America, but there was no engine available until the reheat version of the Avon was fitted into the Swift F.3. When the Variable-incidence tailplane and saw-toothed wing leading edge were fitted to WK198, making it into the prototype F.4, an aircraft had arrived where all of the wishful thinking could now come to fruition, and the end of 1953 was the obvious time. It was first flown by Mike Lithgow on the 2nd May 1953 and fore boded well for the new Swift, now up to the required standard.

The next problem was to select a place where the record could be attempted. It had to be flat, and very hot in the day, with a hard runway, with the necessary facilities. This resolved itself to an RAF airfield in Libya called Castel Benito, but now called Idris el Awal, where the temperature was known to have got to 139 degrees F, and the temperature at Idris for the speed runs would be about 105°F, which would give the speed of sound of about 790mph, and the maximum Swift speed of about 743mph. On the 7th September 1953 Neville Duke set the World Absolute Speed Record in the Hawker Hunter, WB188, at 727.6mph (M=0.943).

On the 11th September 1953 four wives, who were married to test pilots, attended the Farnborough Air Display and were :- Mrs "Mike" Lithgow, Mike was flying the Swift F.III WK195, Mrs "Jock" Bryce, whose husband was flying the Black Valiant WJ954, Mrs Frank Murphy, her husband was flying the Hawker Hunter and Mrs Leslie Colquhoun, Les Colquhoun was on stand by with Supermarine.

September Colquhoun did no flying until the 16th, when he took Swift WK197 for a continuation of the intensive flying on the type, and on the 17th he collected Attacker WZ286 from South Marston and flew it to Chilbolton taking 1.10hrs, where on the 18th he took it up for a consumption test for 1.10hrs. He flew Attacker WZ286 on the 22nd to Nice in 1.05hrs, escorting Mike Lithgow in Swift F.4 WK198, both continuing on to Tunis in 0.50mins and then to Idris in Libya in 1.10hrs. Whilst there he was in charge of a survey party to select a suitable course, including aircraft maintenace and the ground party under Mr Charles Barter, of 12 from Supermarine, that arrived on the 22nd. He selected a main road 50 miles southwest of Tripoli, that run straight for 10 miles over the Aziza Plain to Bur el Gnem, and really showed up well even to a pilot traveling at 700mph. The course ended up between the 81st and 84th kilometer stones along this road.

The Royal Aero Club observers, Major Bob Mayo, Col. Preston, Philip Mayne and Capt. Hubert Broad, at the 81st kilometer stone on the Speed Record course.

Colquhoun flew the Attacker on the 24th in support of the Swift for Record Practice liaison, when it was found that the radio reception from Idris to the local ground station was not possible, so the Attacker was used flown at a height of 5,000ft for the job. On the 25th, Colquhoun went for an air test with the Swift, followed by another flight in the Attacker for R/T liaison record attempts.

This flight by Colquhoun in the Attacker, was for R/T messages from Lithgow back to the ground base and was carried out on the 26th twice more when the record attempt was flown. The Swift F.4 WK198 broke the World Speed Record at a speed of 735.7mph as an average of its four runs over the course of 3 kilometres, at a height of less than 500 metres (1640ft). One more flight on the 28th to better it but it was not possible. The Attacker flew again on the 29th twice, for timing gear calibration. During the record flight Lithgow's refrigeration suit was not functioning and he had trouble with his oxygen mask, also he could not use the reheat for as long as he had hoped so his speed was down, and he had the worst time flying a Swift that he would ever have. The wing fences had been removed just prior to the attempt for the best results. The resultant speed, being only 8mph less than the least that they had hoped to achieve.

Swift F.IV WK198 taking off for the World Speed Record attempt.

Colquhoun flew WZ286 again on the 2nd October and the 3rd as R/T Liaison Record attempts, but the original result was taken. Then on the 7th he carried out a demonstration in the local area. Then on the 8th he flew Idris to Tunis in 50mins, Tunis to Nice in 1.15hrs and Nice to Chilbolton in 1.35hrs. The World Speed Record did not hold for long before the Americans broke it.

Fly High ~ Fly Low

WK198 demonstration above Tripoli Harbour after the event.

During the rest of October Les flew Swift WK197 on intensive flying 7 times, on the 16th it was WK195 for Mk.II handling and 4 more for production testing. November was very quiet with only 6 flights, one with Attacker WZ299 on the 2nd for 1.25hrs, Swifts WK194 on the 2nd for gun firing 1.00hr, WK195 Mk.II handling 20mins, WK197 intensive flying 45mins and WK200 for handling with a PR nose of 50 and 45mins. December only 4 flights with Swifts, WK200 for FR handling on the 4th, WK201 on the 29th for stalling tests twice of 1.05 and 0.55 hrs and WK202 for production tests.

Top picture shows Supermarine fitters forcing compressed air through dry ice into the ventilated suit to cool the cockpit for Mike Lithgow before the record attempt and below the Swift flying so fast that the pressure wave is disturbing the sand on the ground as it passes over, because it is so low.

January 1954 was just Swift testing, WK195, 7 times for Mk.III handling and WK197 four times for generator cooling tests. February, was an eventful month, because some of the Supermarine test pilots were invited to participate in the Coronation Cup (Handicap) down the Cresta Run, St Moritz, on the 7th February 1954.

The test pilots L-R F/Lt CNC Mitchell, S/Ldr N Duke all kitted out and ready to attempt the run, F/Lt LR Colquhoun and Lt/Cdr M Lithgow.

The Cup was really a work out between the Americans and the British with 16 British, 6 American and 6 other nationalities taking part. However they allowed 7 others to take part in a practise run, namely:- S/Ldr Neville Duke, F/Lt LR Colquhoun, Lt/Cdr Mike Lithgow with the experienced person of F/Lt CNC Mitchell as the Cresta Run expert. There were three other novice riders:- JR Heaton, P Arnold and EG Nelson of the USA. All of the main bunch were handicapped varying from scratch to 3.5 seconds, and had three runs each, with the top three ending up being:- EG Nelson (USA) with 136.4, A Vatimbella (GR) with 136.8 and M Muller also on 136.8 seconds. The average time per run varied from being from 45.9 to 55.9secs. A total of 23 persons succeeded in getting times with 4 others (all GB) not recording three finishes, one of these was Lord Brabazon who fell on the first run, and did not try again. Our intrepid aviators recorded the following times:- N. Duke 63.7secs, M Lithgow 70.6secs and LR Colquhoun 83.0secs

When they returned it was back to test flying as usual. There were just 10 flights on production tests and Attacker WK302 the same on the 27th.

> *Groundabout*
>
> **The Name's the Same.** I'm afraid Leslie Colquhoun (pronounced "Cahoon," as if you didn't know), Supermarine test pilot, has got himself a nickname. While with Mike Lithgow's record-breaking Swift team he was reported in the local North African paper by the name of "Ali El Kahoun."

A humorous cartoon from the time.

March it was Attacker WA520 on the 5th and four Swifts on production tests. However April had improved to 12 fights, all Swifts, 7 on production tests and WK200 on the 8th with camera tests in 1.05hrs, WK201 on the 22nd handling with drop tank on the 22nd and WK215 on the 23rd for Mk.II handling tests of 1.00, 1.00 and 0.40hrs duration. May there were 21 flights with one Attacker WZ286 being delivered to South Marston, the remaining 20 are Swifts. All of them being flown on:- Mk.II handling, WK201(2), WK214(5), WK215(3), WK216(2), WK217(3), WK218(5).

May was a very nostalgic month for Les Colquhoun, when the RAFA (Royal Air Force Association) organized an Operation "Malta Pilgrimage". This was when more than 500 relatives and comrades went to Malta on the 3rd May 1954 to meet HRH the Queen and HRH the Duke of Edinburgh, when she unveiled an RAF Memorial at Valetta of 2,300 officers and men of the Commonwealth who had lost their lives in the defence of Malta. All of the 500 had been transported to Malta by the T.S.S. "Mediterranean" and six aircraft, one of which was an Avro York of Hunting Airlines which carried 55 of the pilgrims of the 214 that flew out to the island. The other five were four Vikings and a Dakota and the time taken was about seven hours. These were the mothers, fathers, wives and children and ex serving personnel who had flown or been there during the axis period. The Queen gave an address to the crowd and in it she said:-

"To you I would give this message of hope – if we show in all our dealings the same integrity of purpose, and the same resolution in fulfilling it as was shown by them in the war, then surely we shall be able to extract from the dark and desperate difficulties which still beset us, a victory no less glorious than that which we commemorate here today."

The Air Forces Monument is a 50ft high column with an 8ft gilded bronze eagle, and the Queen laid the first wreaths at its base. After the Ceremony the Queen did a walkabout among the attendees with the Duke of Edinburgh who had accompanied her on the visit. The amazing thing about this pilgrimage was that though it cost about £30,000, a lot of money at this time, the pilgrims had all their expenses paid by contributions from the public, £5,000 from RAFA, £969/0/4d from the Maltese themselves, £990/0/10d from other Overseas areas. £750 from the British Legion, and smaller amounts from almost all of the other RAFA Organisations, like the £5 from Calne British Legion, but only £2/2s from its neighbour Chippenham.

The month of June was fairly busy in comparison to the last few months when he flew 26 times. The first flight was in Spitfire 504 on a production test on the 3rd, followed by Swift WK214 on Mk.II handling and 12 others later. WK195 was on reheat tests on the 15th and six later flights. WK196 was flown from South Marston on the 26th and WK219 was flown to South Marston on the 29th, WK197 was on generator cooling tests on the 26thwhilst WK218 was on air test on the 30th. July was a rather quiet one with only 8 flights, WJ960 on hood tests on the 2nd, WK195 on reheat tests same day, and 6 flights on Mk.II handling.

August 1954 was another typical month, flying 18 times with 7 production flights, four reheat tests on WK195, 6 Mk.II handling tests and WK221 to RAF Waterbeach on the 30th. September, the total flights were 19, 5 were production tests, 2 reheat tests on WK195, WK214 on Mk.II handling on he 9th. WK247 was delivered to Chilbolton on the 3rd and return to South Marston on the 13th. WK239 was delivered to Waterbeach on he 2nd, WK206 and WK211 testing at Waterbeach on the 16th. WK195 for the SBAC Show on the 8th and return Chilbolton, 9th air test and 10th to Farnborough and then flown at the show, and also on the 12th. October only 4 flights WK211 testing at Waterbeach on the 1st, WK245 to Waterbeach on the 21st, and WK248 production tests and fly to Boscombe Down on the 27th.

The Swift F.IV WK195 that was at the 1953 Farnborough Air Display as in photograph, but also appeared in the 1954 show.

In November, 7 flights of WK249 to WK255 between the 13th and 30th, of production tests. December only 7 flights, WK248 Mk.III handling 6th, WK218 Mk.II handling on the 17th and 18th, and production tests for WK254 18th, WK253 20th, WK257 22nd and WK252 on the 30th.

On the 1st January 1955 the name changed to Vickers-Armstrongs (Aircraft) Ltd. but the Supermarine name did not go into history until later.

January 1955 only six flights, WK215 on the 19th on handling with link collectors, production tests of WK252 20th and 24th, WK255 24th and WK251 on the 27th. In between these Swifts, he flew a Hawker Hunter Mk.II on the 25th for 40mins. For February it was all Swifts again, with WK272 for Mk.IV handling on the 2nd with delivery to Boscombe Down on the 7th, WK217 for surge tests on the 10th, 16th (2), 17th and 28th(2), WK273 RR Avon 116 assessment on the 17th and 20th. . .

March 1955, and he carried out 21 Swift flights, WK196 on the 2nd for cabin conditioning and again on the 18th for drop tank handling. WK217 on the 4th for surge tests, WK274 to South Marston 7th, but he flew it again on the 10th 3 times for handling with drop tank and twice for performance, and on the 12th and the 14th (2), 15th, 16th and the 30th, WK273 he flew fitted with wing tips on the 14th, WK272 on the 17th for Mk.V handling, WK219 on the 17th (2) for gun firing. April, and he flew 21 times, all Swifts, WK274 he flew 16 times on performance, take off tests and roll measurements, WK275 flying tail tests on the 3rd, WK197 on brake tests on the 4th and WK219 to Boscombe Down on the 6th. May he only flew the Swift 4 times, WK276 on the 11th from South Marston, WK273 on the 16th for vibration checks and two on production tests. June he flew Swifts 9 times, WK275 on the 8th for flying tail tests, WK216 for gun firing on the 16th and 7 for production tests.

July 1955 it was only 6 flights, WK273 on the 4th as a target aircraft, WK195 on the 5th to Warton, WK273 on air test on the 7th, WK274 for performance on the 25th and 26th and WK297 on production test on the 13th. August it was 9 flights, WK196 on the 2nd and 5th for demisting trials, WK248 on the 15th for weapon air supply tests, WK273 and WK275 22nd air test, WK279 23rd and 31st for Mk.7 handling, XD904 and XD905 31st practice for SBAC Show (these two were the first and second of the production contract of 58). September flights increased to 23 with:- XD904 to Farnborough on the 4th, and Farnborough to South Marston on the 8th with a return to Farnborough for a display at the SBAC Show later that day.

WK198 on ventilation on the 19th, also WK 248 on weapon air supply, WK274 was flown 12 times on performance, WK279 for Mk.7 handling and WK278 on anti 'G' tests on the 17th (2) and the 20th.

October he flew 13 times, XD904 on the 3rd South Marston to Chilbolton, WK278 on the 7th anti 'G'tests, WK308 to Chilbolton on the 11th, WK279 27th to South Marston 27th, WK277 on the 27th, 28th

(2) and 31st on autostabiliser tests, XD905 5TH, XD906 20th, XD908 10th, XD909 28th and XD910 on production test. November was similar with:- WK277 on autostabiliser tests on the 1st (2), XD907 9th, XD909 11th, XD912 15th, XD914 21st, XD916 26th and XD911 all on production tests. December XD907 8th deliver South Marston to Boscombe Down, XD911 an air test 16th and 19th deliver South Marston to Aldergrove, the following Swift FR.5 aircraft were all on production test on the dates shown, XD917 10th, XD919 21st, XD915 23rd, XD921 29th and XD920 on the 30th.

Swift FR.5 XD904 with everything down at Farnborough 1955.

January 1956 was really quiet, Colquhoun recorded 2.15hrs flying the Rapide G-AHJA and 50mins the Auster G-AHLK. Also he flew Swifts XD922 on the 9th and XD924 and XD915 on the 13th for air tests. February was slightly better, Swift PR.V WK274 on the 2nd, WK308, WK275 (2) air tests on the 10th and XD909 reheat development on the 15th. The test flights were XD923 6th, XD930 23rd, XD925 21st and XD949 on the 28th. March the weather must have been improving because he accomplished 34 flights, WK196 F.IV test flight 8th, XD909 reheat development flights on the 13th, 14th (3), 21st (3) and 23rd, and production tests with XD925 21st, XD925 (15) in 6.35hrs, XD949 26th, XD928 27th, XD950 27th and XD948 28th. [The ( ) are the number of times flown

April he flew Swifts XD909 on the 6th from Chilbolton to South Marston, Swift FR.7 XF774 (4) (this was the prototype Blue Sky missile launcher) F.7 and flew from South Marston to Chilbolton on the 11th.

He test flew WK279 on the 16th and 17th, XD954 (2) 30th, and XD954 (2) 19th production tests, XD903 and XD914 test flight on the 20th. May he flew almost all of the aircraft many times as shown:- XD958 (2) 1st, XD903 Chilbolton to Boscombe Down, WK294 (7) and XD957 (2) 4th, XD956 (5) 10th, WK293 (2) 16th, WK310 (2) 17th, Spitfire AB910 South Marston to Chilbolton 18th, XD955 (3) 23rd, WK309 (7) 24th, XD954 (3) 29th and WK312 (4) 30th. June he flew Swifts on production flights:- XD959 (5) 5th, WK298 (2) 13th, XD960 (3) 19th, WK315 (3) 20th, and on the 22nd XF780 (2nd prototype F.VII) (4), WK292, and XF774 on the 22nd, 26th, 27th, 28th and 29th.

XD905 was flown at the display on the 9th, believed to be the one in the water colour picture taking off and just airborne.

In July 1956 Les flew 18 times but with only 5 Swift Vs, WN124 (this should have been the first of 58 F.4 but all were cancelled except it, and that had to be completed as an FR.5) 2nd test flight, WK291 (9), WK311 (1), WN124 (5) and WK290 (2) on production tests. August was about the same with: Swifts WK303 (2) 14th, XF113 FR.7 (3) 14th and WK300 (3) on production tests, WK308 and XD904 20th, WK308 (2) 21st and XD904 on tests flight, and WK275 Chilbolton to South Marston 30th, XD904 Chilbolton to Boscombe Down 31st. September was the same pattern except that the SBAC Show came at the start of the month, XF113 F.VII flown South Marston to

Farnborough 2nd, carried out 6 flights between the 3rd and the 8th. WK296 FR.V flown to Farnborough 11th. An F.VII flown on Radar cooling tests on the 28th and 30th (3) for 30mins and 3 for 3hrs. Production tests were carried out with WK296 (3) 13th, WK287 (4) 23rd, WK288 (6) 24th, WK301 (7) 26th and WK314 (4) 27th. October 3rd and Swift F.7 XF780 was on radar cooling trials, and all of the following were on production test:- WK513 and XF114 (11) 4th, XF113 20th, WK307 (3) 23rd, WK306 and WK295 (2) 25th, WK281 26th and XD962 30th. November only three on production test WK297 (3), XF117 (3) and WK302 (8). December was also quiet with only 3 Swifts flown, XD904 South Marston to Wisley (Vickers airfield near Weybridge), WK289 10th and XF116 (3) on the 29th.

Swift F.7 XF774 fitted with dummy Fairey "Fireflash" guided missiles.

10. South Marston and Scimitar testing

In 1956 Les went to the Vickers factory at South Marston, near Swindon, where all of the work and staff were moving to, from all of its factories in Hampshire, and its Headquarters at Hursley Park. It was having to contract, and move into more up to date premises for the wooden huts at Hursley Park had outlived their usefulness.

Les Colquhoun in the process of climbing into a Scimitar aircraft. (K. Colquhoun)

1957, January the start of a new year, and it must have been a fine clear month, because he flew a total of 28 flights. 26 of these were his normal production testing of Swift aircraft:- XD965 (4) 7th, XD963 (3) 9th, XF119 (3) 16th, XF120 (3) 17th, XD966 (3) 22nd, XD964 (3) 26th, XD970 (1) 26th, XF117 (2) 28th and XF116 (2) 29th. To finish the month off he flew a familiarisation flight in a twin engined Scimitar F.1 WW134 for 1.00 hour. (This type was used by the Royal Navy, this aircraft is the third production prototype). February was also flyable and he flew 26 times in Swift aircraft, XF119 (3) 8th and

XD968 (1), XD972 (3) 15th, WK278 (5) 20th, XD973 (2) 22nd and XF121 (3), WK277 (4) 25th and WK274 (5) 28th. March a very similar month of Swift flying of 34 flights:- XD967 (5) 1st, XF118 (1) 4th, XD969 (2) 11th, XF114 (14) 14th, (the (14) is suspect but it is written), XF117 (1) 20th, XD974 (5) 22nd, XF116 (1) 25th, XD976 (5) 27th and XF115 (1) 30th.

Scimitar F.1 XD212 first production flown on the 13th April.

April was a similar flying month to March with XF116 flight from South Marston to RAF Valley, followed by production flights XD965 and XD974 on the 4th, and Scimitar F.1 XD212 (the first production aircraft) on the 13th for 35mins.

Swift FR.V WK276 (2) 15th, XD975 (4) and XF123 (3) 25th and XF122 (3) on the 29th. May there were only two Scimitar F.1 aircraft flown, XD213 (3) 4th and XD216 (3) 25th on production flights. There was however 14.05hrs of Rapide G-AHJA, ferry flying. June was another very quiet month with only two days flying of:- XD212 Scimitar F.1 flying from South Marston to Wisley near Weybridge, and 10 flights in Swift F.1 XF124 on production flying. The Rapide flying was 7.20 hours.

July Colquhoun started off the month flying Spitfire AB910 on the 4th on air test, on the 12th he flew it from South Marston to Wisley, on the 22nd he flew it from White Waltham back to South Marston, finally on the 29th he finished off by giving it another air test. Back to testing, on the 10th he flew Scimitar F.1 XD215 on 4 production tests, then delivered it from South Marston to Boscombe Down the same day. Scimitar F.1 XD214 19th and 20th on production tests. On the 20th he carried out C.A. tests with WT854 and with WT859 on the 22nd (these were the first and second production prototypes of the Type 544 Scimitar). He delivered XD214 South Marston to Wisley on the 20th and on the 29th, so that someone else flew it there in he first case. The only Swift he flew this month was a Mk.IV WK275 on 5 production flights on the 24th. AUGUST, and he flew Scimitars XD215 on 3 production tests, on the 17th XD219 from South Marston to Boscombe Down, on the 25th it was production test on Swift F.4 WK275, then fly it South Marston to Boscombe Down, followed by Mk.V XD903, and finally for the month fly Scimitar XD221 on production test. To get from A to B he flew Rapide G-AHJA for 3.35hrs and Rapide G-AHKB for 11.45hrs.

September 1957 and he flew Scimitars, XD220 12th on production test but landed at Boscombe Down, returning to South Marston on the 15th. On the 21st it was XD220 (6) and XD220 (7) on 29th for production tests, then it was fly XD221 from South Marston to RNAS Ford on the 25th and XD222 (5) on production tests on the 29th.

October it was Scimitars XD222 (1) 9th, XD220 (2) 10th, XD223 (6) 23rd and XD224 (1) on the 26th for production tests. NOVEMBER he flew XF113 (4) on the 1st, XD906 (2) 22nd, WK291 (3) 26th with Scimitar XD224 (4) and XD225 (4) 29th all of these on production flights. DECEMBER he managed Scimitars XD226 (3) 20th, XD227 (3) 25th, XD224 (5) and XD225 (2) on the 29th and XD228 on the 31st, on production tests.

January 1958 the Scimitar production was now in full swing, and they dominate the flight testing and production flying with XD227 on the 8th, XD228 (6) 13th, XD226 16th with delivery to Boscombe Down the same day, XD227 also to Boscombe Down on the 18th, XD230 (3) 21st and XD231 on the 27th. FEBRUARY XD228 (4) 13th and on the 14th from South Marston to RNAS Lee-on-Solent (a main FAA station), XD230 South Marston to Boscombe Down 17th but returning the same day, then back on production testing on the 24th, XD231 South Marston to Boscombe Down 26th and return the same day and finally XD232 production testing on the 19th. To fly these 8 aircraft he flew the new DH Heron G-AHGW for 35mins and the Rapide G-AHJA for 5.15hrs, and he had to carry out an ARB (Air Registration Board) on Auster G-AHLK. MARCH was really quiet with XD231 (1) on the 15th for 1.05hrs and XD232 (6) 22nd 5.05hrs total on production flying, and even 7.25hrs on the Rapide G-AHJA.

April 1958 was a normal month with XD231 being delivered from South Marston to RNAS Ford on the 1st, XD234 (5) 14th, XD236 (8) 22nd, XD232 (4) 24th, XD235 (7) 25th with XD237 (3) and XD238 (5) 26th. MAY he flew XD234 (3) 2nd, XD236 (2) 7th, XD238 15th, XD237 (6) 22nd and XD240 23rd, with Swift FR.5 XD912 also flown on the 22nd.. JUNE it was all Scimitar production flying XD242 (2) 18th, XD238 (4) 19th, XD237 (5) 20th, XD239 (8) 26th, XD240 (5) 27th and XD241 (2) 30th.

July 1958 was XD241 (2) 1st, XD240 (2) also XD242 2nd and XD243 on he 4th. AUGUST was not much better with Swift XF113 (3) 14th, Scimitars XD244 (3) 20th, XD245 (2) 27th, XD247 (3) 28th, XD246 (6) 29th and XD243 (5) 30th. SEPTEMBER was Scimitars XD249 (4) 19th, XD247 (5) 24th, XD246 (3) 25th, XD238 (5) 29th and XD250 30th.

October 1958 flights were all listed on the 28th XD248 (6), XD250 (6) and XD264 (7). NOVEMBER was XD264 on the 3rd and XD265 (3) on the 20th. DECEMBER were six production flights with XD267 (2) 12th, XD265 (7) 14th, XD266 (2) and XD268 (2) on the 19th and XD269 (4) and XD270 on the 31st.

January 1959 again only production flights of XD269 (3) 12th, XD272 23rd, XD270 (6) 26th and XD267 (2). FEBRUARY Colquhoun had to take an Instrument Rating test on DH Heron Mk.2 G-AOGW on the 18th, with Scimitar production flights of:- XD267 (2) 2nd, XD268 4th, XD266 (4) 19th, XD269 (3) 22nd, XD271 (7) 23rd, XD272 (6) 25th and XD273 (6) 27th. MARCH with XD273 3rd, XD272 (3) 5th, XD271 13th and XD274 (7) on the 19th.

April 1959 was about the least busy on record with Scimitar XD213 flying to Boscombe Down in 10 minutes and a 3.50hrs Ferry flight in a Rapide. MAY was slightly busier with Scimitars WW134 being flown from Boscombe Down to South Marston on the 5th, XD217 on air test and delivery to Boscombe Down on the 6th, and

XD276 (9) 28th and XD277 (3) 29th on production tests. JUNE little flying again as XD278 (6) 15th, XD279 (3) 23rd and XD277 (9) on the 24th. On the 19th Swift F.7 XF114 commenced Runway Friction Coefficient trials, or in plain language, how long it takes to stop on a runway.

July 1959 he flew Scimitars XD 280 (9) 11th, XD275 (9) 20th and XD265 (4) 24th on production tests, with XD219 being flown from Boscombe Down on the 22nd. Swift F.7 was in use on the 3rd and 15th on runway friction tests, and being flown to RAF Pershore from South Marston on the 15th. AUGUST had XD217 (3) for fin flutter tests 27th and XD281 (6) production tests 28th. Swift F.7 XF114 was also on air test possibly on the 28th. SEPTEMBER was a bit more busy with Scimitars XD 212 4th , XD282 (4) and XD316 (5) on production tests, XD217 on fin flutter tests 4th, and Swifts F.7 XF114 flown South Marston to RAF Coltishall on the 24th, followed by runway friction coefficient tests there, and then it returned to South Marston on the 26th. He also flew DH Dove G-AKSV from Little Staughton to South Marston on the 8th and South Marston to Cambridge and return on the 21st and the 23rd. The first time he had flown this type of aircraft.

October 1959 he flew Scimitars WW134 2nd and XD266 5th on air tests, he flew XD318 3rd, XD317 (6) 14th, XD316 19th, XD219 (3) 24th, XD319 (4) and XD320 (4) and XD321 (2) on the 26th, XD318 (6) 28th and XD319 (2) and XD275 (4) 30th on production tests. Swift F.7 XF114 from Wisley to South Marston 13th, Swift F.7 XF114 was flown on the 15th, XF114 South Marston to RAF West Raynham 19th, XF114 on runway fraction Coefficient trials 26th. The DH Dove G-AKSV, was now part of the family and was a comfortable aircraft to fly, and just to show the work of a Ferry aircraft I put down its flights with Colquhoun for October, on the 1st South Marston to Cambridge and return, 7th South Marston to Shoreham and return, 8th South Marston to Hurn (instrument take-off, Hurn to Eastleigh, Eastleigh to South Marston, South Marston to Eastleigh, Eastleigh to Hurn, Hurn to South Marston, 19th South Marston to Hurn, Hurn to Eastleigh, Eastleigh to South Marston, 20th South Marston Wisley, Wisley to Hurn, Hurn to South Marston and return,Hurn to Wisley to South Marston. 27th for a radio test, 29th South Marston to Cambridge and return, twice that day, and finally South Marston to Hucknell and return. Total flying time in the Dove was 14.00hrs. One last aircraft that he flew this month was one that he had flown at the commencement of his flying career, a DH 82A Tiger Moth G-AOES (ex RAF T6056) for its ARB CofA (Certificate of Airworthiness) test flight.

Swift F.7 XF114 at Filton on wet runway trails with the undercarriage fairings removed, and making the spray rise from its wheels.

November 1959 was a bit less hectic than October and he only carried out Ferry trips in the DH Dove G-AKSV, a total of only 10, with a total flying hours of only 11.50hrs. DECEMBER he did some test flying, XD320 10th, XD318 16th, XD275 (3) 17th, XD322 (5) 23rd and XD321 (4) on the 31st, all on production tests.

January 1960 he only flew three Scimitars, XD275 (2) 11th, XD228 (3) 19th and XD323 (3). He flew Swift F.7 XF114 on runway trials on the 20th (2), 26th, 27th and 29th. FEBRUARY he tested XD324 (6) 10th, XD225 (4) 15th, XD323 (9) 19th, XD230 (9) 23rd and XD222 (4) 29th on production tests. Also Swift F.7 XF114 on runway friction coefficient trials on the 2nd and 4th, and then flying it from RAF West Raynham to Coltishall. His ferry flights totalled 16, all in the DH Dove. MARCH he flew XD325 (3) and XD326 on the 16th, XD222 (2) 21st and XD223 (5) 28th for production flying. Also Swift F.7 XF114 for runway coefficient trials of 20mins. Ferry flights seem to be mounting up because he carried out 36 using the DH Dove, and on the 28th he flew it from South Marston to RAF Lyneham to Dublin, returning on the 30th to Eastleigh, and on the 31st flew it to Wisley, then on to Barrow and back to South Marston, taking off again the same day for RAF Upper Heyford and returning, another 10 flights, now making 46 ferry flights.

April 1960 and he only flew the Scimitar 7 times, XD326 (6) 20th on production test and XD218 on the 22nd for an air test, total flying time Scimitar 5.05hrs. He however flew the DH Dove for a total of 24.10hrs, flying to strange places like Barrow, Manchester, Newcastle, and the usual BAC sites. May followed a similar pattern with 4 Scimitar flights, XD227 5th on flight refuelling trials, XD325 6th and XD327 (2) 24th for production tests. DH Dove flights were a total of 44, with a total flying hours of 32.55hrs.

June he only flew two Scimitars XD328 27th and XD329 29th on production tests, total flying time 3.15hrs. Once again his ferry flights were way above 'normal' with his flying time being 23.15hrs. It was during this month that the old Vickers-Armstrongs (Aircraft) Ltd. name was superseded by Vickers-Armstrongs (South Marston) Ltd. Which was still a subsidiary of Vickers-Armstrongs Ltd. JULY he flew Scimitars XD 329 (2) 6th, XD328 (4) and XD330 (3) on production flights, his flying time was 4.35hrs. His ferry flights this month were reduced to 17 only. AUGUST he flew on the 31st XD227 on Flight Refuelling tests for 1.05hrs and XD327 and XD331 (6) on production tests. His ferry flights were reduced to 9 only.

September was just a Scimitar month with XD327 and XD331 on the 1st, also XD332 on the 20th on production tests, and XD227 on Flight Refuelling tests. OCTOBER was quiet with only XD214 (4) and XD332 on production tests. NOVEMBER On the 10th he flew XD212 to Wisley, then XD216 on the 14th, 16th, 22nd, 24th 28th and 29th on relight trials, and single engined landings, total flying time being only 3.40hrs.

11. The VA-1 Hovercraft

In 1959 Saunders Roe demonstrated their SR-N1 hovercraft on the Solent; it was a limited success but was the first manned machine to fully show off the hovercraft principle.

At the end of 1959 Vickers, based at South Marston in Wiltshire, turned their attention to the design of an Air Cushion Vehicle, with the main board of Vickers approving the scheme, which was to be undertaken in collaboration with Hovercraft Development Ltd (HDL). Mr S.P. Woodley, assistant Managing Director of Vickers-Armstrong (Engineers) of South Marston was in overall charge, with L.R. Colquhoun as his chief pilot.

At this time Colquhoun was living in Grove House, an old farmhouse in 5 acres of its own ground at Blunsdon, 3 miles from the South Marston works of Vickers-Supermarine. At one time during his stay here, he became chairman of the Swindon Gliding Club and gliding became his hobby until the hovercraft came into his life and overtook all other interests.

The V.A.1 in its original condition as G-15-252 with Les Colquhoun battling with the controls of a new system.

The VA.1 with Les at the controls and a good clear but cold view.

Now with the hood of the fan gone, and looks like a tarpaulin covering the panel.

A Permit to Fly had to be applied for from the Civil Aviation Authority because they considered that the machine came under the aircraft category, before it could attempt to fly, or hover as promised.

On or about 29th November 1960 Les Colquhoun had his first taste of hovering flight in the Vickers-built Hovercraft No.3038, when he 'flew' this machine for 4.05hrs; its registration was G-15-252 and its name was the Vickers VA-1 Research Hovercraft. This had been built in conjunction with Hovercraft Development Ltd, with Mr S.R. Hughes of Vickers-Armstrong (South Marston) Ltd as Chief Designer. A great deal of development had already been accomplished with model tests over land, water and in the wind tunnel. This machine weighed 3,500lb, had a length of 25ft, a width of 13ft and a hover height of 4.5 inches. It was powered by a Gypsy Major lift engine and a 90hp Continental engine for propulsion; it had a top speed of 35-40 knots.

Another view of G-15-252, now with a steel protective frame around the pilot.

In December 1960 Les flew XD216 on the 1st, 2nd and 22nd on re-light trials, also XD333 on production tests lasting 1.55hrs. H e also flew 3038 again but this time he had some free runs lasting 2.35hrs and some tethered tests of 3.55hrs.

January 1961, he flew XD216 on relight trials on the 5th and 25th and XD333 on the 3rd for his only production test. He flew 3038 on the 31st on tethers and on three free runs for a total time of 8.25hrs.

In February he flew XD216 on the 2nd, 3rd, 6th and 20th for Sidewinder Handling trials, total flying time of 4.20hrs. He continued with relight trials on the 20th, 23rd and 28th.

G-15-252 now with VA1 on the rudder and nose boom enetering the water.

G-15-252 now modified with a forward boom and undergoing water trials still fitted with a huge rudder. (K. Colquhoun)

Fly High ~ Fly Low

His Hovercraft activities were now increasing as follows:-

1st	Handling	50mins
2nd	Demonstration to Mr Hennessey	50mins
3rd	Handling	40mins
5th	Handling	30mins
8th	Handling and demonstration	30mins
9th	Handling	25mins
9th	Demonstration to Sir Dennis Byrne	20mins
9th	Handling	50mins
10th	Training	25mins
13th	Demonstration to A/Cdr Noel	20mins
14th	Demonstration to Shell/BP Representatives	50mins
15th	Demonstration to Mr Aidan Cranisy	35mins
21st	Training	40mins
22nd	Demonstration at Woodley to Lord Knolly	2.30hrs

The VA1 under trials in the Test Pit, with the crane to lift it in and out.

March 1961 and he flew 3038 on the 1st for handling and demonstrations for 8.15hrs. The rest of the month, and the beginning of the next it must have been modified. His Scimitar flying was with XD227 Flight Refuelling on the 10th for 3.55hrs, XD216 13th, XD213 23rd and XD330 30th were production tests, also XD228 13th air test and XD268 21st for handling. APRIL and recorded for the 13th were:-

XD212 on Flight Refuelling, XD216 (3) handling trials with Sidewinder missiles, XD227 (5) Flight Refuelling trials as Tanker in 4.35hrs, and XD330 (3) productions tests.

Hovercraft operations continued with:-

13th	Handling	30mins	
14th	Demonstration		1.25hrs
18th	Water trials lateral instability	0.20hrs	
19th	Engine check	0.10hrs	
20th	Water trials at South Cerney	1.00hrs	
21st	Stability check on static water tank	0.20hrs	
24th	Cushion pressure measurements	1.50hrs	
26th	Water trials at South Cerney	0.55hrs	
26th	Demonstrations to Mr & Mrs Pearce	0.25hrs	
26th	Cushion pressure measurements	1.00hrs	
27th	Demonstrations	0.35hrs	

May 1961, I continue with his Scimitar flights of:-

- 9th XD216 Relighting and Static Vents (4), XD243 (3)
- 31st production tests, and XD268 24th flight to Boscombe Down.

G-15-252 in all its glory showing its streamlined cabin, and small rudder, and hovering at about 8 inches above the ground.   Via K. Colquhoun

Hovercraft operations were:-

1st	Demonstrations	1.00hr
3rd	Demonstrations to Cdr Sweny	0.20hrs
8th	Demonstrations to Mr Donnett, Mr Fraser	0.40hr
9th	Demonstration to Mr Roxbee Cox	1.00hr
10th	Demonstration to Gen Sir C.Dunphie	0.45hrs
12th	Flexible skirts fitted	0.45hrs
12th	Familiarisation for A Luscombe	0.20hrs
19th	Handling with Continental engine	0.35hrs
24th	Test prior to water trials	0.30hrs
26th	Water trials at South Cerney	0.45hrs
30th	Water trials at South Cerney	0.40hrs
30th	Water trails at South Cerney	0.35hrs
31st	Handling with 'Y' skirts removed	0.45hrs

June 1961 Scimitar flights were all on the 30th XD216 (7) on relighting tests 5.00hrs, XD243 (2) production tests and XD268 flown to Bedford.

Hovercraft operations were;-

2nd	Water trials at South Cerney	0.40hrs
5th	Thrust measurements	0.40hrs
6th	Demonstration	0.30hrs
7th	Water trials towed over hump speed	1.30hrs
8th	Rudder efficiency trials	1.00hr
16th	Handling with twin fins	0.30hrs
16th	Water trials South Cerney	1.40hrs
20th	Water trials South Cerney	2.20hrs
21st	Static tank thrust measurements	0.45hrs
26th	Water trials South Cerney water skis	2.00hrs
27th	Demonstrations	0.40hrs
30th	Demonstrations	0.25hrs

The Hovercraft that Colquhoun called 3038 was modified several times to test several different lift curtain systems and stability devices such as compartmentalisation of the cushion and associated controls. Different fairings and individual crew cabins for the later crew of two added for protection whilst travelling over water. This increased the weight by 200lb and reduced the hover height to 4.1 inches.

The Hovercraft front view with Les and his assistant in separate cabins.

JULY 1961: the only activity was to fly XD268 on a delivery air test of 40mins on the 17th and XD216 on the 21st for handling with B.P. missiles, total time of 4.45hrs.

AUGUST 1961: he flew XD216 on the 18th for an air test of 40mins, and XD268 on the 30th on delivery to Boscombe Down in 25mins.

SEPTEMBER 1961: he only flew one Scimitar XD226 on the 31st on production tests for 15mins.

Hovercraft operations in September were:-

1st	Handling after widening modification	1.30hrs
1st	Demonstration	0.30hrs
4th	Water trials at South Cerney	2.25hrs
6th	Demonstration	1.05hrs
6th	Static hovering	0.55hrs
12th	Water trials at South Cerney	2.25hrs
14th	Exercise "Unison"	1.35hrs

A discussion on the VA-1 with from l to r:- Sam Hughes designer, Stan Woodley, Managing Director, LR Colquhoun and another, taken on the 26th October 1961.

Serial number XS798 was allocated for official trials, but it was not carried.

19th	Slipway trials at Itchen	0.20hrs
20th	Sea trials at Itchen – Calm water	2.35hrs
21st	Sea trials at Itchen	1.50hrs
22nd	Sea trials at Itchen – Calm TV cameras	1.35hrs
25th	Practise demonstrations	0.25hrs
26th	Press demonstrations	1.10hrs
26th	Press demonstrations	0.30hrs
27th	Demonstrations	0.45hrs

OCTOBER 1961: Colquhoun flew two Scimitars on production tests XD226 and XD214 for a time of 4.45hrs, but no dates are given.

His next flight was in December when he flew XD226 on a production test of 10mins.

He flew a Scimitar in February 1962 for 1.55hrs but no serial number or date given. There were more flights in March, April, May, August but no information on them.

Les had elected to stay with Vickers until the Scimitar contract was phased out, and the flight tests show that now was the time when this occurred.

The V.A.1 now modified with a Land Rover front end and a completely different skirt and under control of Soil Fertility with their crop spraying mode.

12. The VA.2 Hovercraft

Another hovercraft, the VA-2, capable of carrying 4-5 people, was under construction, but still primarily for trials and demonstrations. It was powered by two Rolls-Royce/Continental O-300-B aero engines as 135hp lift fans and propulsion was by a Rolls-Royce/Continental O-470-l, 230hp engine, driven by a two-blade McCauley fixed-pitch tractor propeller of 7ft 6ins diameter. This last engine was replaced by the summer of 1963 by a 310hp Rolls-Royce Continental GIO-470A driving a reversible-pitch propeller. It length was 30ft 4in, its beam 15ft and height over the fins 11ft, with a loaded weight of 8,300lb. Its top speed was 69mph and it could cover an operating range of 86 miles.

The Vickers VA-2 on the 8th May 1963 tied up to the jetty in Amsterdam with Les Colquhoun looking from the jetty down on the havercraft. Via K. Colquhoun.

It was first flown in the autumn of 1962 by Les Colquhoun and in January 1963 it saw service over snow and ice in England and was taken to the continent in March 1963 for demonstration purposes. In mid-1963 it was modified and fitted with a new type of skirt consisting of an inflatable rubber structure fitted to air nozzles under the craft which gave it an improvement of about 200% in ground and wave clearance.

The VA.2 was exhibited at the NATO exercise "Realist" on the river Danube at Ingolstadt, Germany, by Colquhoun, who reported back that the VA.2 had been extremely successful. It was one of a series of demonstrations of new types of ground forces' military vehicles and equipment from all of the NATO countries, the idea being to attempt to standardise some of the equipments in service. It was demonstrated before an audience of senior NATO officers in conjunction with the IHTU (Interservice Hovercraft Trials Unit).

The V.A.2 coming up the ramp in Amsterdam, with its original type of skirt. [K Colquhoun]

On its return from the NATO Exhibition the VA.2 stopped off in Amsterdam. BP were sponsoring the fuel and oil of the VA.2 on its initiative but with the co-operation of Vickers, the VA.2 was taken to Amsterdam where it stayed for a full fortnight. One of these days was a "Hovercraft Information Day" on the 17th April, when it was demonstrated to the Dutch press, by LR Colquhoun and Raymond Old, with trips on the hovercraft by Prince Bernhard of the Netherlands, who even took over the controls for a brief time, other VIPs followed by demonstrations to the press. It had been a near thing however because at the BP harbour installation where the VA.2 was parked on the 16th April 1963, a road fuel tanker went up in flames, and with millions of gallons of petroleum in nearby storage tanks it was rather a distracting situation. Everything was however under control and the catastrophe did not happen. In all, there were nine prototype machines on display and demonstrations were carried out in the harbour at Amsterdam. The final day of demonstrations was on the 23rd April, when they experienced the strongest winds, which slightly curtailed the flights, and it was considered too rough for the hovercraft to be operated. What they had come out to accomplish had already been successfully carried out.

The VA-2 was then packed on board ship again and returned to Vickers at South Marston for a check up and servicing before proceeding on some more tests and demonstrations.

After the above water tests and demonstrations and in conjunction with the IHTU the VA-2 was taken over a "Salting Area" on the south coast of England, and following this it was taken over a service obstacle course, which had been constructed to really test the craft, which it successfully accomplished. The service number XS856 had been allocated for these trials, but it was not taken up.

At the end of September 1963, VA.2-001, as it had on it then, was transported to the Kockums shipyard at Malmo in the south of Sweden on the SS *Frey*, for demonstrations on the Oresund between Sweden and Denmark It arrived at Malmo on the 16th September 1963. As usual senior government officials, senior service officers and major shipping companies not only from Sweden but from her neighbouring countries as well, were invited by BP and Vickers to attend. The demonstration was to make the crossing from Kockums shipyard to a patch of open ground in the Amager Strandpark just outside Copenhagen. The weather however made the crossing very choppy with strong winds and steep seas, that the VA.2 had difficulty coping with the size of the waves. Waves up to 2ft high were coped with but with a following wind of 20 knots it was extremely difficult to make a decent turn, especially if the speed of the hovecraft was about that speed also. The new type skirt, which was called by Vickers, "The Flexible Skirt", had been fitted for this trip, which considerably increased the hover height, and the machine could now cross objects of 18 inches in height with no trouble. It crossed the 2ft high sea wall at Copenhagen with ease, over the grass and up the slope under the skilful hands of Les Colquhoun. Also fitted new was a Rolls-Royce Continental GIO-470A engine delivering 310hp.

Les Colquhoun at the "steering wheel" of the VA-2. [K. Colquhoun]

Demonstrations to personnel of the Swedish Navy took just about one whole day, which was windless and very calm, not the sort of day that Colquhoun really wanted for a naval testing. He gave a great deal of dual control instruction to quite a lot of then, and the conditions gave promise to two admirals, a captain and a commander who showed an excellent knack of picking it up. He followed this up with a quick dash to Copenhagen and return, accomplishing it in a time of only 36 minutes, five minutes less than the hydrofoil could accomplish it. Colquhoun accepted a challenge from the hydrofoil captain and after a short distance the hovercraft started leaving the hydrofoil behind, and Colquhoun was "justifiable elated". The pilot of the hydrofoil eased off, and backed down to normal cruising speed.

Under test below the towering cranes of the Kockums shipyard at Malmo, Sweden. [K. Colquhoun]

The last four days of the visit were really not suitable for any ship, let alone a small hovercraft, but a Swedish admiral wanted a demonstration and Colquhoun took the VA-2 out for the demonstration. When he drove into the wind the ride was acceptable but he could not achieve, what he termed "hump" speed, and the spray stopped his propulsion engine, which had him worried, but it restarted first go. To keep it stable he decided to keep the lift engine throttled back and to return to base as a displacement craft, or in plain language, as a ship. He turned downwind with difficulty and made headway slowly towards the shipyard. Just off the yard basin, local eddying effects of the wind made directional control impossible and he had to call for assistance. This was a Dowty speedboat, which took a brave man to defy the sea at that time, and managed to take the tow line from the VA-2. With this assistance the hovercraft managed to make it the 100 yards back to base, any more and the VA-2 might have been rescuing the Dowty boat. The passenger however was a proper seaman because his faith in this new form of transport was increased with the seaworthiness characteristics of the hovercraft.

One odd feature not fitted in the later hovercraft, was the retractable undercarriage that was fitted on the VA-2, that enabled it to turn in very sharp circles, and it could even be taxied on its wheels if necessary, and using reverse thrust a controlled descent of a moderate hill could be also accomplished.

The VA-2 descending the 7° ramp slope at the Kockum shipyard in Sweden, which the hovercraft took in its stride.   [K. Colquhoun.]

Following all these trials VA-2 was shipped to the shipyard of Stalangens Mek, 120 miles south of Stockholm, Sweden, the shipyard being on the Molastron, a small channel off the Braviken where it arrived in early February 1964. It was assembled in a small workshop from which it was driven through a 90 degree turn on its wheels of course, and then onto a 20ft wide road to an open slipway where it was parked. At this time of year the outside temperatures went down to −15°C, so that any maintenance was carried out in these temperatures and at night time lead lamps were provided to light the area. Refuelling was carried out from 50 gallon drums by an electrically driven pump. The hovercraft stayed here for trials for a period of 25 days, and would pass over any of the sheets or blocks of ice that appeared on the river at speeds of up to 45 to 50 knots. A lot of flights were made over the different types of ice floes with some being 2 feet high, moving ice, that this was a demonstration with some meaning. Another time the water was flat calm, like a mirror where there was no indication of speed, and the speed indicator was the only means of checking forward travel, and turning and stopping were difficult to carry out accurately. Over flat snow, this sensation was the same as well, a question of disorientation.

At the end of the trials it was decided that a visit to a small fishing village, Arkosund, at the edge of the Braviken and the Baltic Sea, would make a good exercise, and be of interest. This was about 33 miles from where the hovercraft had its base, alomg the Braviken, and took Colquhoun 40 minutes to cover the distance, averaging 49.5 knots, and returned at a slightly faster speed. The surface that the hovercraft was taken over included concentrated ice blocks, pack ice with large floating ice floes and ridged flat ice. Whilst at Arkosund a trip was carried out into the Baltic with the final accolade being on the last day when H.R.H. Prince Bertil of Sweden visited the base, and went on a demonstration trip taking over the controls for a short period.

The "Ice" tests whilst at Braviken, Sweden over the broken ice floes. Via K. Colquhoun.

13. The VA-3 Hovercraft

In 1962 also, Colquhoun was put in control of the World's first Hovercraft service between Wallasey and Rhyl. For this service Vickers had produced the V.A.3 Hovercoach, which was powered by four 425hp Blackburn 603 Turmo gas turbine engines, two providing lift and the other two mounted high on the chassis for forward propulsion. The length was 54 feet 9 inches (55ft 7in with the new flexible skirt) and the width 26feet 11 inches, (27ft) with an all up weight of about 13.5 imperial tons or 30,150lb, and the ability to hover on a cushion of air 8 inches above the sea/earth. The cushion pressure at the maximum all up weight of 28,400lb was 31.7lb/sq.in. Construction of V.A.3 commenced in March 1961 at South Marston, but it did not first hover until the 25th March 1962, with Les Colquhoun at the controls. For it to carry out its trials it was allocated the Class B Registration G-15-253 and a Permit to Fly, was issued by the Ministry of Aviation, service number XV366 was allocated but not used.

First flight of the VA-3 at South Marston, showing at least a 6 inch hover height. [K. Colquhoun]

Fly High ~ Fly Low

The VA-3 on the runway at South Marston on the 20/3/1962 almost ready for flight with a few people at the side having a looksee. [K. Colquhoun]

It was being shipped to Birkenhead as deck cargo in early July 1962, and deposited on the dock. On the 15th July 1962 the V.A.3 had a trial trip with its pilot, Capt. Leslie Colquhoun and assistant Capt. Raymond Old as his co-pilot, they went from Birkenhead to Wallasey from where the ferry would be operating, and then continued on to the other operational base at Rhyl. The companies operating this experimental for a period of six weeks service, were British United Airways, who had Mr F.A.(Freddie) Laker as the Managing Director, who were in charge of the organizations, with the B.P. Company providing the fuel and lubricants. On the 20th July the first full passenger service with a full load of Press and other invited guests, totalling 24 people, commenced from Rhyl. They were seated in a comfortable cabin with four groups of three on both sides of the central aisle, all seats were facing rearwards for maximum safety. The crew were the same as before except that now there was a steward, Mr Christopher Ashby. The trip to Wallasey took 33 minutes with a top speed varying between 40 and 55 knots. On disembarking these passengers, the Hovercoach was loaded again and returned to Rhyl in 34 minutes, the windscreen wipers going unserviceable and slowing up the journey.

Fly High ~ Fly Low

This service was only experimental and ran from the 20th July to the 16th September, having six return trips each day except Tuesdays, but operating at a loss because they only charged £2 per head return. The fuel consumed with four engines operating, worked out at about 1,200 gallons per day, then add the crew's wages, maitenance, mooring and storage, so that the revenue of £48 was ludicrously low, but Vickers-Armstrongs were obtaining the necessary experience before embarking on a 100 seat hovercraft which would be profitable.

The VA-3 with the families of the two pilots from top to bottom are:-LR Colquhoun, Mrs K Colquhoun, Sally Colquhoun aged 4, Helen and Jane Colquhoun the twins aged 13 and Peta Colquhoun aged 12, Raymond Old, Mrs Old, Patrick and Madelaine Old, probably on the 20th July 1962. [K. Colquhoun]

Fly High ~ Fly Low

The Vickers VA-3-001 on the 20th July 1962 on the Rhyl-Wallasey run. [K. Colquhoun]

This was a new industry and because of this, new rules and regulations were required and so "The Hovercraft Policy Committee", combined with "The Technical Steering Committee" and "The Design Requirements Panel" together with "The Operational Requirements Panel", on the latter were SR Hughes and LR Colquhoun of Vickers and the above were formed in 1962.

A WORLD FIRST ~ 16/9/1962

This is Les Colquhoun's own story of the events of this day.

This particular story covers the conclusion of the world's first ever fare paying passenger hovercraft service which ran from Wallesey to Rhyl across the Dee estuary in the period July- September 1962. The service was backed by Vickers, British United Airways (Freddie Laker) and BP. Such was the confidence of the three Companies that all the planning and setting up of the Service was completed some three months before the Vickers Hovercraft VA.3, a 36 seat hovercraft had even commenced it's trials. These trials began in March 1962 at the Vickers airfeld at South Marston. When these were completed in May, the VA.3 was moved to Southampton for it's first water trials. The scheduled start for the passenger carrying operation was July so the time scale was exceedingly tight. Suffice it to say that the trials went as expected and the VA.3 was taken by a small coaster to Liverpool where it was unloaded by crane into the docks where the engines were fired up and the VA.3 proceeded to it's maintenance base at Rhyl to be prepared for entering service some 7 day later.

The Vickers VA-3 control room or cockpit showing the instrument panel.

The VA.3 was powered by four Bristol Siddely Turmo 603 free turbine engines. two powered the two lift fans and two, the two propulsion propellers. The passenger terminal at Rhyl was on the main beach but at Wallesey things were more difficult as they had to land on the very steep sea wall. Six return schedules per day were planned and BUA set up a special booking office for the purpose of ticketing passenger. There was no shortage of these, the hovercraft was a unique form of transport and everybody was keen to try it. However the summer of 1962 was disastrous, there was a persistent northwesterly wind blowing on shore at both terminals, causing quite steep waves. As a consequence of the above, on only six days was it possible to operate the full schedule, cancellations being caused by sea conditions and maintenance problems. The service carried some 3,600 passengers out of an expected 10,000. It was certainly a very harassing eight weeks. By the 14th of September, we had made 13 engine changes and had reached the situation where there were no more spare parts available and the VA.3 had to be left on the open beach at Rhyl as both the lift engines had failed.

Mr SP Woodley (left) the General Manager of Vickers South Marston with the Chief pilot Leslie Colquhoun at the front of the VA-3.   [K. Colquhoun]

This was the World's first scheduled ACV (Air Cushion Vehicle) passenger service and on its six weeks trial it carried 3,765 fare paying passengers and covered 4,000 miles (6,500 km).

It was unfortunate that the Spring tides were building up and with the wind still from the NW, the tides were higher than normal. On Friday night, the 14th September 1962, the hovercraft was secured by digging an anchor into the sand so that as the tide came in and floated the hovercraft it was safely anchored, No problems were experienced on Friday but on Saturday, one tide nearer the full spring tide and with the wind a little stronger the hovercraft broke loose and Ray Old my second in command had to start the propulsion engines in order to keep the VA.3 from hitting the sea wall.

The forecast for Sunday was for a severe N Westerly gale gusting to Force 9. This was grim news and a second anchor was dug into the sand to secure the VA.3. At about 7 o'clock I boarded the VA.3 to maintain a watch throughout the night. With me were Ray Old and a cruise liner officer Captain Banbury, who had been seconded to the trials for experience. The wind was blowing a gale and the incoming waves looked ominous. Soon they were lashing the VA.3 and as the waves passed under the hovercraft, it was lifted up, only to be bounced back onto the sand followed by the next wave, which would burst over the cockpit and superstructure. All this was very frightening and very unpleasant. I was in the captain's seat and Ray Old and Cpt. Banbury were monitoring the passenger cabin keeping an eye on the structure. The noise was horrendous and it was now dark and lashing down with rain, not that that was important, as there was more than enough sea- water, which by now, with the VA.3 floating on the end of the anchor chains, was smashing onto the windscreen.

Suddenly there was a tremendous crash, and the nose of the VA.3 swung round violently and we were off towards the sea wall. I hastily started up the two propulsion engines and was able to steer the hovercraft away from the wall and out to deeper water. We had broken loose but had no idea why. It was later discovered that the whole anchor fitting in the bow had been torn out. From the passenger cabin Ray old reported that the lining amidships and on the sides and ceiling of the Hovercraft had torn apart indicating substantial bending moments in the structure. In the confusion we could not establish whether or not the main structure had failed but I was sufficiently alarmed to ask the lifeboat crew who were standing by to launch their boat and come alongside. By this time the tide was at it's maximum height and was running across the promenade. The risks involved in launching the Rhyl Lifeboat, were indicated by the fact that the Coxswain, Mr Harold Campini, was awarded the Silver Medal for his efforts that night. A commemorative plaque is now displayed on the wall for all to see, and is the only known event when a lifeboat was launched to rescue a hovercraft.

With the lifeboat launched I considered the situation. Ray Old was still doubtful about the cabin structure and to add to the problems Cpt. Banbury was very sick. Fearing that the VA.3 could break in two, I requested the lifeboat to come alongside and take us off. However there was no way that the lifeboat could come alongside with the propellers whirling round, so the engines had to be stopped, where upon the VA.3 swung round beam on to the sea which added to the difficulties of the lifeboat corning alongside. In fact with the sea running it was impossible. I had to restart the propulsion engines and pull away from the sea wall again and review the situation. During all of this fracas I had told Ray Old and Cpt. Banbury to inflate their mae-wests. I inflated mine only to find that I was jammed between the back of the seat and the control column. I had to deflate my mae-west and cursed my stupidity in inflating it in the first place. However it was agreed that the lifeboat would he just astern of the starboard side of the VA.3. I would then stop the starboard engine and keep the VA.3 into wind using the port engine. When the lifeboat crew reported that Old and Banbury were safely in the lifeboat I stopped the port engine, scrambled out of the cockpit through the passenger cabin and out on the deck where brave men that they were the lifeboat was ready and waiting for me to jump in, and safely in the cabin. I was relieved to gulp down the traditional tot of rum.

So ended a brave enterprise. The VA3 left to it's own devices went alongside the seawall under the influence of the now ebbing tide and some of the engineers jumped on and secured ropes to the engine support struts and lashing the other end to the promenade railings (of Rhyl's West Promenade). Which in the event was most fortuitous since a couple of heavy lift cranes were able to lift the VA.3 onto the promenade the following morning. It was then dismantled and returned to the Vickers factory at South Marston. Here it was completely reconditioned, including any repairs found necessary, and then had a series of trials before it was classified as fit for service. Six months later it was operating with the US Marines at Long Island USA.

If you are ever in North Wales go into the Rhyl lifeboat House and you will see recorded the dramatic and unique events of the night of 16th September 1962".

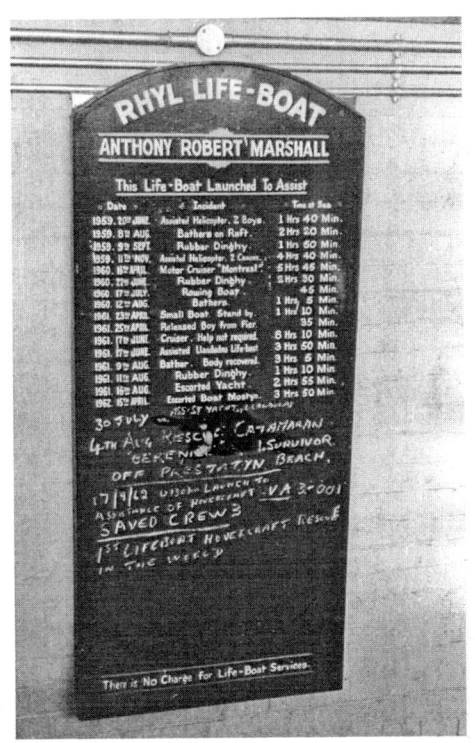

Plaque commemorating the Rhyl Life-Boat Rescues. [K. Colquhoun]

Some of those involved on the VA-3 project, names unknown other than Les Colquhoun, who is third from left. [K Colquhoun]

Now back to his mundane job at Supermarine flying the Scimitar fighter. 1963 was Les Colquhoun's swan song – he flew a Scimitar in March, no serial number stated, for 2.35hrs. In April he flew XD215 1.15hrs and XD270 2.05hrs on production tests, May only the one, XD216 for 1.05hrs, and the last one recorded is XD216 in June for 35 minutes, so it can be assumed that he had got to the end of his contract with Vickers about the Scimitar testing.

The VA.3 was taken to South Marston where it was repaired and again thoroughly tested on Southampton Water, completing its trials by the 24th March 1964. It was then transported by ship to the Republic Aerospace Corp. of America as VA.3-001, for their evaluation, early in 1964 with the improved flexible skirt extensions of 3ft long fitted, giving an improved wave-riding capability and obstacle clearance of 3.5 feet, and two Artouste 2C engines of 400hp for propulsion in place of the others. Because it was for use in America the craft had to be fitted with American instrumentation to Republic requirements in the center of the passenger compartment with the loss of one seat. This ACV was 55 ft 7in long and weighed in at 30,150lb and had a speed of 63mph. The final test run on the River Itchen to the foreshore at Lee-on-Solent was accomplished with the chairman of Vickers-Armstrongs (Engineers) Ltd. Mr W.D. Opher.

The VA-3 for the Republic Aerospace Corp. now with a modified skirt and without the two front fins, and looking better for it. [K. Colquhoun]

Mr Opher had never been on the hovercraft but still wanted to know what it was like, how it travelled, was it really suitable for carrying passengers and what its prospects were. His impressions of the trip however are not known so we can only theorise what they actually were.

The method of loading and unloading the VA-3 onto a ship. [K. Colquhoun]

The VA-3 was transported to the Republic Aviation Corp. marine base at Montauk, Long Island, New York, which is on the North-East tip of the island. Republic had obtained a licensing agreement with Vickers for patent rights and technical support to develop their types of hovercraft on the VA-3 principle, hoping for contracts from the US Office of Naval Research for the US Marines. It "landed" in the US on the 10th March 1964 via the ss "Pioneer Cove" in the Port of New York, being off-loaded on the 14th onto a lighter and then onto the beach. It was checked, a quick run over the bay and then into a hangar to be updated to American standards, with the fitting of radios etc.

Amphibious operations over the sand dunes and sea to land transfers in August 1964. [K. Colquhoun]

The trials were carried out with 16 people of which three were from Vickers, Frank Wells for design matters, Cyril Mayers for servicing and Colquhoun the pilot. Bob Lewis was the American pilot who after 10 hours piloting was in full control. Henri Bourque was the US maintenance man. In these tests the VA-3 was being tested alongside two other hovercraft, which were:- the Bell Aerosystems' SKMR-1 Hydroskimmer 1 and the Westland SR.N5.

It was here that the real advantage of the deepened skirts were proved in practise. Tthe craft was frequently called to operate in sea conditions where the wave heights measured up to 6 feet, and on occasions in conditions where the wave height could not be measured, and the launch that was supposed to maintain station was unable to do so. The Grumman hydrofoil team, were taken out in 4 feet seas by Dick Sage, another American taught by Colquhoun, and were very impressed and had a more comfortable ride than in their hydrofoil.

Negotiating a landing IN the dock ship USS "Fort Mandan" ,which was said to be "not too difficult with reverse thrust available".   [K. Colquhoun]

Amphibious operations over the sand dunes were interesting, when it was found possible to drop down off sand cliffs 6 – 8 feet high without striking the hard structure. It was this exercise that made the US Marine Corps start to reconsider the uses of the hovercraft. It was about when the VA-3 landed, that they had thought to leave a decision for twelve months about acquiring some for the Corps. Colquhoun however gave a USMC officer a "full" amphibious demonstration, which I expect was as hair raising as possible over real obstacles at speed, which up to now no US built hovercraft could achieve. A follow up demonstration piloted by Dick Sage, carrying a brigadier general and an admiral encountered high seas with a surf height of 8 – 10 feet and riding the surf in was achieved successfully, and the general was really impressed, and he called for another series of tests in USN waters at Norfolk, Virginia.

In January 1965 the VA-3 was skimming over the ice-laden water of Long Island Sound to New London, and it was a completely different series of demonstrations to what Colquhoun had even thought of before. Here the US Navy had a dock ship USS "Fort Mandan" and had a programme of amphibian exercises and an instruction programme aimed at establishing a possible level of acceptance for prospective pilots.

In charge of these tests was Dick Sage, the maintenance person was a Republic engineer, Henri Bourque with two ex-USN engineers, and an assistant pilot was Tom Brazier also of Republic. Its one main exercise was to drive into the dock ship, and this was achieved 15 times in conditions of the ship varying from zero to 15 knots, with Dick Sage as the pilot. He was very apprehensive at the start because he only had 10ft clearance, i.e. 5ft each side whilst driving something that had no positive steering and was bobbing about like a ball on a water spout. At 15 knots the wake did cause considerable difficulties, but with more power it was accomplished. It was concluded however that the exercise was a tremendous success. One conclusion was that the use of reverse thrust was very beneficial. Another course on land was a hurdle race over two specially constructed sand walls 30 to 40 ft apart, which the VA-3 passed successfully.

On the 30th July 1964 the VA-3 was operated for 40 minutes from a concrete pad at Montauk, going easily over the water at a speed of 57 mph, as also the sand bars, sand dunes, marshland, a pond and a rocky beach. Colquhoun flew the hovercraft at just below the top speed of 65 mph, to ensure better serviceability.

14. Hoverlloyd and other Business Ventures

In June 1965, the Swedish Lloyd Line and the Swedish American Steamship Co. signed a contract for a five-year charter of two of the biggest hovercraft from Westlands – the 165-ton SRN4 – for a passenger service across the English Channel from Ramsgate to Calais. This pair would be owned by Westland Charters and operated by Hoverlloyd Ltd, a British subsidiary of these two firms. The Managing Director of Hoverlloyd was Mr T. Christoffersen, Hovercraft Commercial Director James Hodgson, Hovercraft Commercial Manager Stevenson Pugh, Traffic Manager Stanley T Dailey, and in daily charge of the affairs was Mr Arne Glucksman, who took on his Operations Chief, Leslie Colquhoun and seven other drivers. Also recruited by Leslie Colquhoun were six maintenance staff, with a former Vickers hovercraft service manager, Mr Emrys Jones in overall charge. The distance between Ramsgate and Calais was 27.5 miles and the fare was worked out at £2/5/0d single. An added bonus of the run was that the route was directly over the Goodwin Sands, and even when they were exposed the route did not alter but gave the passengers something to look out for. With the time of the trip being a mere 45 minutes it was reckoned that they could get in 10 round trips in one day.

Goodbye to Vickers

In 1966 Les decided to leave Vickers completely after 21 years with them and was appointed operations manager of Hoverlloyd when Hovercraft commenced operations at Ramsgate. He operated the company's car ferry between Ramsgate and Calais using two Westland SRN6 Hovercraft. This service was inaugurated on the 6th April 1966 by the SR.N6 "Swift", with the second SRN6 "Sure" still being built. Les also organized the first hovercraft commanders training course at Cowes, I.O.W. and Ramsgate during March 1966.

Fly High ~ Fly Low

The SR-N6 on the "beach" at Calais in April 1966.　　[K. Colquhoun]

The SRN6s were equipped to carry 36 passengers only but absolutely ideal for pioneering a route like this over the English Channel. It was not until the 30th April however that the official passenger service commenced. In August 1966, Mrs Joan Haley was presented with a bouquet of flowers by Les Colquhoun, the Operations Chief of Hoverlloyd, because she was the 25,000th traveller on the service from Ramsgate to Calais.

Mrs Joan Haley, the 25,000th passenger to use the Hoverlloyd passenger service Ramsgate to Calais in September 1966, with Les Colquhoun presenting the flowers.

During the years 1967 and 1968 Colquhoun was the key figure in a planning application for a new purpose-built hovercraft terminal or 'hoverport' at Pegwell Bay. This generated a lot of hostility and controversy in the local community and had to go to appeal. The appeal application was finally approved early in 1968, and actual building work commenced at Pegwell Bay in July 1968.

On the 9th August 1967 a new service was commenced of a day-trip journey between Ramsgate and Deal with a time of only 10 minutes between the two towns as against an hour on a bus. The fare was set at 12s 6d for a return ticket and 7s 1d for a single. At Deal the craft would operate from the beach with tickets obtainable from a typical beachside kiosk

Hoverlloyd spent two years carrying out an SR.N6 cross-Channel operation in order to assess the requirements and problems likely to be encountered when they started the route. This involved maintenance, number and type of staff, also weather conditions together with sea state conditions and a full understanding of the risks of collision. By September 1967 Hoverlloyd had carried out about 2,000 Channel crossings between Ramsgate and Calais and with radar and knowledge of the traffic, the hazard of a collision had been greatly reduced. (They even studied all the collisions that had occurred in the Channel, with the conclusion that the route from Dover to Calais was outside the area of greatest risk.) The schedule crossing time of 40 minutes between Ramsgate and Calais was worked out allowing for a 40 knot block speed in slightly worse than average sea and wind conditions. Hoverlloyd had decided to purchase two Westland SRN4 hovercraft for this important crossing. They had an all-up weight of 165 tons and were capable of carrying 256 passengers and 30 cars and could travel at up to 77 knots in ideal conditions, or 70 knots on maximum continuous power. They were powered by four Bristol Siddeley Marine Proteus 15M/529 gas-turbine engines of 3,400shp maximum continuous power, with 4,250shp maximum permissible at a shaft speed of 1,500rpm.

A trip to the Goodwin Sands, showing the puddles behind the hovercraft, in the Autumn of 1967.   [K. Colquhoun]

A brand new terminal was also built at Calais for the hovercraft (which the French called *aeroglisseurs*) where the municipality were charging £7 for every landing, whilst, at Dover the charge was only £1. The first hovercraft service was inaugurated on 30th April 1966, with the fare set at £4/10s return or £3/7/6 from Dover single.

It was also brought home to the company that they would not be able to operate from Ramsgate and that Pegwell Bay would be an ideal place. The company commenced operations from here in 1968 with Colquhoun being made Managing Director in 1969.

Just to show that hovercraft travel was safe, on the 13th September 1967 Mr Christopher Cockerell (designer of the hovercraft principle) presented a silver salver to one of the family Mr & Mrs Head and son Jonathan for being the 1,000,000th passenger carried since hovercraft operations began on the 24th July 1965.

A caricature of Les Colquhoun and dignitaries, including the Duke of Edinburgh and the Mayor of Ramsgate at the Opening of the new Hovercraft Hoverport at Pegwell Bay, Ramsgate, Kent. From the *East Kent Critic* of May 1969.

Another view of the SR-N6 leaving the Goodwin Sands. [K. Colquhoun]

Fly High ~ Fly Low

The SR-N6 inward bound for its base at Ramsgate, returning from a scheduled trip to the French port of Calais.   [K. Colquhoun]

In January 1969, Mrs Mary Wilson, wife of Prime Minister, Harold Wilson, christened the first Hoverlloyd SRN4, naming it "Swift". Shortly afterwards, in April 1969, the second SRN4 "Sure" was delivered to Ramsgate. Such was the progress on the Hoverport that it was officially opened in May 1969 by HRH the Duke of Edinburgh.

The SR-N4:

Fitted with four Bristol Siddeley "Marine Proteus" gas turbines, each driving a variable-pitch propeller mounted on a pylon, interconnected with the propellers are four centrifugal fans for the cushion air. The craft is controlled by varying the propeller blade angles, and by swivelling the pylons to change direction. If up to two engines fail then the craft is completely buoyant, it can move as a displacement vessel on the remaining two engines. The SR-N4s are of the "Mountbatten" Class designed for all the year round services on open coastal waters and waves up to 8 to 12 feet high, they weigh 165 tons and can carry 174 passengers and 34 cars or 254 passengers and 30 cars.

Seaspeed took over Hoverlloyd but Colquhoun was not out of a job – he was appointed to run the company's jetfoil service from Brighton to Dieppe. He and his family duly moved to Brighton.

The massive SR-N4 Ramsgate–Calais Cross Channel Ferry. [K. Colquhoun]

During April 1972 Hoverlloyd received their third Hovercraft, another SR.N4, which they named "Prince of Wales", at Ramsgate.

Later in 1972 Les left Hoverlloyd and started his own consultancy for high speed marine craft. He also worked with Bell and Rhor of America, on surface effect ships in the USA.

Fly High ~ Fly Low

A show of strength with two SR-N4s at speed. via K. Colquhoun.

Les later became involved with the London Hovercraft Service, that ran between Greenwich and Westminster using a Vosper sidewall hovercraft.

In 1978 Les joined Jetlink Ferries and ran a Brighton–Dieppe Boeing Jetfoil service, sponsored by Associated Newspaper Group, but striking French fishermen blocking the port of Dieppe and withdrawal of sponsorship caused this company to close in 1981.

The SR.N4 at rest on the beach [K Colquhoun]

Les Colquhoun when Managing Director of Hoverlloyd. [K. Colquhoun]

It had been started on the assumption there would be two Jetfoils operating, but in fact only one was ever delivered and it proved impossible to run a satisfactory service with just one craft

Retirement at 61

After all these setbacks, Les decided in 1982 to retire from business life at the relatively young age of 61. He and Katie were also elected to be the custodians at Chiddingstone Castle and held this position for four years. They both found this interesting and rewarding but not in the financial sense. The 'Chiding Stone' stands in a 30 acre park of the 18th century castle. The castle contains the Royal Stuart and Jacobite Collection, with superb lacquer and swords. All this is displayed in a superior country house setting, which sets off each collection. It is open to the public between March and October, and also, limited opening in the winter months.

Chiddingstone Castle, near Edenbridge, Kent. A castle only in name though.

Les retired to Broadstairs before they retired to live in Broadstairs in Kent, an attractive village located NW of Tunbridge Wells with half-timbered houses and a perpendicular Church Tower. in 1984 and as an ex-Spitfire pilot joined the Spitfire Society in Southampton and went on to become chairman of the Southern Region and later Chairman of the Society.

He finally made a return trip to Malta in 1999.

A final farewell

Leslie Robert Colquhoun died on the 27th April 2001 aged 80, and as a final gesture of the esteem in which he was held, a lone Spitfire PR.XI, PL983, from The Battle of Britain Flight, flew over the church during the burial service, in a final farewell.

The last picture of Les Colquhoun wearing his Spitfire Society tie, at Eastleigh for the Spitfire window celebration, that I also attended.

APPENDIX 1 ~ AWARDS

To 126118 F/Lt LR Colquhoun:
- 1939/45 Star
- Italy Star
- Africa Star
- Clasp to Africa Star
- Air Crew Europe Star

Items 1, 3 and 5 were to be issued when supplies were available dated 4/2/1946.

To 1377233 Sgt L Colquhoun

3rd July 1942 DFM (Distinguished Flying Medal).

To 126118 F/O LR Colquhoun

DFC (Distinguished Flying Cross)

To 126118 F/Lt LR Colquhoun (Retired)

27th July 1950 GM (George Medal)

APPENDIX 2 ~ GEORGE MEDAL

10, Downing Street,
Whitehall.

Personal and Confidential   27th July, 1950.

Sir,

I have the honour to inform you that The King has been graciously pleased to approve the Prime Minister's recommendation that the George Medal (G.M.) be awarded to you. Your name will therefore appear in a list of awards to be published in the London Gazette of Tuesday, the 1st August.

You will understand that this letter must be treated as strictly confidential until the 1st August.

Yours faithfully,

Anthony Bevin

L. R. Colquhoun, Esq., D.F.C., D.F.M.

Fly High ~ Fly Low

CENTRAL CHANCERY OF
THE ORDERS OF KNIGHTHOOD,
ST JAMES'S PALACE, S.W.1.

(OFFICES—3 CLEVELAND ROW, S.W.1. TELEPHONE: WHITEHALL 0792)

22nd January, 1951.

SIR,

I have the honour to inform you that The King will hold an Investiture at Buckingham Palace on Wednesday, 21st February, 1951, at which your attendance is requested.

I am desired to say that you should arrive at the Palace between the hours of 10 o'clock and 10.30 o'clock a.m., and this letter should be shown on entering as no other card of admission is issued.

Two guests only may accompany you to watch the Ceremony and their tickets may be obtained by making application on the enclosed form which should be returned as soon as possible. It is regretted that in no circumstances may this number be increased.

DRESS.—(a) Serving Officers of the Royal Navy, Army and Royal Air Force should wear the dress laid down in the regulations of their respective service. No Orders, Decorations and Medals should be worn, nor should swords be worn.

(b) Retired Officers who are not in possession of the dress described in (a) should wear Morning Dress or Dark Lounge Suit. Orders, Decorations and Medals should not be worn.

(c) Civilians should wear Morning Dress or Dark Lounge Suits. Orders, Decorations and Medals should not be worn.

I am, Sir,
Your obedient Servant,

De la Bere
Brigadier
Secretary.

Leslie R. Colquhoun, Esq.,
D.F.C., G.M., D.F.M.

The Buckingham Palace Command

L to r Katie Colquhoun (wife), Les Colquhoun and Edith Colquhoun (mother).outside Buckingham Palace.

APPENDIX 3 ~ Supermarine Swift Flight Tests

Here are a few Flight Test Reports from some of Colquhoun's Swift tests, exactly as they were written at the time. They cover the first two prototypes of the Supermarine Swift, WJ960 and WJ965. [Flight No. 74 = the 74th flight of WJ960.]

Flight No. 74 ~ Swift WJ.960 ~ 18th July 1952

First flight was devoted to recording some engine bay static measurements under conditions of flight. The results were passed to the Technical Office.

Some throttling back was done at high altitude and high Mach Nos. and at high A.S.I.'s at low altitude. The intakes were fitted with flush louvres and bulges. It is some time since this pilot flew this aircraft but it was definitely thought that the throttling back characteristics were much more noticeable. There was no severe buffeting as experienced on VV.119 but the general effect was of roughness which felt unpleasant. It was thought that under all throttle conditions the engine seemed rougher than when fitted with the divider plate. This was particularly noticed on the climb at 7500 r.p.m. and when above 2,500 ft. there was a definite beat to the engine and one almost expected to see a propeller on the front.

The aileron servodyne was thought to be very poor and flying the aircraft straight and level was rather like trying to balance on a tight rope.

Flight No. 75 ~ Swift WJ.960 ~ 18th July 1952

Raised louvres were fitted for this flight the purpose of which was to take some elevator angle measurements at high Mach Nos. and generally to assess the intake characteristics. With regard to the latter the changing of the louvres did not make any appreciable difference to the roughness experienced on the previous flight. The beat above 2,500 ft. was again noticed.

The elevator angle measurements were carried out up to an indicated Mach of .92. During this last dive very severe buffeting was experienced when endeavouring to recover from the dive by merely pulling back on the stick. The airbrakes had to be extended and the engine throttled to initiate recovery. This buffeting in a much milder form was experienced during a steep turn at about .76 I.M.N. at 37,000ft. It was not thought to be in any way connected to a 'g' stall.

It is interesting to record that even apart from the aileron servodyne characteristics the fore and aft control of this aircraft is not to compare with VV.119. The trim change with Mach No. around .8 indicated is very disconcerting when manoeuvring at high altitude.

Also may a pilot plea for just some small amount of pressure in the cockpit!!

Flight No. 76 ~ Swift WJ960 ~ 18th July 1952

This third flight was devoted to further measurements of engine bay static pressures and elevator angles at high Ms. The results were passed to Technical Office. Even after three flights all the odd noises and vibrations that seem to occur on this aircraft have not been discovered.

Flight No. 33 ~ Swift WJ960 ~ 7th May 1952

The purpose of the flight was familiarization and general handling combined with some auto observer short of intake conditions.

The general impression gained was that the aircraft is not pleasant to fly, particularly at altitude as VV.119. The fore and aft control at 35,000ft at between .84 and .88 I.M.N. was thought to be very touchy. The highest Mach No. attained was .9 indicated at about 34,000ft. At this mach number the starboard wing dropped but could be held. When the Mach No. dropped to about .88 - .89 the wing drop disappeared very suddenly.

Up to the highest speed attained 460 knots the ailerons were thought to be very good. It was noticed initially that there was a tendency for lateral rocking during the climb. This seemed most noticeable between 20,000ft and 30,000ft and was very difficult to stop. However, this may have been due to lack of familiarity with the light control.

The engine handling was considered good. The acceleration both on take-off and in the air when he throttle is fully opened was most impressive. The throttling back at 35,000ft at an I.M.N. of between .88 and .9 was good, there being no intake buffet or other noise. The lowest revs attained were 5,400 at about 28,000 ft.

Flight No.3 ~ Swift WJ.965, 22nd July 1952

The purpose of this flight was general handling with particular regard to snaking and stick thumping at increasing A.S.I's. The take-off with maximum fuel was trouble free; the nose wheel was lifted at 110-120 knots and the aircraft became airborne at 120-130 knots. The initial acceleration was slow to 250 knots but seemed to pick up as speed was increased. The retraction of the wheels was very speedy and was thought a great improvement on previous Supermarine aircraft.

The stick thumping was carried out up to 420 knots and was O.K. The elevator appeared completely dead beat and the ailerons produced a short sharp oscillation which immediately died out. This was sufficient however to shake the instrument panel.

It was thought that generally the ailerons were heavier than on WJ.960 or VV.119 and this became more pronounced at altitude. At .88 indicated Mach No. at 32,000 ft. they were thought to be very heavy. From the point of view of control feel however they were much superior to any flown on WJ960 by this pilot. There was no tendency for servodyne hunting. The elevator control was good but seemed considerably lighter than on WJ.960 or VV.119.

Rudder free the snaking started at about 325 knots and was quite pronounced. However by putting pressure on the rudder pedals it was possible to increase the speed to 430 knots before snaking became apparent. At 450 knots under these conditions it was considered uncomfortable.

Some slow speed handling was carried out between 10,000 and 15,000 ft. wheels and flaps down. With 200 gallons remaining the aircraft was flown down to 115 knots there was no buffeting or unpleasant feel about the aircraft at this speed. The elevator trimmer was almost fully down at this stage.

It was thought that operation of the undercarriage caused a noticeable amount of lateral rocking of the aircraft until it was down and locked. It was also noticed at this stage and particularly on the final approach to land that the aircraft was very right wing low. After landing it was found that there had been a failure of the starboard wing tank transfer.

The aircraft was trimmed at 250 knots at 6500 r.p.m. and the engine then opened up to full throttle the resultant nose up trim change when the speed had increased to 350 knots was estimated at 5-10 lb. push force.

A climb to 34,000 ft. was made indicating about 0.7 I.M.N. At this height the aircraft was levelled out and pushed into a gentle dive until the Mach No. had increased to .88 indicated. At this Mach No. the elevator was beginning to feel touchy and directional snaking was starting. An A.S.I. and height were recorded at .87 indicated, they were 310 knots at 31,500 ft. For a similar manoeuvre on WJ.960 the change of trim with increasing Mach No. is much more noticeable. However as mentioned earlier the ailerons were very heavy on this aircraft at this Mach No.

The airbrakes were operated up to a maximum speed of 575 knots. The nose down attitude change seemed much more severe than that experienced on the other prototype Swifts and there was a very noticeable nose down trim change. The stick force to hold this was estimated to be 5-10 lb. There was also quite a lot of aileron buffeting which is not a characteristic of the other prototypes.

The tail parachute was successfully streamed on landing.

The new nose wheel was considered an improvement in that the castoring action was improved.

Flight No. 4 ~ 22nd July 1952

The purpose of this flight was to carry out some preliminary stalling tests and slow speed handling.

The first stalling tests were carried out immediately after take-off when then fuel remaining was estimated to be around 400 gallons.

There did not seem to be any warning of the stall in the form of buffeting, especially in the all up case, but at about 2 - 3 knots above the stall the aircraft started yawing from side to side and was very difficult to control. Reducing the speed farther caused the port wing to drop. The stalling characteristics were not explored beyond this stage. It was thought that the yawing characteristic could have been caused by the tail parachute cone. The stalls were repeated at a later stage in the flight when the fuel had been reduced to 250 gallons.

Results:

ASI Conditions	Stall warning	Wing drop speed	Fuel
All UP	128	126	About 400 galls.
AU UP Air brakes out	117	115	About 400 galls.
All Down	125	117	About 400 galls.
All UP	123	121	260 galls.
All UP brakes cut	114	111	250 galls.
All down	116	114	250 galls

In the last stall the aircraft was very right wing low possibly am to a further failure of the starboard wing tank.

Flight No. 5 ~ Swift WJ965 ~ 22nd July 1952

The tail parachute and cone were removed for this flight to check their effect on the directional characteristics of the aeroplane.

The snaking which had been present on the previous flights mesa gone completely and the speed was increased to 450 knots with no unusual characteristics. The controls felt smooth and very pleasant.

The aircraft us climbed to 38,000 ft. and some general handling carried out. It was thought that there was a lot of back lash in the rudder circuit at this height.

Two Mach No. runs were carried out, the first to .92 I.M.N. and the second to .93 - .94 I.M.N. During the first run the nose down trim change started about .86 - .87 I.M.N. but was not very great and could be easily held without retrimming. The aircraft became right wing low at about .9 but it too could be held and about .92 the aircraft seemed laterally level once more. The aircraft was pulled into a climb without using airbrakes or retrimming.

The second dive was started at or about 40,000 ft. and was slightly steeper. The starboard wing drop stage was encountered at about .91 I.M.N. as before and the dive was continued until the I.M.N. was .93 - .94. At this stage it seemed that the control control column had been pulled back quite a lot in an effort to counter the nose dawn trim change. Further backward pressure on the stick started off a fairly severe elevator buffet as on WJ960. The air brakes were extended and the pressure ceased on the control column until the aircraft had decelerated to .91 when the aircraft was pulled out of the dive.

It was thought that this aircraft was a lot more pleasant to fly under these high I.M.N's than WJ960. The controls at all times were smooth and the longitudinal trim change with Mach No. was not so apparent. It was thought that serious attention will have to be devoted to the nose down trim change with air brakes. This definitely felt unpleasant especially when they were operated at .94 I.M.N.

Flight No. 80 ~ Swift WJ.965 ~ 26th May 1953

This aircraft now has the fully modified ailerons with full power and spring feel. It was this pilots second flight in an aircraft thus modified.

First impressions of the control before joining up with the Lancaster were that the ailerons did not feel as good as those experienced on WK.198. They appeared to lack positive centring and it was found difficult to accomplish accurate turns or to stop the rate of roll exactly where one wished.

Formating at 160 knots was hard work at first and forces of up to 20 lb for aileron control gave the aeroplane an unusual feel. However, after 20 minutes of this the pilot was feeling happier with the aircraft.

On completion of the photography speed was increased up to 400 knots. It was found very necessary to adjust the spring feel with increase of speed. It was still felt that the ailerons were not as good as those on WK. 198, primarily due to poor self centring. If the stick was displaced to nearly full aileron travel and then released it did not find its neutral position as on WK.198 but went beyond it and then back again to an inch or two in the direction of the original displacement.

When altitude was increased to 35,000 ft. the ailerons were not liked at all. Accurate turns were found to be difficult and the behaviour of the aircraft at times could only be described as wallowing. A check on the lateral rocking was made, locking the stick by bracing ones elbows against the sides of the cockpit. Under this condition at 34,000 ft. slight lateral rocking was apparent. As far as could be judged from the cockpit the ailerons did not appear to be moving. With the stick still firmly held the rudder was very slightly displaced and released, this caused a very marked increase in the lateral rocking and lends weight to the belief that the directional stabilizer may go a long way towards curing lateral rocking.

With 258 gallons gone some stalling all down was carried out. Buffeting started at 117 knots and the aircraft felt very right wing low at 115 knots, which with the spring feel required quite a stick force to hold but it was felt that there was more aileron available.

The fuel system showed consistently tail heavy from 195 gallons gone and the rear tank blinker also showed empty at this stage.

The nose wheel was again causing severe vibration after take-off.

The trimming controls on this aircraft are now very badly grouped. The elevator trim in particular is out of sight when setting normally and completely equipped with oxygen mask.

Flight No. 81 ~ Swift WJ.965 ~ 26th May 1953

This second flight was entirely devoted to photography and after an hour and ten minutes at 160 knots the pilot felt quite at home with the spring feel ailerons.

Just before landing a stall all down was carried out with 350 galls gone. A speed of 102 knots was recorded at which point the aircraft was dropping alternate wings and much hard work was being done on the ailerons in correcting this tendency.

A dive to 578 knots was accomplished over the airfield at 1,000 ft. it was thought that at speeds above 550 knots the ailerons are becoming very light.

Flight No.82 ~ Swift WJ.965 ~ 26th May, 1953

This third flight was for the purpose of further investigating the stalling characteristics of the aircraft and also to carry out same high Mach Number runs.

All up the aircraft was stalled at 119 knots with 61 gallons gone. At this stage one had to work hard on the ailerons to keep the aircraft laterally level. Buffeting had started at 128 knots and increased in intensity as the speed was further reduced.

All down with 65 gallons gone the aircraft became right wing low at 120 knots. This out of trim feel was wound out on the spring feel and the speed was further reduced. At 117 knots mild buffeting started which increased as speed was further reduced. At 105 knots a mild port wing drop occurred and it was thought that the true stall had been reached. At speeds between 117 knots and 109 knots both the ailerons and rudder had been used to keep the aircraft laterally level.

At 38,000 ft. on the climb mild buffetting started at 2 g at .75 I.M.N. The aircraft was climbed on to 42,000 ft. The first dive was to .94 I.M.N. and up to this Mach Number the aircraft was extremely smooth. No wing drop was noticed on this dive.

On the second dive starting at 42,000 ft. and 83 I.M.N. the nose down trim change occurring at between .89 and .92 I.M.N. was trimmed out. At .94 I.M.N. the push force increased a lot and it was thought that even pushing very hard the Mach Number was not going to increase further. However, .95 was eventually reached before recovery. As recovery was started a jolt was felt on the elevator and slight elevator buffet was experienced during the pull out. A slight port wing drop had been experienced during this dive at around .92 and .93 I.M.N.

A third dive was made starting at a slightly higher indicated Mach Number .86 at 41,000 ft. During this dive the nose down trim change was not entirely trimmed out but again the push force increased at .94 I.M.N. and with a very hard push force, .96 I.M.N. was reached. A jolt on the elevator was again experienced when the engine was throttled and recovery initiated. The slight port wing drop was also experienced on this dive. Observers at Chilbolton reported hearing two faint sonic bangs during this dive. It was thought that both these last two dives had reached Mach One, evidence being the increase in push force and the jerk on the elevator.

The fourth dive was abandoned because of a fuel gauge defect, the highest I.M.N. reached was .935. The airbrakes were extended and height was rapidly reduced. Below 5,000 ft the airbrakes were closed and the speed increased in a slight dive to 590 knots at 1,000 ft. This was an I.M.N. of about .9 or just under. The nose down trim change was not fully trimmed out but the aircraft felt quite comfortable to fly. It was noticeable at this speed that the ailerons were becoming very light. At 570 knots it was possible to apply full aileron but the force required to cause the deflection was not thought to be 20 lb. It was thought that the ailerons had an overbalanced feel at these speeds but as this was a first impression and the first time a Swift had reached these speeds this opinion might not be substantiated during further tests.

The airbrakes were operated at Mach Numbers of .94 indicated and apart from a nose down altitude change which seemed rather more than when operated at high

ASIs were without comment.

[This was Les Colquhoun's first supersonic flight. Supermarine's first ever had been by D.W. Morgan on the 26/2/1953.]

BIBLIOGRAPHIC SOURCES

- Air 27/607   69 Squadron ORB January – December 1942
- Air 27/2203 682 Squadron ORB September 1942 – June 1944
- *Air-Cushion Vehicles* magazine.
- *Warburton's War* by Tony Spooner, 1987, Kimber.
- *The Maltese Spitfire* by Harry Coldbeck, 1997 Airlife Publishing.
- *Supreme Gallantry* by Tony Spooner. 1996 John Murray.
- *Never a Dull Moment* by Denis Le P Webb. 2001 J&KH

INDEX

Aberdeen 85
Abery Mrs F.L. 119
Agrigenta 61
Air Cushion Vehicle 173
Air Gunner 11
Ajaccio, Corsica 88, 99
Albert, HRH Prince of Belgium 144
Aldermaston 105
Alesion 94
Alexandria 38
Algeria 68
Alghero, Sardinia 94
Algiers 74
Allach 100
Alpha Romeo 52
Altmark 5
Amsterdam 183
Ancoma 98
Andover 144
Anlong, Way 91
Anson, Avro 80
Anthorn RNAS 119
Antipaxes, Greece 63
Anzio, Italy 91
Apatin, Yugoslavia 90
Arcidosso, Italy 93
Argus 24
Arkosund, Sweden 189
Arena Aerodrome 54P
Argentinian pilots 118
Argus HMS 26, 34
Arno, River, Italy 91
Arnold P. 158
Arthur W/Cdr 11
Artouste 2C engines 200
Asciano, Italy 88
Ascoli, Italy 88
Ashby Christopher 190
Associated Newspapers 213
Athenia s. s. 3
Attacker prototype 118, 122P
Attacker F.1 132P
Attacker R4000 139P

Augsburg 97
Augusta 29, 37, 51, 61
Aulla 97
Auster, Taylorcraft 97, 141
Austin Mr 135, 146
Austria 92
Aviano 91, 94
Awards 217
Avro York 160

Baghdad, Iraq 137
Bailey Lt. 129
Baja, Hungary 98
Ball, S/Ldr A.H.W. 87
Ballater 85
Baltimore, Martin 43, 53
Banbury, Capt. 194
Bari, Italy 42, 67P
Barret F/Lt 12
Barter Charles 154
Barton Sgt 11
Bastia, Italy 90
Battle of Britain 8
Battle of Britain Flight 213
Baum Sgt 43
Beaufighter, Bristol 39, 80
Beaufort, Bristol 38, 40
Beer Mr 124
Belgium 148
Bell SKMR-1 Hydroskimmer 200
Bell & Rhor of America 210
Belluno, Austria 97
Belpasso 60
Belson Capt. 131
Benghazi 47, 68
Benson RAF 17, 21, 76
Berica Aerodrome 47
Berka 44
Bernard Prince, Netherlands 185
Bertil Prince of Sweden 189
Birkenhead 190
Biscari 29, 36, 41, 56P
Bizerta 74, 90

- 228 -

Black F/O J.A. 40
Blackburn 603 Turmo 190
Blackpool 10
Bleiburg, Austria 93
Blunsdon 104
Bocco di Falca 47, 51, 64P
Boeing Jetfoils 211
Boeizzo 29
Bolana, Italy 96
Bologna, Italy 92, 94
Bolzano 96, 97
Bone, Aleria 75
Borg, Sir George 59
Borizzo 31, 47, 51
Boscombe Down 111
Bourque, Henri 200
Boute, General Le 144
Boyd W/Cdr 114
Brabazon Lord 159
Braemar 85
Brag, Yugoslavia 92
Branksome Avenue 119
Braviken, Sweden 189
Brazier, Tom 202
Brighton - Dieppe 211
Brindisi 38, 58
Bristol Siddeley Marine Proteus 206
Bristol Siddeley Turmo 603 193
British Embassy 145
British Lion 144
British South African A/W 115
British United Airways 190
Brize Norton 108
Broad Capt. Hubert 154P
Broadstairs, Kent 213
Brussels, Belgium 144
Bryce Jock 153
Bucari 56
Buckingham Palace 134, 217
Buckstone F/Lt 16
Budapest, Hungary 97
Buenos Aires 123
Burnett, Charles 140, 146
Burrows 'Bill' 26
Bush Sgt Cyril 16
Byrne Sir Dennis 177

Cagliari 42, 46, 74
Cairngorms 84
Cairo 18
Calabria, Reggio de 31

Caltanisseto 61
Camera Installation 27, 28, 72P
Camfuglia, Italy 88
Campini, Harold 195
Canilatti 61
Cangola 95
Cannes, France 99
Cantania 100
Cantanzaro Marina 64
Cape Granitola 58
Cape Hawk SS 22
Cape Orlando 62
Cape Passero 34
Cape San Vito 50
Cape Santa Maria 62
Capodichina Aerodrome 55P, 66P
Capodistre Gulf, Yugoslavia 98
Capronica, Italy 88
Casablanca 74
Casaibianco 97
Cassino, Italy 86
Castel Benito, Libya 153
Castel Vetrano Aerodrome 29, 47, 51, 76P
Castle Bromwich 111
Catania, Sicily 29, 36, 41, 53P
Catterick RAF 16
Celina Bridges 92
Celje, Slovenia 97
Cephalonia 47
Chamberlain Neville 2, 3, 6
Chattis Hill 105
Chiddington Castle 212
Chilbolton 117P
Chobham, Surrey 13
Chocolate 34
Christofferson, T. 204
Churchill, Winston 10, 99
Civalivecchio, Itlay 96
Cockerell Christopher 207
Colbeck F/O 20, 52
Colerne RAF 105
Colquhoun, Edith 218
Colquhoun, Helen 104, 191
Colquhoun, Jane 104, 191
Colquhoun Katie M. 119, 191, 218
Colquhoun Les 147P, 148P, 150P, 158P, 193P
Colquhoun, Peta 104, 193
Colquhoun Picture 5
Colquhoun, Sally 104, 191P
Coltishall RAF 170

Colvin F/Lt H. 32
Combo 41
Comiso 29, 36, 41, 60P
Como Lake, Italy 91
Compoformion 99
Constanzaro Marina 43
Consul, Airspeed 121
Continental engine 179
Continental 0-300-B 183
Continental 0-470-1 183
Continental GIO-470A 183
Convoy Patrol 15, 16, 17
Copenhagen, Denmark 185
Corfu 56, 63
Corsica 90
Cotrone 59
Cowes IOW 204
Cox Roxbee 179
CR42s 23
Cranisy Aidam 177
Cresta Run 158
Croskell F/Lt 121
Crown Film Unit 142
Cruxall 26, 31
Cubb 83
Cullen W.H. 1
Cunningham W/Cdr J. 125
Curtis Lettice 125
Cygnet, GAL 97
Czechoslovakia 2

D-Day 89
Dailey Stanley T. 206
Dailey F/Sgt J.O. 27, 38, 43, 45
Danube 184
Denedet, Italy 90, 91
Derry John S/Ldr 117, 136
Devas F/Lt 11
Devechia, Italy 90
Dickinson Mr 115, 135
Djerba 57
Dolgano 99
Domine D.H. 108
Donawitz 93
Donnett Mr 179
Douglas-Hamilton S/Ldr D 17
Dove DH 170
Downing Street No. 10 216
Drayton Manor School i
Dubrovnik, Yugoslavia 92
Duke of Kent 151

Duke, Neville record 153, 158
Dunkirk 10
Dunlop Rubber Co. Ltd. 125
Dunphie Maj/Gen C.A.L. 151, 179
Dyce RAF, Scotland 15, 16, 80, 101

Eagle HMS 23, 24, 33, 34, 36, 39
Ealing 103
Eastleigh 105, 129
Edenbridge, Kent 215
Edinburgh, Duke of 159, 209
18 EFTS 14
Eisenhower, Lt/Gen Dwight 74
El Adjina 87
El Aouina, Italy 90
Elana Island 89
Elba 96
Elmas Aerodrome 46, 71P, 76P
Emelia 95
Empedocle 61
Etienne, France 88
Exercise 'Realist' 184

Fairchild 24W-41A 91, 97
Fairlop RAF 15
Fairoaks RAF, Surrey 14
Farli 96
Farrell 31
Ferrara, Italy 100
Fielden, Sir E.H. 152
Filton 171
Firth of Forth 17
Fishington 41
Fiume, Italy 90, 92, 96
Flight Test Reports 219
Florence, Italy 88
Foggia, Italy 42, 90
Fordown, Scotland 85
'Fort Mandan' USS 201
Fraser Mr 179
Fraserburgh RAF 84
French Morocco 68
'Trey' SS 185
9 FTS 15
'Furious' HMS 51, 68
Furlong, Frank 112
FW 190 93

G-suit tests 162
Gabes 25
Gaetta, Italy 83

Gammon T. 152
Garda, Lake, Italy 91
Gasgoine 26
Gedi 94
Gela 29, 33, 36, 41, 47P, 48P
Genoa, Italy 96
George Cross 22, 29, 34, 59, 134
George Medal 124
Gerbini Aerodrome 29, 36, 41, 72P
German Air Force 24
Germany 12
Gibraltar 18, 80
Gilliams (Gillions) Sgt Frank 27, 38, 62
Gladiator, Gloster 21
Glorious HMS 5
Glucksman, Arne 204
Gnonne 94
Goldbeck F/Lt R.G. 74, 79
Goodwin Sands 207
Gorgoua 88
Gorizia 100
Gort, General 59
Gozilia 95
Grada, Yugoslavia 100
Graf Spee 5
Graud 100
Gravedonna 100
Graz, Austria 97
Greece 20
Greenwich-Westminster Service 211
Greta 88
Grotaglia Aerodrome 71P
Grove House 161
Guildonia, Italy 90, 91

Haley, Mrs Joan 207
Harvey R.A. 124
Hawarden RAF 13
Hawker Fury 2
Hawker Hunter 153
Head Jonathan 207
Head, Mr & Mrs 207
Heaton J.R. 158
Hennessey Mr 177
Heron DH 169
Herschel Raymond 32
High Post 103
Hitler 14
Hodgson James 146, 204
Hoggett Cpl 31
Horns 56

Hornchurch RAF 14, 15
Home Chunky 117, 152
Hornet Moth 97
Hovercraft Development Ltd 173
Hoverlloyd Ltd. 294
Howard F/Lt 12
Howard Sgt 81
Hughes Sammy R. 175
Hullavington RAF 12
Hunter HMS 101
Huntley 85
Hurricanes 12
Hurst F/Sgt Johny 16
Hydrofoil 187
Hyres, France 91

Idris el Awal 153
Imperia 96
Indian Trainers 126
Ingolstadt, Germany 184
Innsbruk, Austria 97, 98
Insch 85
Ionian Sea 60
Isle of Rab 96
Italian Air Force 23
Italy 86 Itchen Works 124, 181

Jablanac 100
Jaffarano 60
Javelin, Gloster 134
Jemmitt P/O FCM 76
Jesemce 100
Johnson P/O S.T. 40
Joine 95, 96
Jones, Emrys 206
Jones Yankee 16
Ju.52s 65P, 81, 86
Ju.87 30, 33
Ju.88 17, 30, 64, 68
Judge Pee Wee 117, 152
Justin John 143

Karachi 146
Katakolo, Greece 72
Keevil 105
Kerkenna 57
'Kimberley' HMS 99
King George VI 57, 134
Kiriloves 100
Kirton RAF 16
Klagenfurt, Austria 93, 95, 97

Knolly Lord 177
Kockums Shipyard 185P
Korda Alexander 143
Kotor 92
Kralovdc, Slornia 97
Kurit 57

Lake Guardia 97, 99
Laker FA (Freddie) 190
Lalero, Italy 83
La Goulet, 90
La Marsa, Tunisia 86
Lampedusa 37, 46
Lavariana 99
Laviano 99
Lean David 143
Lecce 61P
Lee-on-Solent 100, 118, 148
Le Luc, France 91
Lecce, Italy 42, 59P
Leghorn, Italy 92, 93
Leuben 93
Levigaldi 97
Lewis Bob 200
Licata 61
Lifeboat Rescues 188
Life-Boat Plaque 198P
Linz, Austria 99
Lithgow Mike Lt/Cdr 112, 114, 151 P, 158P
Lloyd, AVM HP 25
Lloyd Line 204
Locata 60
"Littorio" battleship 58
Local Defence Volunteer 4
Lockie S/Ldr 151
London 12
Long Island Sound 202
LST427 90
Ludlow Ernest 26
Luqa, Malta 31, 65P
Luscombe A 179
Lympne 125
Lympne Trophy 125, 126P
Lyon 94

Macchi 202s 37
MacKay S/Ldr R.C. 85
MacLean W/Cdr 22
Maestre 96
Magister, Miles 97

Magettino 56
Maison Blanche 86
Makarska, Yugoslavia 92
Malignano, Italy 88
Malmo, Sweden 185
Malta 18, 20
Malta Pilgrimage 159
Maniago, Italy 93, 94
Manston RAF 80
Map of Malta Area 35
Marsala 29
Master 1, Miles 12, 85
Master II, Miles 102
Mauripur 139
Mayers Cyril 202
Mayne Philip 154
Mayo, Major Bob 154P
Mazzaro 54
McNillan F/Lt 93
Me. 109 23, 24, 34
Me.323 64, 65P, 86
Meadows 26, 31
Medenine 25
Messina 31, 36, 41
Messina Straits 38
Medenine 27
Meteor F.IV 128
Meulebroeck M. Van De 144
Mijet Island 92
Milan, Italy 91, 94, 95
Miller Mr 146
Mitchell F/Lt C.N.C. 158
Mohal, Hungary 98
Molastron 189
Monfalcone 100
Monofallone 96
Monserato Aerodrome 58P, 74
Montauk, NY 200
Monte Cassino, Italy 92
Monte Castrelto 93
Montrose 16
Morgan Guy 117
Morgan S/Ldr Dave 114, 117, 145
Morgan S/.Ldr J. 90
Morizia 96
Morton Cpl 31
Mosasc 91
Mosquito, DH 80
Moth Minor DH 85
Mount Etna 78, 79P
Mudie Cdr I.M.N. 119

Muller M. 158
Munich 100
Murphy Frank (Hunters) 153
Murray F/O 16
Mustang, IIIF N.A. 106

Naples, Italy 33, 38, 74
Natal 123
Natal 9
NATO Competition 184
Navarino 48, 58, 63
Nelson E.G. 158
Neuberg, Germany 100
New York 200
Nice 154
Niece 95
Noel A/Cdr 177
Nota Arga 45

Oberhosdorf 100
O'Duffy F/O 12
Opher, W.D. 189
'Ohio' SS 49, 50P
Old, Madelaine 191
Old, Patrick 191
Old, Raymond 185, 192, 191P
Operation 'Torch' 74
Oran 74
Orbetello, Italy 95
Oresund, Sweden 185
Oristano Aerodrome 71
Orr-Ewing, Lt/Cdr M.R. 147
57 OTU, Wrexham 16
Orvieto, Italy 88
Ossoppo 93, 94
Oxford, Airspeed 131P

Pachino Aerodrome 34, 36, 77P
Padua 97
Painter A 119
Pakistan Attackers 146
Palermo 36, 37, 42, 51, 60, 74
Palermoand 47
Palma 38
Pantelleria Aerodrome 29, 35, 37, 66P
Papas 44
Parenzo 100
Parish Councillors 118
Parker 31
Patraf, Greece 63, 72
Patras 45

Patrick F/O 43
Patrick Nigel 143P
Paverazzi 100
Pegwell Bay 208
Penn Acres 110
Penty, Katie 103
Perranporth 80
Pershore RAF 170
Perugia, Italy 88, 93
Pianosa 96
Piastoia, Italy 88
Picento, Italy 88
Piacenza, Italy 88, 95
Pien del Lago, Italy 88
Pileocia 62
Piomouino, Italy 88, 90, 93
'Pioneer Cove' SS 202
Pisa 88, 93
Pistoia, Italy 92
Plesi 96
Ploesti, Rumania 88
Po Valley, Italy 98
Pola 91, 93
Pomigliano, Italy 92, 94
Portoforram, Italy 90
Portreath RAF 87
Powell Brian 137
Preston Col. 154
Prince of Wales 212
Prometheus 143
1 PRU 18, 84
2 PRU 18
4 PRU 86
Pugh, Stevenson 204
Pula, Yugoslavia 93

Queen, HRH The 159
Quill, Geoffrey 103, 114

Radlett 112
RAF Memorial Malta 159
Ramsgate, Mayor of 210
Ramsgate to Calais SR-N4 200
Rapide DH 137P
RATOG 118
Ravager HMS 108
Ravenna, Italy 85, 100
Razanas 100
Redman F/O D. 40
Reggio di Calabria 29, 42, 95
Republic Aerospace Corp 198

Rheim, Germany 100
Rhyl 195
Richardson Ralph 143
Rieti 93
Rimini 94, 100
Riposto 44
Royal Oak 3
Robarts P. 117, 140
Rolls-Royce/Continental 183
Rome 88, 95, 96
Rommel General 22, 37
Roosevelt, Lt/Col Elliot 86
Royal Oak HMS 8
Royal Swedish Air Force 118
Royal Thai Air Force 140
Rhyl Lifeboat P
Rhyl, Wales 190

Sacarda 55
Sage, Dick 203
St David, Hospital Ship 91
St Etienne 94
St Meryn RAF 21
St Moritz 158
St Tropez bay, France 90
San Guisto 88
San Pietro, Sardinia 98
San Severo 99
San Stefano 88
Sardinia 38, 47
Sarsamo 88
Saunders-Roe 173
Saw tooth leading edge 153
Scarrott Air/Cdr G 119
Schlosheim 100
Schom 94
Schweinfurt 94
Schwind Major F.L. 119
Sciacca 47, 51
Scimitar F.1 166P
Sea Hawk 136
Sea Otter, Supermarine 108, 128
Seafang 111
Seafang F.32 112, 116P
Seafire F.III 118
Seafire F. XV 107, 149
Seafire F.XVII 107
Seafire F.45 103
Seafire F.46 110P
Seafire F.47 110
Seagull ASR. 1,

Supermarine 128P
Secimomrino 75
Sergnano, Italy 88, 94
Serte 57
Sfax, Tunisia 73, 76, 86
SheIIBP 177
Sherburn-in-Elmet 136
Sheridan Dinah 143
Sibenick 86
Sicily 22, 86
Sidi Amor 88
Sienna, Italy 83, 93
Sirte 56
Skopje, Yugoslavia 87
Smart G 119
Smith Joe 152
SM.79s 23
Smoke bombs 112
Soil Fertility 182
Sorizzo 60
Sound Barrier 143
Souter 31
South Cerney 179
South Marston 104, 173
Spain 22
Speed Record in TS409 121
Speed Record in PA147 I
Spezia, Italy 96
Spiteful Prototype 112
Spiteful F.14 111
Spiteful F.16 109
Spitfire F.1 85
Spitfire IIA 13
Spitfire VC 68
Spitfire F. VIII 115
Spitfire T. VIII 115, 116P, 125P
Spitfire PR G 84
Spitfire PR.IV 18, 84
Spitfire H.F.IX 103
Spitfire PR.XI 87
Spitfire F.XIV 106
Spitfire F.XVIII 103
Spitfire PR. XIX 103, 127P
Spitfire F.21 103
Spitfire F.22 108, 110P
Spitfire F.24 120
Spitfire Society 215
Spurgeon F/Lt 93
69 Squadron 20, 87
680 Squadron 82, 87
682 Squadron 86, 87

683 Squadron 87
800 Squadron 123
SR-N6, Westland P
St Tropez 99
Stalangens Mek Shipyard 189
Stewart Mr 134, 140
Steyk 95
Stone "Stoney" 16
Supersonic 150
Swedish Air Force 126
Swedish Lloyd Line 206
Sweny Cdr 179
Swift from Seagull 129
Swift prototype 129, 149P
Swift WJ960 221-222
Swift WJ965 223-229
Swift F.4 152P
Swift FR-5 163
Swift F.7 165P
Syracuse 29, 61

Tara, Yugoslavia 86
Taranto, Italy 38, 42, 51
Tarrant Rushton 151
Tekkarch 100
Tenca 85
Teramo, Italy 88
Terni 93
Thomas Sgt 16
Thomas F/O 16
Tiger Moth 11, 171
Tito, Marshall 100
Tivat, Yugoslavia 92
Todd, Ann 142P, 143
Torquay 13
Toulouse, France 94
Trapani 29, 36, 37, 56P
Trebelzue, Cornwall 19
Trento 96, 97
Trieste 91, 93, 96
Tripoli 25, 66
Tripoli Harbour Swift 156P
Trondeim 9
Tunbridge Wells Kent 215
Tunis 73, 78P, 90, 154
Tunisia 81
Turin 94
Turkish Prime Minister 152
Type 322 Dumbo 118
Type 508 VX133 148
Type 535 VV119 143, 148

Type 541 WJ960 145

Udine, Italy 96
Ulijan 92 VA.1 173P-182

VA.2 183P-190
VA.3 191P-198
Vala Luka, Yugoslavia 86
Valance 94
Valetta C.1 137, 138P
Valetta Harbour 39, 49
Valiant B.2 WJ954 153
Vatimbella A. 158
Valley RAF 167
Vampire F.1 117
Vampire F.3 119P
Vapuror, Yugoslavia 98
Variabke Incidence Tail 149
Vasta, Italy 91, 93
Vega Gull, Percival 97
Vela Luka, Yugoslavia 92
Venice, Italy 91, 93, 96
Venegona 100
Vericelli 94
Vetrono 60
Vicenzo 97
Vienn, France 94
Vienna, Austria 97
Viking, Vickers 123
Vilena 97
Villach, Austria 97
Villacidea 75, 80P
Villaoba 93; 94
Viareggio 88
Villafrana 94
Villeoma 99
Viscount 700 151
Vitro Valentia 29
Vologna, Italy 96

Waddy Sgt 16
Wade S/Ldr T. S. 136
Walrus, Supermarine 120P
Wall Map of 69 Sqdn 78
Wallasey, England 191
Warburton Adrian, S/Ldr 53, 62, 78, 82
Warner, Christopher Sir 145
Wasp USS 29, 33, 36
Waterton Bill 134
Webb, Denis Le P. 133, 137
Webb S/Ldr 121

Wellington X 121, 124P
Wellingtons 22
Wells Bob 31
Wells Frank 200
Westland SRN4 294
Westland SRN6 204
Westland Charters 204
Wet Weather Trials 171P
Wilson Harold 209
Wilson, Mrs Mary 209
Wing tip up landing 123

Wisley 108, 123
Woodley S.P. 196P
World Speed Record Amphibians 136
World Absolute Speed Record 153
Wrexham RAF 13

Yugoslavia 98

Zagreb, Yugoslavia 97
Zante 44
Zara, Turkey 92